Oysterville

OYSTERVILLE

Roads to Grandpa's Village

Willard R. Espy

Illustrations by Earl Thollander

 Clarkson N. Potter, Inc. / Publishers   NEW YORK

DISTRIBUTED BY CROWN PUBLISHERS, INC.

Published by Clarkson N. Potter, Inc., 225 Park Avenue
South, New York 10003 and simultaneously in Canada by
General Publishing Company Limited

Manufactured in the United States of America

CLARKSON N. POTTER, POTTER, and colophon are
trademarks of Clarkson N. Potter, Inc.

Designed by Ladislav Svatos/Graphicon Ltd.

Library of Congress Cataloging in Publication Data

Espy, Willard R.
　　Oysterville: roads to grandpa's village.

　　Includes index.
　　1. Espy family. 2. Espy, Willard R. 3. Oysterville, Wash.
—Genealogy.
CS71.E72 1976　　　979.7′92　　　76-40227

ISBN 0-517-52196-2 (cloth)
ISBN 0-517-54913-1 (pbk.)

10　9　8　7　6　5　4　3　2　1

First Paperback Edition, 1986

To my sister Dale;
my brother Edwin;
the memory of my sister Mona;
and my surviving uncles,
Willard and Cecil

Scotch
Broom
Oysterville,
Washington

The Federal Government declared Oysterville
a national historical site in 1976.

Contents

Acknowledgments

With thanks to:

✢ My first cousin, Julia Hurtt, and my second cousin, Ethel Jones, for anecdotes and documents that threw new and sometimes disconcerting light on certain forebears;

✢ Ruth Dixon, editor of *The Sou'wester*, and Roger T. Tetlow, for illuminations of early days on Shoalwater Bay;

✢ Dr. John Niven, Professor of History at the Claremont Graduate School, and John B. B. Trussell, Jr., Associate Historian of the Commonwealth of Pennsylvania, for references on Indian fighting during the eighteenth century in Pennsylvania;

✢ Mrs. A. V. Hall and Colonel Harold B. Limpson (Ret.), for helping me clarify the Civil War record of Captain Richard Taylor;

✢ Adrian Berwick, for providing detached professional criticism despite the inhibitions of an old friendship;

✢ Mignon Franco, first because she is a paragon of typists, and second because she is Mignon Franco.

Introduction

It was not irrelevant to papa, nor is it to me, that he was conceived and born in grandpa's village in the centennial year of our nation. He concluded in his dotage—missing the correct date by a mere century—that his birth year literally coincided with that of the Republic. "It is astonishing to reflect," he would say, propped up in bed, his head shaking slowly, "that if I am still here on November 5, 1976, I shall be two hundred years old."

I wish he had made it.

The genes that he commingled with mama's carried coded instructions from three hundred years of American preachers and farmers and tanners and doctors and beggars and plantation owners; from sergeants, politicians, Indian fighters, haywards, storekeepers, and witches. An astonishing number of these genes were out in the open, waving hello, calling attention to themselves by name; thus it was our custom to say, "Papa's long nose has appeared with puberty for a hundred and fifty years in the Apperson line; and Aunt Shae's honking voice was reported by Sam Richardson in the 1640s; and mama's inability to pronounce her medial r's dates back to the Taylors' transition days in Texas." Had I been born with abnormal extremities, these would have been attributed without a second thought to Abigail Kimbell, a forebear notable for her "unusual number of fingers and toes."

"A child," said playwright Peter Shaffer, "is born into a world of phenomena all equal in their power to enslave. Suddenly one strikes. Why? Moments snap together like magnets, forging a chain of shackles. Why?"

Which moments snapped together for the Espy children? Why this for my brother Ed, and that for my sister Dale, and the other for me? Were our genes the magnets? Or our surroundings—our neighbors, perhaps: the Andrewses, or the Christies, or the Nelsons, or the Wirts? Or is our nature simply the result of our confinement in the blue-green bottle of grandpa's village, with parents who interpreted according to their own needs the meaning of the shadows outside?

The bottle was a dozen well-worn houses and barns on the peninsula side of Shoalwater Bay, an estuary of the Pacific Ocean. Shoalwater Bay, now called Willapa Harbor, occupies the bulk of Pacific County, in the southwestern corner of the State of Washington.

Four hundred feet of salt meadow separate the main street (once called Territorial Road) of grandpa's village from the bay; but the protection is porous. A hundred years ago there was a street between our house and the mudflats; but the tides gnawed until the street fell in and drowned. (The door that was the front door of our house in 1869 is now the back door, and the erstwhile back door is the front.) Swollen morning tides in December turn our meadow into an archipelago of gorse-topped islands. The place I grew up in seems afloat then: on some winter mornings, even the road becomes a waterway for rowboats and rafts.

In an ordinary year, a hundred inches of rain fall on grandpa's village; we have mutated until we breathe with comfort air that is half water, or water that is half air. I suspect that if the peninsula were to sink beneath our feet, a mishap that in some downpours seems imminent, we could live submerged without serious inconvenience.

Even today, we of Oysterville are a far reach from the rest of the world; but when I spent my knee-pants years there, in the first quarter of the twentieth century, we were all but totally isolated.

I was more than six years old when the first automobile coughed its way up the lane past our house, and more than ten before we Espys had a car of our own. I was eight before we could boast a phonograph—a wind-up contraption that pitted a revolving black cylinder against a scratchy, grimly determined, diamond-pointed needle. I was fourteen when we blew out our last coal-oil lamp and flushed our first toilet.

Nor am I yet an old man.

During those early years we stayed still while the seasons revolved around us.

In January, tens of thousands of brant, a seaweed-eating goose, lined the edge of the tide. Their quacking was as mournful, ominous, and interminable as a Greek chorus.

In February, herring swarmed over Leadbetter Bar from the ocean in such quantities that they must have raised the level of the bay. The retreating tide left them thrashing in shallow backwaters; we scooped them up in buckets, sieves, sou'westers, and, if necessary, in the sweaters off our backs.

By March, lovesick frogs were calling in the marshes, and tadpoles

in stagnant ponds were dreaming of the high-jump records they would break once their hind legs had grown out.

In April, leaves replaced the pussy willows, and a green haze blurred the silhouettes of the alder trees.

In May, lilacs, azaleas, hydrangeas, and rhododendrons caught fire in the rain; the brown gorse turned to gold, and the Scotch broom to the color of canaries.

In June, when the salmon berries ripened to a watery yellow, we sometimes saw hints of sun. The following month, a northwest wind would come up in the afternoon to spin the vanes of the windmill standing beside our house; the mill pumped water into six barrels lined up on the roof, whence gravity pulled it down in iron pipes to dribble out of the kitchen taps. If the wind did not abate, the water eventually overflowed and drenched the shingles. If the wind died down, we children did the pumping.

August was a time of dahlias, marigolds, and chrysanthemums. In September, the Virginia creeper that blotted out the chimney of the Wirt house across the lane became a scarlet cascade. In October, the villagers harvested the cranberries on hands and knees, straddling rows of plants that were low and red and wet. In November, ducks and geese cried in the flyways, marshes, and lakes.

December was the month when the old folks generally died.

Grandpa's village was named Oysterville because oysters had been its reason for becoming. By the time of my childhood, however, the oyster industry was dead and most of the oystermen were gone. The popula-

The Cannery

tion consisted of subsistence farmers, clam diggers, hunters, cranberry growers, bachelor-hermits — and, of course, Espys.

Grandpa stayed, I suppose, because he *was* the village, and saw no reason to become anything else. For papa, the reasons were more complex. In the first place, he did not exactly stay; rather, he returned. He had ventured into the outside world; had studied engineering, Latin, and Greek, in California, and nursed one of grandpa's ailing gold mines back to health; and he had married a wife who knew dishwashing only as an unmentionable word. Papa was persuaded to return to Oysterville at the turn of the century to watch over his father's property; the old man was dipping his toes into the chilly water of dying. As it turned out, grandpa kept pulling back his toes until 1918, when one morning he felt too tired to get up for breakfast, turned on his side, and quietly expired at the age of ninety-one years, eight months and eight days. By that time I assume that papa took for granted, as his father had before him, that *he* was Oysterville.

Nor did there seem to be any resentment of this point of view among his neighbors. If there had been, I think I should have known, because there were a number of children around my age in the village, and children are accurate barometers of their parents' feelings. They got along fine with the young Espys. The only concern I felt lay in myself — a feeling of inferiority, occasioned largely by lack of physical prowess. I suspected, too, that our playmates, for all their tolerance, considered us Espys in some ways "simple."

They would ask what it felt like to be rich, and whether papa kept gold coins in his rolltop desk as his own father had before him, and — a far graver matter — why we did not contribute the gloves, bat, and ball needed for games of one-old-cat. At the age of ten, I laid out a ramshackle golf course in the meadow between our house and the bay. I used coffee cans for greens cups and cut tree limbs into an elaborate assortment of clubs. My lofter, shaped from a crooked alder branch, proved more useful than any eight-iron I was to own in later years. Why, asked my schoolmates, didn't papa simply send away for a set of store-bought clubs? Yet they knew as well as their parents that the demise of the oyster industry had left my parents as poor as anyone else in the village. Minnie Andrews, the postmistress and storekeeper, had no reason to keep secret the times when for lack of requisite pennies the Espys had to put off buying coal oil, coffee, and even postage stamps.

The myth of our wealth was simply persistent, like the rain. I now think this was because we owned land. It may have been axiomatic in those days that any landowner was wealthy. And there is no denying that most of the fields, meadows, forests, and swamps surrounding the village, not to mention sand flats and oyster beds as far as the eye could reach at low tide, were ours.

Let me be clear: this property was utterly worthless. The upland was wilderness and swamp; the tideland and oyster beds were in effect 18 papa's by default, he having bought them for a dollar an acre after previous owners let them go for taxes. Every Oystervillean, adult or child, knew, and freely proclaimed, that papa had to be tetched in the head to pay a dollar for nothing.

But such realities had no effect on the legend. We Espy children came to half believe it ourselves. We considered ourselves a special sort of rich people — the sort without money. I sometimes think of myself that way still.

One more factor may have set us apart. After all, grandpa *had* founded Oysterville. He *did* run it. He took his dominance for granted. I recall the day — I was six or seven, and grandpa was ninety — when he decided to leave church in the midst of a hymn. As he walked down the aisle straight as a sloop's mast on a calm day, his attention was caught by an amiable matron, a row of shiny-faced offspring beside her and a new arrival asuck at her breast. "How many does that make?" demanded grandpa. All singing in the congregation ceased as he spoke; only the organist continued bravely to pump and wail. "T-twelve, Major," replied the red-faced mother. "Good number to stop on, good number to stop on!" boomed grandpa, stamping out the door. Whether through coincidence or obedience, the woman never bore again.

Grandpa was accustomed to being obeyed; and I suppose that in papa's turn he was too. But papa was far more willing than his father to render service in return. When not mowing hay, patching fences, or milking cows, he was running the school board, or serving in the state Senate, or acting as justice of the peace. He performed more marriages than anyone in the history of the county. He fought rearguard battles to protect the property of the remaining Indians. If a widow was being tricked out of her property, papa went to court for her. If a Chinese could not write English, or a Swede could not write at all, they dictated their letters to papa. If sickness struck a preacher, of whatever denomination, our telephone would ring — a short, a long, and a short — and papa would hurry into his second best suit and ride horseback to fill the empty pulpit. Sometimes the round trip came to eighty miles. Baptist though he was, even the Catholics called on him to preach.

If a neighbor pounded on the door at three in the morning to report someone gravely ill, papa, who was probably still reading or writing by the nursery stove, would harness Empress and Dolly, arrange a mattress in the back of his wagon, and take the sufferer to the hospital. During the Great Depression, when no one in the community had money for a driver's license, papa persuaded the authorities to let everybody go on driving their pickup trucks, unreproved and unfined. Nor would he accept pay for any of this, much as he could have used the money. His services were reflexive: Oysterville was papa, and papa was Oysterville.

Mama's case was different. She was a city girl, and her emotion on first regarding Oysterville was one of astonishment and disbelief, like that of the fabled farmer looking at his first giraffe. Her loyalty was en-

19

tirely toward her husband and children, not their village. Were it not for leaving her family behind, I doubt whether she would have stayed in Oysterville overnight. Even after fifty years, though by then she had long since become beloved of the villagers and they of her, she confessed that when she heard the clang of her doorbell her first impulse was still to run the other way.

For this very reason, her achievement in Oysterville may have outshone papa's. He, after all, was among folk he had known all his life. He enjoyed people whatever their station; indeed, when no one was around at milking time, he talked to the cows. However he may have regretted the loss of the outside world, he was at least in Oysterville, where he was born and shaped. My mother, on the other hand, whose life was confined to her family and books, who was terrified of strangers and started at a raised voice as at a clap of thunder, found herself exiled overnight from surroundings that stimulated her mind and suited her sense of the fitness of things, and set down in a midden of emptied oyster shells.

She adjusted, though she never quite learned to let her neighbors' minds alone. She had a persistent notion that if once she could expose them to *Evangeline,* or *Idylls of the King,* an inner radiance would be added to their lives. So she insisted on lending them books. After keeping each borrowed volume, doubtless unopened, for a polite period, they would return it, declaring they had never enjoyed anything quite so much.

Yet she carved out for herself a lasting place of honor and affection in Oysterville. These decent, gentle people sensed that hers was a decent and gentle heart.

No woman in the village could surpass her tender skill at bandaging a hurt child. She kept iodine, bandages, cotton, and pills in a tin box in the nursery bureau, next to a cracked leather kit filled with allopathic medicines. Doctors then were still of two fiercely competing breeds: the allopaths, who treated fever by putting ice on the forehead, and the homeopaths, who treated fever by throwing on more blankets. From that tin box and that old leather kit came all the medication some Oystervilleans ever knew before their hands were finally folded across their chests.

Gradually even I, a small, self-centered boy, could sense the reconciliation, the acceptance, between mama and the village. How could she resist a child who offered her a woven grass basket filled with daisies, and ran away without waiting to be thanked? How could she disdain a neighbor who, plowing in his potato field, dropped the reins and rushed over to help when the chimney pipe of her kitchen stove collapsed? Or an old bachelor who tendered amber, thin-shelled razor clams, fresh from the cold waters of the Pacific, and refused to take pay?

Yet she was never quite at home in Oysterville. Perhaps, of us all, only papa was. Papa had lived in Oysterville most of his life, and mama much of her life, and we children all our lives; yet I well remember waking on blustery nights, pulling the quilts higher about my chin, and wondering seriously whether I was not living out a dream in grandpa's village.

We perched at the end of the known world, and could go no farther without dropping off. So we simply sat there in the black winter evenings, talking about where we began, and the roads that had brought us in the end to grandpa's village.

"Bay V", Oysterville, Washington

Family Album

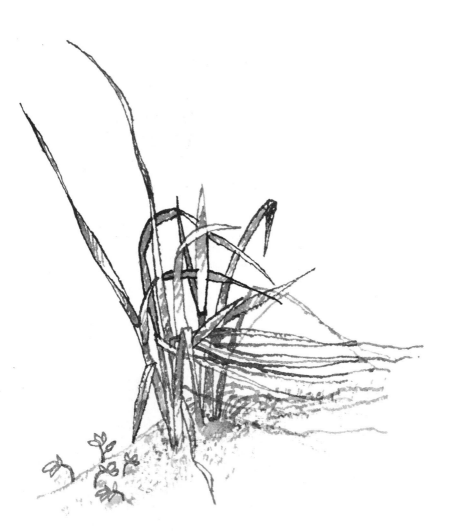

Grandpa Espy's mother, Elizabeth (Carson) Espy.

Deacon Elisha Rand, grandfather of Grandpa Richardson.

Grandpa and Grandma Espy at the time of their marriage.

Grandpa Richardson in his middle years.

Grandma Richardson in her middle years.

Pop and Mom with their first three children.

Grandpa Espy shortly before his death.

On August 7, 1895, Aunt Dora Espy, twenty-three,
was married at Oysterville to A. King Wilson,
an attorney of Portland, Oregon.
In this picture of the wedding party in front of the Espy home,
to the left in the rear row, is Uncle Ed, twenty-one,
separated by two bearded gentlemen from his brother Harry
(with pensive expression
and drooping white breast kerchief), eighteen.
Seated almost in front of Harry is the bride,
her mustachioed groom glowering at her side
and her arm around her six-year-old sister, Verona.

Kneeling in the foreground, again to your left, is Uncle Will,
only in his twelfth year but already looking disillusioned.
Immediately in front of the groom,
peering around a woman in a dark straw hat, is Uncle Cecil, seven.
He is leaning toward Aunt Susy, seventeen.
To the right of the pillar
sits the true focus of attention, grandpa Espy,
showing the inside of his hat.
Grandma is resting her right arm on his knee.
Family friends and Jefferson, Apperson, and Wilson relatives
make up the remainder of the party.

Oysterville
and
Surrounding Areas

1.
*The beach where grandpa
hauled his new
clinker-built boat home
through the surf.*
2.
*Grandpa logged here
through
the winter of 1852–53.*
3.
Bruceport. The Bruce *burned here.*
4.
*The Palix River, where grandpa met
Chief Nahcati.*
5.
*Oysterville, founded by grandpa
and Isaac Clark in 1854.*
6.
*The isthmus between
Shoalwater Bay and
the Columbia River.*
7.
*Point Ellice, where grandpa
beachcombed during
the winter of 1853–54.*
8.
*Astoria, where grandpa
sold the logs he gathered
at Point Ellice.*

Papa's Road

1

The Weaklings Died along the Way

GEORGE ESPY begat
HUGH;

Hugh begat
JOSIAH;

Josiah married
JEAN TAYLOR
and begat
JOHN;

John married
ANN MONTGOMERY
and begat
THOMAS;

Thomas married
ANNA HAMILTON
and begat
ROBERT HAMILTON;

Robert Hamilton married
ELIZABETH CARSON
and begat again
ROBERT HAMILTON;

Robert Hamilton married
JULIA ANN JEFFERSON
and begat
HARRY ALBERT;

Harry Albert married
HELEN MEDORA RICHARDSON
and begat

. . .

My grandfather, Robert Hamilton Espy, followed the Oregon Trail to the West Coast in 1852. The sole remaining memento of his trek is a beehive clock on the chest of drawers behind my study desk. The clock has just struck three. It is made of the cheapest kind of laminated wood, glued and screwed together.It is twenty inches high, ten inches wide, and four inches deep. Its hands are encircled by Roman numerals. The glass door beneath, which opens to reveal a pendulum and a key hanging from a nail, is decorated with an oil painting of a red and yellow bird, species unknown, sitting on a green branch.

According to the solemn asseverations of papa and Aunt Dora, Grandpa Espy brought that clock west with him. But papa and Aunt Dora are long dead. Uncle Will and Uncle Cecil, still decidedly alive, insist that grandpa lost all his domestic possessions, including a bureau and a plate-glass mirror, somewhere around Fort Laramie in a fire that consumed his wagon. They insist that he arrived at the Columbia River with only such essential gear as an axe, knife, frying pan, blanket, and rifle.

After losing the wagon, grandpa had to travel afoot. It must have been awkward to tramp well over a thousand miles with a beehive clock on one's back. Yet the clock has been around far longer than I have; and though I have total confidence in the word of Uncle Cecil and Uncle Will, I prefer in this case to believe the version handed down by papa and Aunt Dora, who were as honest as their brothers, even if they did exaggerate once in a while. There is even physical proof of the odyssey of the clock: throughout my boyhood it never ran. What better proof of the joggling it took, riding grandpa piggyback over the gravel and around the boulders of the Blue Mountains? Let it then be stipulated that grandpa brought that clock with him over the Oregon Trail.

Papa sometimes recapitulated the trek for us as it had been described to him years before. Unfortunately, there were inconsistencies in his account. As will become evident, Grandpa Espy was not a loquacious man. When tricked into telling a story, he generally left the best parts out. Papa was the opposite. When a fact was missing he tended to fill the gap, if not by inventing, at least by approximating how he thought matters probably came about, or should have come about. He had, moreover, a detailed and circumlocutory mind; someone once said that if a cow walked past the house papa would be likely to spend half a day describing the cow's yield of milk, the butterfat content of the milk, the cow's age, the details surrounding its birth, and the names and natures of its forebears going back fifty years.

When leading up to a new run-through of grandpa's migration west, for instance, papa frequently began by announcing that the Espys were, had always been, and probably always would be, a pretty poor lot. The Espy contributions to the building of the American nation, he would remark, took place more or less by accident, at times when our conscious minds were probably on how to get a baby over the colic or a mare over the heaves.

Since he was by no means insecure about himself—he never, for instance, felt the need to boast—this sort of self-deprecation may have been his way of protecting his children from the sin of pride. My own belief, though, is that he was teasing mama.

"Now, *your* family, Helen," he said one winter evening, brushing his hands vigorously after positioning a gray-bearded alder log on the fire in the library, "is different from mine; yours are almost-somebodies, and an almost-somebody is the unhappiest person in the world. In the old days the Espy men were perfectly satisfied to be nobodies and to marry nobodies just like themselves. Back in 1610, when my six-times-great-grandfather George came from Scotland to the Plantations of Northern Ireland, his wife was such a consummate nobody that no one even bothered to write down her name. Our minds worked so slowly that it took us a hundred and fifteen years to decide to cross the Atlantic from Ireland to Pennsylvania. The Espys in those days were a very happy clan."

"You know perfectly well that James Pollard Espy was no nobody," said mama stoutly.

(This was the cousin who announced in 1835 that moist air, as it moves higher, expands and cools until it comes down again as rain. In my boyhood, I never considered that much of a discovery; I myself could look out a window any run-of-the-mill day and watch the moist air rise and the rain fall. Still, scholars got excited at the time, and wrote books about James, and called him the Storm King, and there is no question that he was the nearest thing to a famous Espy we had ever had.)

"But he was certainly an aberration," insisted papa, settling himself in his revolving chair, his back to his cluttered rolltop desk. "He must have known it himself—at least he had sense enough not to have any children of his own. Suppose his children had turned out to be smart, like him. It would have spoiled the name of the family. . . . But you know perfectly well that I didn't set out to talk about Jim Espy, Helen. I was talking about Espy wives. My point is that the most satisfactory wife is a nobody, and that fact the Espys have been proving for three hundred years."

"But you did marry me," said mama, rather complacently, "and you admit I'm at least *half* a somebody."

"I hate to say it," said papa, "but I've got to lay the fault at the door of my own father. One of the few mistakes he ever made in his life was to marry above himself. And what happened? Naturally, all his children had to marry above themselves too. Every one of them, except for those who didn't marry at all." He stood up and kissed mama lightly on the top of her dark hair. This was his way of saying that he was only joking; but of course she knew that already.

It is perfectly true that since grandpa's day the unspoken rule of all male Espys has been: Marry your better. In this way, we gradually improve the bloodline. But there is a price to pay; not only are the husbands aware of the wives' superior qualities, but these soon come as well to the attention of the wives, who occasionally remind us that we are a lesser breed. Such reminders strain any marriage. Moreover, in view of the fact that our wives put us in our place even when we are around to argue back, we are justly concerned over what they may let out about us once we are dead and unable to defend ourselves. For this reason every male Espy from grandpa on has made a point of outliving his wife.

I used to wonder why papa teased mama about the difference in their backgrounds. I am sure now I have the answer. It was papa's way of saying, "I'm well aware of the amenities you gave up to marry me and come to this wilderness. I want you to know I understand your sacrifice, and am grateful that you love me so."

He worshipped mama too much to realize she would have given up far more, and still have thought she had the better of the bargain.

"You know," she said, "I have often wondered why father (for so she referred to Grandpa Espy) felt he must marry someone with a better —what would you call it? social? educational? cultural?—background than his own. He was the superior specimen in this part of the country. Why, he was the Patriarch of Oysterville for more than fifty years."

Papa pulled at his goatee. "I think that was just the problem," he decided. "Father had succeeded, and he was determined that his children were not going to drop back to where he had started. You've got to remember that as an unschooled man he had an almost superstitious reverence for education.

"Oysterville is primitive enough, I admit. But by comparison with what father had known as a boy, Oysterville was a New York City—yes, or a San Francisco, Helen. Don't forget he came from generation after generation of Scotch-Irishmen, who had hacked farms out of forests populated largely by Indians and Espys. Father's forebears had no time to be concerned over gratifying their egos; they were preoccupied with survival. His grandfather Tom served in the Revolution, but the last thing in the world Tom wanted was to be a hero. He aimed to attract as little attention as he could, in camp or on foray, so as not to get scalped. Father was born in 1826, but his earliest memory was that the skin on the faces of the couple on the next farm came down in folds, like an elephant's, because they had been scalped alive a quarter of a century before.

"No, father didn't start life with a silver spoon in his mouth. Any spoon he had was wood, or at best tin. That's what the Espys ate with, when they weren't using their fingers. Their pitchers were made of leather, and their bowls were gourd and melon shells.

"His mother was a widow before father was five. In a way, that may have been a lucky break for him. At ten, he was apprenticed to a tailor, and got the idea he didn't have to live out his life on a farm. Father used to consider that tailor his true parent. By the way, he must have learned the tailoring trade pretty well. He was an expert judge of a bolt of cloth   38 all his life. When it came to cutting fabric on a bias, or selvaging the edge of a skirt, even mother deferred to him."

After these preliminaries, papa would launch on his father's trip across the plains.

In 1845, grandpa bought his freedom from the tailor for a fifty-dollar promissory note, which he paid off ten years later. Now his own master, he moved with his sister Margaret and her husband, Elias Medley, from Pennsylvania to Wisconsin. There he was converted from the Presbyterian to the landmark Baptist faith; learned to break up lead ore underground; and became a skilled feller of trees.In 1850, he rode a lumber raft from the Big Bull Falls down the Wisconsin and Mississippi rivers to New Orleans, where his head was set abuzz with stories of a western Beulah Land called Oregon, the Algonquin word for beautiful water. One informant declared that spruce trees in Oregon grew three hundred feet high and forty feet around. Nay, said the next; he had seen a tree whose lowest branch was two hundred and sixteen feet high, while its butt circumference was fifty-seven feet. I remember driving our Ford (in the early 1920s) through a gash hacked in just such a tree.

Oregon Territory, went the tales, was a land of clear, fast-running streams, where a steelhead would leap a yard to take a hook. The climate was balmy, except for a phenomenon dismissed with a shrug as "Oregon mist." The soil was so fertile that a farmer who planted an apple had to jump aside lest he be impaled on the up-shooting trunk of the tree. And a man could have all the land he needed, more than he could possibly farm alone, simply by staking out a claim.

Between 1842 and 1852, 20,000 men, women, and children piled their most precious possessions into their sturdiest wagons, harnessed their strongest oxen, rounded up their most valuable cattle, and headed for Beulah Land.

On April 21, 1852, grandpa merged with the westward-flowing stream.

He was then twenty-six years old, slender, wiry, gray-eyed, above middle height, exceptionally erect of carriage, long of stride, and, at least by report, indefatigable beyond the common. He wore a woolen shirt, trousers stuffed into heavy, ankle-high boots, a hat of felt or coonskin, and in cold weather a sweater or mackinaw.

Here papa would begin to speculate on which of us children most resembled grandpa. He usually picked on me, which did not altogether please my mother. She said that maybe I was an Espy on the outside, but I was a Richardson on the inside, while some people she might name — and she nodded portentously at my sister Mona — were Richardsons on the outside and Espys on the inside.

"I could tell better if they grew beards," said papa.

Grandpa, unlike one migrant family he knew, could not boast of a blue game hen that laid an egg every day; but he did start out with a rooster, four hens, two dogs, six cows, and two yoke of oxen. The dogs kept the cows from straying. The oxen worked in shifts; one yoke hauled the wagon, while the other plodded on unharnessed.

Grandpa's wagon was a canvas-covered Conestoga, named after its place of origin in Pennsylvania. Because of their broad wheels, Conestogas were suitable vehicles for travelling in soft soil or on prairies. They were roomier, if less compactly arranged, than most modern motor-campers; a tall man could sleep athwart inside a Conestoga among the towels, clothing, pots, pans, baskets, and rifles. Grandpa filled the chinks between these articles with salt meat, dried corn, apples, potatoes, and flitches of bacon. He covered these again with sacked flour, which also served as his bed. Buckets, churns, lanterns, water kegs, and farming tools hung clanking under the floor. Grandpa kept a sheet-iron cook-stove, small enough so that he could push it out at mealtime on a shelf fastened to the rear axle. Once he reached the Oregon Trail proper, he fueled this stove with buffalo chips, previous wagon trains having stripped the countryside of wood.

Oxen were preferable to horses for crossing the plains. Nothing wore them out; their eating habits were frugal; and their flesh was so 40 tough that no Indian would bother to steal them. They were slow, to be sure—but then, who was in a hurry?

Four of the six cows were dry, but he milked the other two morning and night, skimming off the cream and drinking the milk. By the time the cream had been bumped and jolted all day long, papa said, it generated a respectable lump of butter to go with grandpa's evening meal.

The first leg of grandpa's journey carried him three hundred miles southwest from Platteville, Wisconsin, to Independence, Missouri. As he neared Independence the wagon trains grew more numerous, until they seemed to converge from all sides of the horizon. The trains threw up a dust haze that would have done credit to a twentieth-century smog in Los Angeles.

West of Independence lay two thousand miles of Indian country. The wagon trains averaged about ten miles a day; eight miles was a poor showing, and fifteen a record. The emigrants could expect to reach the Columbia River, those of them who arrived at all, in four to six months. They knew they would have to ford rivers in spate, and surmount almost impassable mountains. Many would die of cholera, scurvy, or Indian attacks. "The cowards stayed behind," said papa, "and the weaklings died along the way." They sought, therefore, to unite their forces under leaders who had already survived the rigors of the trail. Grandpa and a friend, Henry McClurg, bound themselves to a Mr. Whitlock, a middle-aged man of imposing presence; grandpa referred to him in later years as "the great deceiver." Whitlock promised to guide and guard them, taking as payment all their livestock, which they were to herd and drive. His own contribution was to ride in a horse-drawn carriage, wearing a frock coat, along a trail so gouged by earlier wheels that a blind man could have traced it with his white cane.

Whether Whitlock would actually have been of any use in the event of an Indian attack was never put to the test. The nearest they came to confrontation with the savages was at Little Horn, where a band of Indians pressed them for tobacco, flour, and such, but did not molest them.

The journey from Independence began in the spring, with the turf hard enough to sustain traffic and yet easy on the feet of the stock. Game was abundant, and the prairie sparkled with flowers. The heat, however, advanced with the season; the grass turned brown, and the trail became a ribbon of dust that billowed up from under the wagons and settled back on man and beast in a gray powder.

Once papa rubbed his still-brown, side-parted hair in a puzzled way, and said, "I never could learn from father just when the wagon with his possessions in it burned, but it had to be somewhere between Platteville and Fort Laramie. I have always suspected Whitlock burned the wagon himself, to make father more dependent on him. But that is only my guess; father never said so. He did describe the cast-off furniture along the trail—some of it old and beautiful heirlooms, still not ravaged by sun and rain." The pioneers discarded the luxuries first; then heavy stores and feather beds; farther on there were even abandoned wagons, relics of owners who had died of cholera or dysentery. Still farther, the trail was lined with skeletons—mostly of horses, cattle, and hogs, but sometimes of humans, buried once but dug up again by prowling beasts or Indians. To minimize such desecration, the emigrants learned to bury their dead in the road itself, so that the passing traffic, beating the earth hard, would discourage scavengers from digging down to the body. Grandpa waited out two of these middle-of-the-road burials, one of a ninety-year-old woman, the other of a girl who had died in a fall from a wagon. One day a woman riding a cow caught up with the Whitlock train. She stayed with them for the night, but she and the cow were already on their way and out of sight when the others first stirred next morning.

The train crossed more than one hundred streams by grandpa's count, papa went on; several were so deep that grandpa and McClurg had to caulk the wagon beds and pole the wagons to the opposite bank.

The prairie section of the trail west ended at Fort Laramie. Here the emigrants rested their stock, overhauled their wagons, bathed, and became human again for a few days before braving the grim mountains ahead. Papa's voice altered when he began to describe the Laramie layover. The most uxorious and faithful of husbands, he was nonetheless an unabashed worshipper of female beauty; if he had not been a puritan, he would have been a rake.

"Imagine it, Helen," he said (and we children were well aware that this was love-talk; he had forgotten we were in the room), "imagine women who for months had been walking dust pillars suddenly becoming women again. The men must have felt the way Adam did when he woke up and found Eve. There they were—clean-faced, shining, every inch female. Suppose I had been my father, and had come across you at some dance, all squeaky-clean (could he really have said "squeaky-clean" as far back as 1920?), togged out in all the finery you had hidden away in your trunks. What would you have worn, do you suppose? A leghorn bonnet? A finger ring? A breast pin? Would you have been in a blue dress, with tight bodice, collar, and sleeves, and a long skirt and waist?"

Mama lowered her eyes, as was her way on such occasions; I could not tell in the flickering light whether she smiled. Ordinarily, who was less likely than Harry to notice a breast pin, or a blue dress with tight bodice? Yet she knew he was imagining the two of them there together as he described the Laramie dances, and the courting, and the weddings.

From Laramie on, however, practicality again replaced style in women's wear. As the wagon trains threaded northwestward through the Rocky Mountains, skirts grew short not for enticement but for greater ease of movement. When shoes wore out, they were thrown away and the women went barefoot. Patches multiplied under the dust on their dresses. Sometimes these workaday dresses had to be packed away lest they fall apart, and were replaced by the precious party gowns. By the time the trains finally reached the Snake River near its junction with the Columbia River in Oregon Territory, the women were glad to exchange their bedraggled finery for fresh salmon. The Indians were equally delighted with the trade, and flaunted bonnets, bodices, and skirts without regard to the wearer's age or sex.

Papa, my uncles, and my aunts disagreed about the details of the trek after the Whitlock party left Fort Laramie. One thing certain was that McClurg, grandpa's companion from the start, took ill, so that for six weeks the whole care of the stock fell upon grandpa. But none of grandpa's children ever knew whether McClurg recovered or died. Grandpa never got around to telling them. It is clear only that at Fort Hall, Idaho, grandpa severed relations with Whitlock, and continued his journey afoot. He had no stock to encumber him; Whitlock had taken it all, even the dogs.

Papa said grandpa was accompanied in his tramp by three brothers named Hakes. Aunt Dora, on the other hand, insisted that grandpa's youngest brother, Tom, joined him at about this period, though she could not say when or how. Another account does not mention Tom, but says the Hakeses and grandpa came across "a poor woman, Mrs. Boils, who had lost her husband on the way and needed help to care for her stock. Espy was left to help her, and the other boys went on."[*] Aunt Dora had a romantic view of the incident:

"Father and Tom," she said, "tossed coins to see which one would accompany the widow and her children to The Dalles, and which one would turn south to the California gold mines. Years later, I learned from Uncle Tom that your grandfather won the toss, which is why Tom went south. Tom said your grandfather was very much in love with that widow."

Perhaps. But since grandpa managed to avoid any permanent commitment to a member of the opposite sex for another eighteen years, any boiling in his blood for the widow Boils must have quickly simmered down. He sheltered her only as far as the Grande Ronde Valley in eastern Oregon. There he again distributed his gear about his person and made his way alone up the bleak Blue Mountains. From their summit he caught his first glimpse of the green Columbia River Valley, which he finally reached on August 27, 1852, four months and six days after leaving Platteville.

Grandpa's first employer in Oregon Territory was a sawmill owner, "old dad," "dad" being a generic term for anyone whose hair was dropping out or turning gray. Old dad set grandpa to hauling logs by ox sled up the Cascades, along the bank of the Columbia River.

"Whom should he meet one day," said papa, "but that old deceiver Whitlock, proceeding downstream in the same fancy carriage he had

[*]Julian Hawthorne, *History of Washington*. New York: American Historical Publishing Company, 1893.

driven all the way from the Missouri while father herded oxen! Father had the right of way, as he was loaded and heading upstream, but Whitlock ordered him off the road. Father refused, and finally, leaving his ox team standing, walked off into the woods, whistling. When he returned an hour later he found that Whitlock had backed up his carriage and worked it past the ox sled, bumping over the boulders. Perhaps the old man feared father was concealed behind a rock with a gun trained on him, ready to pull the trigger if Whitlock touched the oxen. I think that in truth father was not very far away."

In the spring of 1853, grandpa's employer sent him to Shoalwater Bay to fell and limb trees for the San Francisco market.

On Shoalwater Bay, said papa, grandpa ate his first oyster. He also met the Bruce boys.

2

The Burning of the Bruce

Unless my sainted papa was a liar, San Franciscans in the early 1850s toted such heavy pokes of gold that the city could afford to pave streets with flour at $50 a sack, and sidewalks with sugar at $100 a sack.

Prospectors squatted all day by gravelly streams, patiently swirling the water in their iron pans and watching for a glint of yellow at the bottom. The pans served also as frying pans, plates, and saucers. Meals consisted of hardtack; beans; coffee, roasted and ground on the spot; bacon; and an occasional dividend of venison or bear meat.

When at long intervals the gold hunters flung themselves into San Francisco's easily purchased embrace, they sought out special food even before special ladies of the night. To palates deadened by months of hardtack, the tang of oysters, particularly, was a miraculous resurrection. Had it been otherwise, grandpa would never have founded Oysterville, and I would never have written this book.

The miners' craving for oysters was so insatiable that San Francisco Bay was soon denuded of the bivalves, and a search began for more. The nearest source was Yaquina Bay in the Oregon Territory. Next in order came Netarts Bay, due west of Portland; then Shoalwater Bay, where this chronicle is centered; and, finally, Puget Sound. The oysters in the first two locations could meet only a small fraction of the demand, while Puget Sound, this being long before refrigeration, was so far away that seafood frequently spoiled in transit. Refractory winds in the Sound sometimes added days to the round trip. Besides, the Puget Sound oyster, known as the Olympia, had a coppery taste offensive to refined San Francisco palates.

But the same gourmets who rejected the Olympia oysters sang hosannahs to a bivalve thriving in a barely known estuary just above the mouth of the Columbia River. The native oyster of Shoalwater Bay, they averred, was a taste of heaven locked between shells.

Unfortunately, there were few vessels available to fetch back these delicacies. Almost as fast as ships entered San Francisco harbor, their crews headed for gold country. In the early 1850s, vessels by the hundred rotted at their anchors in the bay.

Enter the Bruce boys—eight East Coast fishermen who, having called on Lady Luck in the gold country and found her not at home, decided their training equipped them better to prospect for oysters than for gold. In the fall of 1851, they pooled their resources and bought the *Robert Bruce*, an eighty-two-foot, two-masted schooner of one hundred and twenty-nine tons out of Sag Harbor, New York.

The new owners considered themselves captains, and expected not only to be so addressed but to be accorded all the deference and obedience that their exalted state deserved. The result was trouble.

The cook of the *Bruce*, a man named Jefferson (some say he was Mexican, but Jefferson hardly seems a Mexican name; maybe he was black) was the only non-captain aboard, and therefore the only crew member who could be safely addressed as "Hey you." He was expected to perform all chores, such as making up bunks, that were beneath a captain's dignity.

Jefferson tucked away these humiliations in his mind until he could think of nothing else. Finally, on an overcast morning with the schooner quartering smartly in a twenty-knot breeze, he refused to bring the helmsman a cup of coffee. "I'll hold the wheel," he said; "you get the coffee." The altercation that ensued was as salty as the spray blowing past them. Captain Winant, the skipper, sided with the helmsman against the cook, whereupon Jefferson rushed to the galley and returned brandishing a meat cleaver. Whether he attempted to use it is not certain; in any event, a belaying pin knocked him flat, and he was confined below in irons.

It did not take long, however, for the Bruce boys to realize that without Jefferson they would have to do all the menial work themselves. They therefore unshackled him on his promise of good behavior, and thereafter hailed him as Jefferson, or at worst Jeff, instead of "Hey you."

Three weeks out of San Francisco they sailed past the efflux of the Columbia River—a discolored Sargasso Sea of drifting roots, logs, timber, boards, chips, and sawdust. Leadbetter Bar, the entrance to Shoalwater Bay, lay thirty miles north of the river mouth.

Since the channel they were following shifted between tides, they crossed the bar at a crawl, alert to tack at a moment's notice. At three o'clock on the rainy afternoon of December 16, 1851, they dropped anchor near the mainland shore of the bay, not far from the mouth of the Willapa River.

With the outward leg of the voyage completed, the captains relaxed. Once the ship was snugged down, they grew high in and on spirits. They smoked their pipes, told jokes, and sang bawdy songs while Jefferson prepared a feast to celebrate their safe landfall.

The feast centered upon lamb curry—a staple of long voyages, partly because its pungent flavor camouflaged the taste of decaying meat. No one knows exactly what the cook put into that dish; perhaps it was laudanum. In any event, the captains all fell sound asleep around the table even before they had emptied their plates.

At this time only one white man lived permanently on Shoalwater Bay. He was Bill M'Carty, generally referred to as old Brandywine by reason of his having once sailed in a frigate by that name. M'Carty, whose father-in-law was Cardowan, chief of the Chehalis Indians, had cleared and drained a farm at the portage between the head of Shoalwater Bay and the mouth of the Columbia River. There he lived happily with his wife and small daughter; but he had an itching foot, and spent much of his time hunting. An expedition with in-laws had taken him to the northeast corner of the bay on the day the *Bruce* sailed in, and he watched her arrival with interest. It puzzled him that she lay so long at anchor with no sign of life; and his curiosity was thoroughly aroused when, just before dark, he saw a man come on deck, throw a bulging   48 canvas sack into the ship's boat, and row off toward the Willapa River.

There are varying versions of what happened next. Papa always said that M'Carty saw smoke seeping upward from the deck, paddled out to the vessel, ran across the hot boards, descended the smoke-filled companionway, and found eight men snoring over an unfinished meal; that he cajoled, prodded, and slapped them into half wakefulness; that he got them one by one up the companionway, and into his canoe; that he brought them safely ashore; and that they then stood watching and swearing as the *Bruce* burned to water level.

According to another account, however, the *Bruce* was set afire at night. An Indian boy, noting the flickering of Jefferson's torch, roused M'Carty. They paddled for the vessel at top speed, but the flames moved even faster, licking upward at the canvas furled about the masts, and leaping aft with each new gust. The captain and crew, according to this version, were asleep not in the galley but in their own bunks. By the time they could be aroused, the smoke was stifling and the air almost too hot to breathe. No possessions but the clothes on their backs could be salvaged.

If this version is correct, M'Carty could not possibly have seen Jefferson rowing away from the vessel. In any event, the cook was never seen again. A white man, Aunt Dora said, appeared a few days later at an Indian encampment on the Willapa; proving quarrelsome, he was expelled; he then made his way northward to the Strait of Juan de Fuca, seat of more warlike tribes, and was again driven away; he started back toward the Willapa River, but on the way embroiled himself in one quarrel too many, this time with the Quinault Indians; and the Indians settled matters by tying him to a tree in the forest and leaving him there, "knowing," as Aunt Dora put it sepulchrally, "that the bears would do the rest."

There are even those who insist that the burning of the *Bruce* was not a simple act of revenge at all, but part of a fiendish plot. According to this theory, the Chesapeake Bay oystermen who had been happily killing one another for generations had simply expanded their theatre of war to the Pacific Coast. One of these rival groups discovered the treasure of oysters hiding in Shoalwater Bay and resolved to make it their own, crushing competition by any means necessary. Jefferson thus becomes a planted spy, placed on the *Bruce* to guarantee the failure of her mission to Shoalwater Bay.

If indeed there was a plot it backfired. Instead of driving the Bruce boys from the bay, it established them there.

Captain Winant, leaving his men to survive as best they could, took a canoe to the head of the bay, portaged to the Columbia, staying overnight at the M'Cartys', made his way across the river to Astoria, and caught a vessel bound for San Francisco. There he hired a second schooner and returned to Shoalwater Bay, where his men had spent their time piling up more prime oysters than the hold of his ship had space for. Before their first season was over, the Bruce boys had their own oyster schooner, *Mary Taylor*. The second year they added the *Equity*. They built a communal lodge on shore opposite the wrecked *Bruce*, starting Bruceport, the first settlement on the bay.

By 1853 a peach basket filled with oysters from Shoalwater Bay brought a dollar in gold on delivery to the schooner, which might hold up to 2,000 baskets. The basket brought $10 on arrival in San Francisco; epicures there would pay a silver dollar for an oyster smaller than the dollar.

Schooners coming north for oysters carried as ballast redwood lumber, fieldstone—for the peninsula was simply a sandspit, without rock, and there was no rock to be found on the mainland either—and any frippery of civilization, from a top hat to a whore, that the fancy of an oysterman could conjure up.

All Shoalwater Bay was the Bruce boys' oyster.

That is, until grandpa happened by.

3

Grandpa Settles with the Bruce Boys-
and the Oysters

Grandpa's logging went on within hallooing distance of the Bruce boys, and he fell into the habit of visiting them on rainy evenings. He referred to them in later years as "very clever fellows," meaning that they were good providers, agreeable hosts, and ruthless poker players.

Their cordiality turned as sour as milk in the sun, however, when one evening grandpa suggested trading his felling axe for a pair of oyster tongs. The Bruce boys desired no recruits, as earlier applicants could have told him. Such found themselves with scuttled boats and missing oysters; sometimes entire crews vanished. Nobody charged that these interlopers suffered irreparable physical harm; doubtless they were simply advised to drift away. The Bruce boys "hinted with some urgency," as papa put it, "that my father's room would henceforth be more valuable than his presence." Grandpa shrugged his shoulders, shouldered his axe and saws, and hiked four miles south to the Palix River, where he resumed felling trees and lopping limbs.

Once, when I was very small, I heard grandpa try to describe the ineffable beauty he found in the Palix country that summer. The sky was as bright as the inside of a silver bowl, he said, even when rain was falling. A few hundred yards from his cabin, there was a clear space where the river joined the bay, and each evening the setting sun dropped into that slot, filling it from bank to bank. As the sun sank, it drew over its shoulders a cloak of many colors, like Joseph's, ranging in hue from blood red to dim violet; when it sloped beneath the horizon, the colors for an instant multiplied, like the last burst of flame before a blazing log collapses into gray ash.

Yet can grandpa have said that? It must have come to me somehow at second hand, for he was so inarticulate that most of the facts of his life have come down to me flat, in two dimensions. If you find me saying that on such a day grandpa shot a crow, that statement is an assumption based on the fact that crow shooting, one of his intermittent pastimes, was not precluded on that particular day. When his own children appealed to him to arbitrate conflicting accounts about his trip over the Oregon trail, his response was simply to stroke his beard. In a vociferous mood he might say, "Ask the Hakes boys; they would probably remember better than I do." The Hakes boys, if not dead, were in any event far from Oysterville.

His children did not press their queries. Grandpa was set in his ways and unresponsive to importunity.

He must have been a difficult subject for Julian Hawthorne, son of the American storyteller Nathaniel Hawthorne. Julian traveled the byways of Washington in the 1890s to turn the recollections of old-timers into a book of biographical sketches.[*] When Hawthorne arrived at grandpa's home, the old gentleman had just settled down to his daily perusal of the Portland *Oregonian*. He waved the visitor to a chair, and

*History of Washington. New York: American Historical Publishing Co., 1893.

returned to his reading. A half hour later, presumably having memorized the paper, he set it aside and said, "I'm afraid that's all I can think of to tell you, young man. But it was good of you to come."

Grandpa would never have mentioned that a notable social event took place on Shoalwater Bay on July 4, 1853, were it not that the event had already been put on public record by a visiting anthropologist, James G. Swan.* Swan's tent happened to be the focus of the celebration, held in honor of the seventy-seventh anniversary of our nation.

Swan was quartered near the Bruce boys, from whom grandpa preferred to stay remote; but this was a special occasion, when animosities were suspended. He therefore baked an oyster pie as his contribution to the festivities, and set out in his canoe for Swan's place. He found himself caught up in a ragged regatta of canoes, rowboats, and sailboats manned by loggers, trappers, oystermen, and Indians, all headed for Swan's, and one and all firing their shotguns or rifles at random by way of celebration. When they were not firing at random, they were firing at wildfowl, the easiest victims being the cormorants that commonly blundered overhead.

Food was prepared by all-male hands, since Mrs. Paulding, a widow with a farm on the isthmus between the bay and the Columbia, near the old M'Carty place, was the only white woman within a radius of fifty miles. Besides boiled salmon, clams, seagulls, seal meat, and venison, there were puddings, pies, doughnuts, and sourdough bread. Grandpa appointed himself guardian of the whiskey, knowing that strong spirits weaken the wits of Indians and whites as well. A side benefit may have been an extra tot or two for himself.

The only information he ever volunteered about that notable occasion was that he had been asked to toast President Millard Fillmore and had refused because he thought Fillmore truckled too much to the South on slavery. But when reminded of that Fourth of July, his eyes would light up. He would shake his head and murmur that it was "something to shoot at—something to shoot at."

Swan's memories of the day are more illuminating. One man, he reported, read the Declaration of Independence; a second recited extracts from Webster's orations; and a third delivered a rambling oration of his own, after which the assembled guests fired off their guns in a deafening salute to liberty.

To climax the day, a hollow cedar stump nearby was stuffed with dry spruce limbs and lighted. The resulting bonfire worked its way into the surrounding forest and continued to burn there until rain extinguished it weeks later.

Grandpa's taciturnity may help explain the quick, lasting friendship that sprang up between him and Chief Nahcati, who with a score of Siwashes

---

*James G. Swan wrote *Three Years on Shoalwater Bay*. New York: Harper & Bros., 1857.

and their families paddled that September from the peninsula to the headwaters of the Palix, where they annually caught and smoked dogfish. Grandpa by then spoke Chinook as well as English—and was equally silent in both languages. The Siwashes, for their part, were so verbally costive that even their tribal history passed from generation to generation through a series of grunts. Since grunts are subject to a wide range of interpretation, Siwash history changed not only from one generation to the next but even from one side of the bay to the other.

Day after day, the red man and the white sat together in silence, watching the sun descend into the mouth of the Palix. At last Nahcati muttered a prime bit of information, one he had withheld from all other whites. The peninsula side of Shoalwater Bay, he confided, was lined with mountainous reefs of oysters—oysters far tastier and fatter than those currently making fortunes for the Bruce boys. If grandpa would agree to hire Nahcati's tribe as crew, Nahcati would personally guide him to this ostreal treasure.

Grandpa may not have replied in words, but I am sure he was moved to nod his head.

The season of deluges being imminent, the two men agreed to postpone examination of the peninsular oyster beds until the following spring, when the Siwashes were regularly camped near the point of the peninsula gathering wild raspberry stalks.

Nahcati's people followed the seasons around the bay: early spring found them on the peninsula; summer, salmon fishing on the Columbia side of the isthmus; fall, dogfishing on the Palix; winter, resting up from their exertions in their lodges at the mouth of the Willapa River. Their departure from the Palix in 1853 coincided with a growing surliness in the wind. Grandpa headed in the opposite direction, proposing to beachcomb through the winter near the Columbia River bar, where the weather might be as bad but there would at least be white civilization within reach.

He left early one November morning, traveling by canoe. By one o'clock he was entering Bear River, at the head of the bay. Less than a mile upstream the canoe began sticking in the mud, the tide being low and the river little more than a tidal slough. He pulled his hip boots to their full length, lowered his legs into the water, pushed his craft to the bank, where he pulled it above reach of high tides and hid it in a tangle of dead limbs, branches, twigs, and leaves rising higher than his head, these being the end product of countless years of tree droppings. He did not turn his canoe bottom side up; on his return he would prefer a waterlogged canoe to one that would not hold water either in or out. After concealing the craft as best he could, he adjusted pack, axe, belt, saws, and rifle about his person. With his gear in approximate equilibrium, he began to tramp the ten miles still separating him from the Columbia. This was none of your jolly picnic tramps; rather, he slipped, slithered, jumped, slogged, and waded. Once, indeed—when a sodden bank disintegrated under his weight—his tramp became a plunge. He dropped five feet, boots first, to the bottom of a slough, and continued an additional eighteen inches or so through the bottom mud, winding up chest-deep in dirty water. He found himself as firmly driven into the muck as a San Francisco piling, and to all appearances as helpless to break free.

But though he had flung his saws from him with one hand as he fell, he had kept his rifle raised above his head. By extending the gunstock he could barely touch and slowly lower an overhanging pine limb, until he could grasp it with his free hand. Flinging the rifle ashore, he pulled the limb toward him until he could obtain a solid purchase on it, and finally, with a Paul Bunyan heave, freed himself from the mud, leaving his boots behind him. He needed those boots, though, so he removed his sopping slicker, pack, mackinaw, shirt, and trousers, gingerly re-entered the slough in his one-piece woolen underwear, and proceeded to duck below the surface and grope about until finally he managed to locate the two water-filled boots and work them out of the mud.

Grandpa had barely reassembled his possessions when the wind swung to the southeast. After a preliminary puff, it blew out the sun as casually as it would have blown out a candle. Genesis repeated itself; the winds of Heaven were open, and a deluge descended.

It was too late for grandpa to worry about getting wet—that issue had been settled—but in the dimness of the driving rain he was uncertain of his trail. His most sensible course, he thought, would be to huddle up against a tree until the tempest abated and he could orient himself. He had just sat down, ready for a wet wait of indefinite duration, when the wind paused to catch its breath, and he heard not far off the excited barking of a dog, followed almost instantly by the crowing of a cock. Having crossed the isthmus in the opposite direction six months before, he knew that he must be near Mrs. Paulding's farm; M'Carty's and Wilson's places were farther on. He sloshed toward the sounds, and in a few minutes found himself in her farmyard. Clearly Mrs. Paulding was hospitable. She exclaimed over grandpa, warmed his heart with whiskey, and hung his clothes, underwear and all, to dry before a roaring fire. It may be assumed that she turned her back politely while grandpa covered his nakedness with a pair of her late husband's overalls. She provided him with a clay pipe, tobacco to smoke in it, and a rocker to sit in. As if that were not enough of Christian charity, she cooked him a meal of fricasseed chicken and dumplings, and he slept that night under an eiderdown quilt, with a pot under the bed. He was duly grateful.

Next morning grandpa set out again, following what was called a cart path, though it is hard to imagine how any cart could travel it, since it consisted mostly of stumps, logs, and knee-deep mud and water. The rain having subsided, he had no difficulty finding the headwaters of Wallicut Slough, a small crooked stream meandering through fertile prairie land to join the Columbia River. He reached the river in the late afternoon, and made directly for Point Ellice, across from Astoria.

Point Ellice was an odd place for a winter retreat. It lies at the area of contact in a never-ending battle between river and sea. Twice every twenty-four hours the Pacific Ocean lies supine, accepting, even drawing into itself, the thrust of billions of gallons of river water. Twice a day it rouses to thrust wildly back. The overall result is a never-ending, mindless frenzy of activity in which driftwood, wreckage, and flotsam are hurled back and forth across the bar until thrown ashore by some vagary of current.

Whatever the drawbacks of Point Ellice as a winter resort, grandpa found it ideal for beachcombing. Here was a farrago of logs of every sort—sycamore, ash, cottonwood, fir, spruce, and cedar. Here were entire trees, uprooted. Here was timber already roughly hewn for the mill.

For grandpa, such an enormity of wood made Point Ellice a Canaan, a Land of Promise where he might happily have put down his roots had it not been for the lure in his mind of another Canaan promised by a Siwash chief. Astoria, just across the river, offered him an assured market for his logs, and the enticements of civilization besides. He built himself a reasonably watertight cabin and began trimming driftwood, binding it into rafts of a dozen logs each, which he kedged across to an Astoria mill.

Kedging is a delicate art. The kedger rows a cable-length ahead of his raft (also called a boom); drops anchor; and lets the current swing the raft downstream and forward as far as the cable will allow. He repeats the process until he lands his cargo at the far bank. Hitting any specified spot is tricky. But grandpa took advantage of the tidal shifts with some finesse and was usually able to reach his millyard destination precisely.

After selling his supply of logs, he ordinarily spent a day or two buying supplies and relaxing. For grandpa, relaxing consisted mostly of playing poker.

In the early winter, with a considerable pot at stake, grandpa's full house fell before the four treys of one Isaac A. Clark. Grandpa set out methodically to avenge himself, and I think eventually succeeded; but meanwhile he and Clark struck up an enduring friendship. They were virtual duplicates in age, height, disposition, background, and, especially, in their passion for poker. Both had been apprenticed to tailors. Clark hailed from grandpa's part of Wisconsin; they had acquaintances in common. Their only substantial point of difference lay in religion; Clark was as fervent a Methodist as grandpa was a Baptist.

By the end of the winter, it was understood that Clark would join grandpa in his oystering venture. Meanwhile, however, grandpa continued to haul, trim, and kedge Point Ellice logs, on the theory that the most torrential rainstorm is less wet to the man who knows he has a few gold coins tucked under a stone of his hearth. Grandpa did well that winter; he tucked enough coins under the stone to tide him over the first hard months of oystering.

On the morning of April 11, 1854, the wind being from the northwest and the outlook fair, the two men left Astoria for their rendezvous with Chief Nahcati. They crossed the Columbia to the bar of the Wallicut in a flat-bottomed ship's boat. They worked the boat across the bar by brute strength, pushing, one on either side, ankle-deep at one moment and breast- deep at another. Once in the deeper water past the bar, they were able to row upstream a couple of miles before the slough petered out. They then abandoned the boat and slogged along the cart path to the home of Mrs. Paulding, who again provided hospitality for the night.

But when they continued to the bank of the Bear River next morning, they could find no sign of the canoe that grandpa had cached away so carefully the preceding fall. Grandpa accepted the setback philosophically. "Finders keepers," he shrugged, and Mr. Clark added, a little ambiguously, "What's sauce for the goose is sauce for the gander."

The problem was not serious. An Indian cemetery was located nearby. It was the Siwash custom to compose a decomposing chief in his best canoe, with his choicest possessions, including perhaps his favorite squaw, slain for the purpose, and to invert his second-best canoe over the first as protection against the rain. Grandpa and Mr. Clark checked the various sepulchers for seaworthiness, and finally appropriated a dugout canoe that had been in residence only a few weeks. This meant that the dead chief had been there but a few weeks also; but they arranged him respectfully atop the tenant of another canoe, assuring both Indians company in the Happy Hunting Ground.

Their new canoe had been stove in to let out rainwater. Grandpa patched the hole with alder bark. He and Mr. Clark then scrubbed the inside of the inner hull, to minimize a lingering mephitis, and carried the craft on their shoulders to the riverbank for launching. They proceeded downstream, surrounded by screaming airborne fowl, until the river became a channel of the bay, the tide being near the low. By noon they were past the north end of Long Island, with three-quarters of their journey behind them. At that point, however, the tide began to flood. The rising water brought with it a smoky nor'wester, loaded with rain as opaque as a heavy fog. Even to confirm the general direction in which they were moving proved next to impossible. At first they used a long pole to measure the depth of the water beneath them; as long as they could not touch bottom, they knew they were in the channel. Soon, however, the deepening of the water made that guide useless. They could only guess whether they were angling westward toward the peninsula; pointing north toward the treacherous ocean bar; or erring eastward toward the Willapa and the scarcely more friendly reception to be expected at the hands of the Bruce boys.

Soon, fortunately, they heard thumping off to port. Veering toward the sound, they came ashore at a salt meadow, where Chief Nahcati sat in the rain, patiently beating a spruce knot against a hollow log, each blow evoking a mighty boom. He had caught a glimpse of the Espy-Clark canoe, a glint of light off Long Island, just before the rain blew in, and had been drumming to guide them ever since. 58

They spent the night at Nahcati's lodge, and examined the oyster beds at low tide the next morning. To reach the beds required a hike in gum boots of nearly a mile to the channel, but the slogging was amply repaid. Captain Kidd, had he wakened on an island where the flowers were emeralds, rubies, and diamonds, could not have been more euphoric than grandpa at the sight of acres of oysters, stretching farther to the north and south than the eye could follow. Others might have seen only millions of prickly shellfish, often united in clumps that a boot could kick apart; but grandpa would not have traded these oysters for anything in the world. It would have taken the combined forces of the Hudson's Bay Company and the United States cavalry to tear his boots from their grip on those oyster beds.

Next day, the two men began cutting alders for a ten-by-twelve-foot log cabin, which the Siwashes helped them set up in the meadow where Nahcati had sat in the rain to guide them ashore.

Grandpa and Isaac Clark were to share that cabin for the next four years. The smoke from their chimney seemed to be the signal other drifting white men had been waiting for. Two arrived within days, and others followed. Cabins popped up in the salt meadows overnight, like molehills. Grandpa and Mr. Clark regarded the influx dourly; they were as intent as their rivals across the bay on keeping every possible oyster in their own hands. With Nahcati's assistance, the two proclaimed that all newcomers were there on sufferance, and that Espy-Clark decisions were to be taken as fiat. The newcomers paid little attention, even in the short run. Willy-nilly, grandpa and Clark had fathered a village.

"We'll call it Espyville," said Mr. Clark.

"We'll do nothing of the sort," snorted grandpa, perhaps recalling that a couple of villages called Espy and Espyville back in Pennsylvania never had amounted to much; "we'll call it Oysterville."

Oysterville it remains to this day. But it remains grandpa's village, too.

The Bruce boys initiated hostilities as soon as they observed that oystermen had moved into territory they considered their own. Actually, the Bruce boys' beds and the Espy-Clark beds were in some cases almost contiguous, separated only by the narrow bay channel itself. Before the end of April the Bruce boys, or someone, stove in the bottom of grandpa's canoe. He patched it, and they stove it in again. But grandpa only made another patch; he was a persistent man. Meanwhile, Nahcati's Siwashes were handpicking the very best of their oysters and transporting them to shallow water for safekeeping.

One morning early in May, Nahcati pointed out a spot of light blinking irregularly seven miles to the north. It was a sail, crossing Leadbetter Bar into the bay. Every available canoe was immediately loaded with oysters, and the Espy-Clark party paddled boldly across to Bruceport to wait for the schooner to drop anchor.

The Bruce boys lay in wait with their own fleet of canoes. The crew of the schooner dropped sail and anchor and then lined the rail cheering both sides—"Go it, husband, go it, bear!"—as the opposing armadas maneuvered for position. Two canoes would bump together; a hand reddened by sun or nature would seize the gunwale, and in a moment the opposing crewmen would be scuffling among their ballast of oysters, bear-hugging or skipping back to evade a roundhouse punch. At intervals, the battlers tumbled overside, sometimes alone, sometimes locked in fierce embrace. There was no serious danger, since weapons were tacitly forgone and the water was only waist-deep, but the battle was in deadly earnest. Eyes were blacked, cheeks bruised; hair was pulled; oaths were hurled. The Bruce boys won; eventually all the oysters of the invading force were dumped overboard, and the Oyster-villeans beat a humiliated retreat.

The next day they returned in greater numbers, but were defeated just as expeditiously.

At this point, grandpa had three choices. He could have abandoned his dream of an oyster empire, and returned to logging. He could have struck a bargain with the Bruce boys to serve as their hired man on the peninsula side of the bay. Or he could have continued to fight.

Apparently, neither of the first two possibilities even entered his mind. Instead, he studied the strategic situation, and decided that there was one major hole in the Bruce boys' defenses. They were still using clumsy Indian canoes to gather their oysters for shipment. If he could come up with a handier and roomier vessel, he could defeat the Bruce boys by superior efficiency; he could ready two bushels of prime oysters for shipment in less time than the Bruce boys could ready one.

Clark and the Siwashes continued gathering and culling oysters, while grandpa rowed across Leadbetter Bar to the North Cove beach and tramped along the sand ten miles to Grays Harbor and the Chehalis River. He was in search of Dad Simmons, who was known to run a small sawmill and build boats on the side. He found Simmons in the village of Montesano. Drawing on the gold pieces accumulated during his previous winter of kedging logs, Grandpa arranged for the construction of a clinker-built ship's boat as large as any two of the Bruce boys' canoes put together. (These clinker-built, or lapstruck, boats were made like a clapboard house—that is, each board overlapped the one below it, the whole being locked together by rivets or clinched nails.) Grandpa's first clinker-built boat, twenty-two feet long, could carry twice as many oysters as a canoe of comparable length. He worked with Simmons for two months to complete the vessel, and then hired two Indians to pole it upriver to the ocean. They retraced grandpa's route along the North Cove beach, walking at the water's edge, the clinker boat angling behind them in the breakers at the end of a long line. Each time a breaker receded, drawing the boat seaward, grandpa and the Indians dogtrotted along the beach, keeping the line taut until the next incoming wave pushed the boat shoreward again. These maneuvers sometimes required that the three men wade a hundred yards offshore, surf breaking as high as their throats, never sure their next step might not be into a drowning hole between sandspits.

But they reached Leadbetter Bar. They rowed the clinker boat across, and found themselves surrounded by a score of canoes filled with wellwishers, the Indians as excited as the whites. Here, all agreed, was a weapon to force the Bruce boys into a truce.

The new boat was solemnly christened "*Stuffy.*" For a time it plied the bay unmolested. When schooners arrived for oysters, nobody tried to dump *Stuffy*'s cargo into the water. All was quiet on the oyster front.

One night, however, *Stuffy* disappeared from its mooring, only to reappear a few days later—in the fleet of the Bruce boys. Now grandpa's case was desperate. He could not appeal to the law; there was no law. He could not do physical battle with the Bruce boys; they would simply toss him into the bay. The war councils among grandpa, Nahcati, and Mr. Clark were long and lugubrious. But finally a strategy was devised.

Grandpa let it be known that he was giving up and going back to the felling of trees for pilings. Isaac Clark announced that he, too, would depart at the end of the oyster season. Defeatism darker than the daily rain clouds settled over Oysterville. When the white settlers woke one morning to find grandpa gone, most of them lost little time in going too.

They had fallen for a sham. Grandpa actually was on his way back to Montesano, where with the last of the savings from his Point Ellice beachcombing he arranged for the building of a new clinker boat half again the size of the lamented *Stuffy*. When he returned to Oysterville aboard an oyster boat almost as big as a schooner, even the Bruce boys accepted the fact that grandpa was not going to quit. There ensued a series of conferences between the two sides, and an arrangement was quickly arrived at. The Bruce boys would no longer interfere with grandpa and Clark; grandpa and Clark would not interefere with the Bruce boys; and both parties would work together to prevent any incursion by other oystermen.

But trying to monopolize all the oyster beds on Shoalwater Bay was about as practical as spitting into a January sou'easter. Within weeks rough-looking adventurers in boots, slickers, and sou'westers were converging on the bay; soon they were piling up heaps of oysters as fast as their tongs could scoop the bivalves in.

The first oyster beds were held by squatter's right. Early in the 1850s, Washington having become a legally constituted territory, the territorial legislature decreed that the beds were to be treated as private property, subject to purchase, sale, and, of course, taxation, provided only that the owners did not interfere with water navigation. Thereafter newcomers could no longer even work as hired hands in the oyster beds, much less acquire beds of their own, until they had been residents for at least six months.

The oystermen divided their property into "whacks" of about five acres each, the exact size of a whack depending on the estimated value of the beds. Cull beds, useful for sorting but not for growing oysters, remained common property. Theoretically the whacks were divided by lot, but by some unexplained tropism the best beds tended to converge into the hands of the larger operators — that is, the Bruce boys on the eastern shore, and the Espy-Clark combination at Oysterville.

Mr. Clark's interests soon broadened to include storekeeping and farming. He became the motivating force behind the establishment, four miles south of Oysterville and just east of the ocean dunes, of a Methodist campground, now the village called Ocean Park.

Grandpa stayed with oystering.

Though the Bruce boys continued to prosper, encroaching tides eventually washed Bruceport itself away. The tides gnawed at Oysterville, too. The early homes, general merchandise stores, and bars, built along the shore, were simple frame structures, supported by pilings or floats to raise them above high tides. These precautions were not always successful. In 1866 an unusually high tide carried away eighteen buildings. The bay continued to gnaw until the whole of Front Street was consumed. Grandpa's village, like some primitive, threatened organism, shrank back as the waters advanced.

But it prospered mightily. By 1855, Oysterville was shipping 50,000 baskets of oysters a year to San Francisco. Three years later, the figure was double that.

Oyster heaps, Nahcotta, Washington

4

Sweet Beulah Land

Imagine it is the fall of 1855. You are a passenger aboard a three-masted, hundred-ton schooner that has been clawing its way north from San Francisco for the past two and a half weeks. Your ship is ballasted with fieldstone that eventually will be dumped to make room for oysters forked from the bay you are about to visit. Five miles to the starboard there is a darker strip against the horizon — low land lying, by calculation of the captain, at latitude 46°43′ north, longitude 124°01′ west. You have been told this is a swampy spit twenty-eight miles long, pointing due north from the bay of the Columbia River, which formed it ten thousand years ago by washing sand into the sea.

The day is sunny. Between you and the land there winks and glitters, under the whisk of a brisk northwest wind, a white turmoil of breakers stretching to a shoreline littered with silver driftwood. An eyeglass, courteously provided by the first mate, brings the shore so close you think you could swing an axe and split the logs flung helter-skelter among ridge after ridge of blindingly white dunes, backed by a crest of evergreens.

Your ship edges landward, until it seems about to blunder like a sick whale into the surf. But somehow the breakers make way to let you pass, drawing you across Leadbetter Bar into Shoalwater Bay as gently as a lover draws his bride to the nuptial couch. The roar of surf diminishes to the sound of a heartbeat; you are sailing up an estuary six to eight miles wide and perhaps three times as long. The mouth of the Willapa River lies behind you; to your port smaller streams — the Palix, the Nemah, the Naselle — are received by the bay and receive it in return. Though twice a day the water drains off to nothingness on either side of the channel, the tide is now approaching full, and the wind is steady from the northwest; you can quarter southward without taking soundings. Your wake follows you past one forest-clad island and then another, the second scarcely large enough to hold an acre of spruce. At the head of the bay, you come about and return with a following wind to the mouth of the Willapa, dropping anchor where the *Robert Bruce* burned four years before. To the east, a few hundred feet away, rise sand bluffs, steep but scarcely taller than your masts. They are topped by evergreen trees that you know stretch endlessly inland. Westward, five miles away, is the North Beach peninsula; the first mate's glass enables you to pick out the scattering of cabins that make up the new settlement of Oysterville, huddled at the bay's edge among salt meadows, huckleberry bushes, wild blackberries, and dense stands of spruce and alder trees. If you could take flight, as swans and seagulls are doing all about you, you would see that the peninsula behind the village is scarcely a mile wide, with a central spine no more than fifty feet high. Its western slope descends to swamps and lakes; these in turn press against the great inner dune that marks the beginning of the ocean beach.

You have been looking at grandpa's village.

In the 1850s, the supply of oysters appeared inexhaustible. At low tide, booted whites and Indians transferred them to cull beds for sorting. The oysters in the early fifties were generally carried in canoes or clinker-built boats like grandpa's. Later, it was more common to load them into strings of bateaux. These were hauled by plungers—fast, narrow sloops, the mast set well aft, with a heavy set of sail, and centerboards rather than keels out of deference to the shallowness of the bay.

The amount of water crossing Leadbetter Bar four times a day varies according to the season and the weather, but averages a formidable seven and a half million gallons a second. The difference between the water level at its highest and lowest may be as much as twelve feet, or as little as half that. The extremes are greatest in December, when peak tides overrun the banks by day, and June, when the tides peak at night. More than half the 70,400 acres in the bay is exposed at extreme low tide—an empty space of sand and mud stretching for miles to the nearest dry land. The tide floods faster than a man can walk.

When the tides did not fall far enough to expose even the shallowest beds, the early oystermen used their spare time to paint, caulk, and scrape their boats and repair their gear. Soon they developed tongs. These consisted of two long handles scissoring on an iron pin, with tines at the end that came together like teeth, so that oysters could be gathered even when the water was too deep for hand-picking. The longer the handles, the deeper the oysterman could reach; the taller the oysterman, the longer the tongs he could use. A man named Rhoades stood six and a half feet in his boots; his tongs were sixteen feet long, and he happily retrieved oysters from beds inaccessible to his competitors.

The Olympic, oyster schooner

Some oysters, concealed in jungles of eel grass, had to be located by feel and guess rather than sight. In winter, when only night tides dropped low enough for oystering, the men worked with lanterns. These, weather permitting, were visible from shore, blinking as their light was occluded or revealed by moving oystermen.

Oysterville was scarcely a paradise at first — or later, for that matter. In the summer of 1860, one John Marshall, from Staten Island, New York, found himself stranded in the village. He sharpened his pencil with his jackknife, got the loan of a piece of ruled tablet paper, and wrote home to his wife:

"This is a hard place. No preaching here no Sunday school [and no commas in his sentences]. Oysterville is a strip of land about 200 yards wide and about a mile long. About 25 houses in it. My little woodshed back home is a palace to some of the houses in this place. The best house in this place would cost about 300$ home. The houses are nothing but boards no wall in them."

Six months later, when the rain began to fall in earnest, he found Oysterville no longer just "a hard place"; rather, it was "the hardest country that I ever bin in."

John Marshall escaped from Oysterville as soon as he could scrape up enough money to leave. Andrew Wirt, who arrived in 1858 and lived there for the next sixty-odd years, remembered the early days of the settlement much more kindly. He described it, indeed, as a "metropolis" graced with "two hostels and a population of five hundred," though admittedly somewhat short of married couples and families. It is hard to see how twenty-five houses could have accommodated five hundred people (the National Historical Register states, more conservatively, that ten or fifteen families and a total of about one hundred fifty people were year-round residents in the 1860s), but there was a large "floating" population, and perhaps the hotels were particularly spacious.

I suspect that John Marshall's principal grievance was the incessant rainfall. Yet what is a hundred inches a year? It rains two hundred inches in some parts of the Olympic Peninsula, upstate. That would make even an Oystervillean feel wet, or at least slightly damp. And I have no intention of visiting Mount Waialeale, on the island of Kauai, where the average annual rainfall sometimes exceeds 460 inches.

Not that there is anything inherently disagreeable about rain; it only takes getting used to. I was astonished, on a visit to California fifty years ago, to see seminudes happily semibreasting the waves of the Pacific until a cloud crossed the sun and a momentary mist thickened the air. The swimmers fled shoreward as fast as overhand crawl and flutter kick could carry them, scurried into beach houses, and hastily toweled themselves dry. They loved the water, but dreaded getting wet.

Raw weather, though, is a different matter, and on some winter days in Oysterville I find myself inching pretty close to the fire. Now that I am past my prime I understand better than I used to what Ernest Warner Lilly, a Shoalwater Bay schoolboy, wrote in his diary back in 1884. "It has been a raw, cold day," he complained. "It would snow if it were a country that it snowed enough to know how. The weather has been changing, as it always does excepting when it is too dry or too wet for comfort; then it will keep at it until everyone is tired of it."

He did not make allowance for the fact that the Japanese current warms the region enough to make winters generally mild, with grass in constant growth, roses abloom until Christmas, and daffodils, tulips, and camellias out in full splendor by March. Indeed, Sitka, Alaska, ten degrees north of Oysterville, is warmer on an average winter day than Washington, D.C.

Rawness or no rawness, rain or no rain, some Oysterville winters go by without so much as frost on a windowpane. In my childhood we had no reason to own skates. When the temperature did drop below freezing, we vied with one another to see how far we could slide across the ice-covered puddles. The winner was the boy whose slide continued until the ice broke and dropped him into a foot of water.

Once every five or ten years, however, there are spells of intense cold; then floes form in the bay, drifting back and forth for days as the tide floods and ebbs.

The worst difficulties of Oysterville in winter are the short days, the pervading dampness, and the violence of the tempests. As compensation, the intervals between storms are marked by subtle shifts of color in sky, meadows, and bay, even in the bluffs on the mainland shore. These shifts are soft, tentative, and continuous, as if God were still experimenting to find some perfect hue.

The wet climate, working on an acid and not particularly fertile soil, has determined the nature of both plant and animal life on the peninsula. The deciduous trees are largely alder, maple, or poplar; the evergreens include hemlock, spruce, pine, cedar, and fir, rising from all but impenetrable undergrowth.

This, then, was the Beulah Land settled by grandfather Espy and Ike Clark in the spring of 1854. After four years, Clark married Lucy Briscoe, daughter of Judge and Mrs. John Briscoe, one of the first white couples in the area. The bride and groom built the first frame house on the bay, measuring a commodious sixteen by twenty-four feet. Unfortunately, it soon burned down.

Grandpa continued living in the original cabin. It was not a bad life. He was out working most of the time. The winter nights were long, to be sure; in the winter he needed a whale-oil candle to read by at three o'clock in the afternoon. In the summer, however, he could still study his Testament and his Shakespeare by daylight at ten o'clock in the evening. And he could usually contrive a poker game if he grew restless of an evening.

He planted a vegetable garden, but that was only by way of propitiating his farming forebears. Most of his food was the bounty of woods, water, and air.

His supply of wild vegetables began in January with raw cow parsnip and wild celery, and proceeded to boiled yellow dock, flavored with sugar and molasses. By late winter he could boil skunk cabbage, which he claimed was tasty, though there is no indication that he ever ate it after his marriage. In the spring he ate wild raspberry stalks, their centers as crisp and tender as cucumbers. In June he picked watery-sweet salmonberries, so called not for their yellow color but because they ripened just as the salmon were beginning to swarm.

The salmonberries were followed in turn by a yamlike root; tiny wild strawberries; a cattail flag, said to be savory with a touch of vinegar; and a species of rush the size of a walnut, growing like potatoes in the sand near the ocean beach. In September and October, the squaws brought him cammas roots, which look like an onion and taste, when steamed until soft and sweet, much like a sweet potato. Baked, cammas is reportedly as delicious as fried bananas; I confess I have never tried it.

Autumn also brought bearberries, currants, blackberries, gooseberries, huckleberries, salal, cranberries, wild crab apple—the fruit smaller than a cherry, coming in clusters of between six and ten—and, finally, shotberries, so perdurable that they sometimes clung to their bushes right into the next growing season despite the pounding of winter rains.

Seafood and meat supplemented the vegetables. The ocean sinks swarmed with Dungeness crabs. The hard sand, exposed at low tide, held an infinite number of slender razor clams, which hinted their presence by the slightest of indentations in the surface above them. Their shells were thin, translucent, the color of amber. One had to dig them fast; once alarmed, they would burrow faster than hand or spade could follow.

The mud flats of the bay concealed torpid mud clams. There were quauhaugs, too, a larger variety living so near the surface that a fast tidal runoff sometimes uncovered them; and there were the still larger smetar that dwelt a foot below the surface and yet managed to extend their snouts to feed.

Fish, from the majestic sturgeon to the sociable herring, passed Oysterville endlessly in their cyclical journeys. In May, salmon began to cross the bar, pausing in Shoalwater Bay to adjust to the change in the temperature and salinity of the water before continuing up the Naselle or Nemah rivers to spawn and die.

There is some evidence that the territory of Washington fell under the American rather than the British flag at least partly because American salmon would not snap at flies. When Americans were shouting "54–40 or fight!" in 1845, Prime Minister Robert Peel sent a frigate to Oregon to assess the situation. In his spare time, Lieutenant William Peel, son of the prime minister, cast hopefully for salmon, which refused to rise. Obviously, a country where salmon will not take a fly is no place for a gentleman. William wrote his father, "This country is not worth a damn!" At least, in Sir Robert's estimation, it was not worth a war. The British relinquished all claim to the area north of the Columbia River.

The Oysterville woods abounded in black bears, wolves, lynx, panthers, elk, deer, and antelope, not to mention rabbits, raccoons, foxes, skunks, squirrels, chipmunks, minks, and martens. Otter and beaver sported in the streams. And all were edible.

The peninsula was infested with fleas, mosquitoes, and tiny gnats called no-see-'ems. Birds hopped through the meadows, swam in the ponds, flew through the air. If the sky darkened, one might look up to find the sun blacked out by clouds of them. There were brant, Canada geese, white geese, ducks of every sort (mallard, canvasback, teal, red-head, gray, butterball); snipe, alternately gleaming and glooming as they wheeled; swans, some black, some white; cormorants, stork, sheldrake, curlew, loon; gulls, wheeling and screaming above a decaying fish. In the woods and meadows there were pigeon, pheasant, quail, woodpeckers; robins, too, hopping about after worms; barn swallows, goldfinches.

Grandpa lived happily off of whatever came along. I do not believe, however, that he ever ate crows. In this respect he was more discriminating than a local captain who was famous for cooking everything that ever lived, including young eagles, hawks, owls, lynx, beaver, seal, otter, gulls, pelican, and, finally—for Christmas dinner, of all things—two crows. As reported by James G. Swan:

They were very ancient, entirely devoid of fat, and altogether presented to my mind a sorry picture of a feast. But the captain was delighted. "I will make a sea-pie of them," said he, "and then you can judge what crow-meat is." The birds were cleaned and cut up, and a fine sea-pie made with dumplings, salt pork, potatoes, and a couple of onions. And precisely at meridian on Christmas day (for the old captain liked to keep up seahours), the contents of the iron pot were emptied into a tin pan, and set before us smoking hot.

I tried my best to eat crow, but it was too tough for me. "How do you like it?" said the old man, as, with a desperate effort, he wrenched off a mouth-full from a leg. "I am like the man," said I, "who was once placed in the same position: 'I ken eat crow, but hang me if I *hanker* arter it.'" "Well," says the captain, "it *is* somewhat hard; but try some of the soup and dumplings, and don't condemn crow-meat from this trial, for you shot the grandfather and grandmother of the flock: no wonder they are tough; shoot a young one next time." "No more crow-meat for me, thank you," said I. So I finished my Christmas dinner on dumplings and potatoes.*

This same captain once tried to bake a skunk, but, not having properly cleaned it, it smelt so unsavory when the bake-kettle was opened

Swan, pp. 325–26.

that he was forced to throw skunk and kettle into the river, which he did
with a sigh, remarking what a pity it was that it smelled so strong, when
it was baked so nice and brown.

*Clamming in the old days
Oysterville, Washington*

This Man Came Out on a Beef

In 1853, when grandpa first gazed on Shoalwater Bay, there were barely a hundred fifty whites in all the thousand square miles of peninsula, salt water, and mainland wilderness that made up Pacific County. They lived in tents, rickety cabins, or lodges vacated by wandering Indians. A few, deep in the mainland forests, or scattered about the fertile isthmus between the bay and the Columbia, dug for potatoes instead of clams. But the oystermen and trappers saw no sense in such drudgery; when the tide was out, they said with reason, the table was set.

Communication between the coast and the interior was so difficult that no one tried it except from necessity, which caused some head scratching when the time came for the first territorial legislature to convene in January 1854. Only sixty-one Pacific County whites had paid the toll that made them eligible for office. But the worst difficulty was not finding a man to elect; it was finding a way to traverse the hundred miles inland to Olympia, the territorial capital.

Five successive delegates were required to keep the area represented at the initial session.

"Joel Brown," papa told me, "was the first nominee, and since no one offered against him, he was considered elected. He was living then on the Palix, about where father had logged the preceding year. Joel thought he'd better figure out a route from the Palix to the capital. Well, he tramped, and he canoed, and he fell through hollow hills of blackberry bushes, and he ran out of shot, and he smashed his leg between two floating logs, and he wore himself to such a frazzle that he came stumbling back to his cabin and fell on his bunk and died.

"So then the settlers voted in Jehu Scudder from Long Beach. Jehu tried to map the Indian trails to Olympia, but somewhere along the way the whole thing got too much for him, and he died too, and the Indians brought his body back to Long Beach, and there he lies in the Lone Fir Cemetery to this day.

"The next man who agreed to try was Henry Fiester. He took another route, generally following the Cowlitz River, and did reach Olympia. On the evening after his swearing in, he was sitting in a saloon, having a nip to restore his strength, when he fell off his chair and was dead before he hit the floor. The newspaper said next day he had been called from time to eternity by a stroke of apoplexy, but everyone knew the trip to Olympia killed him."

Another possible cause of Representative Fiester's demise may be inferred from an Olympia housewife's letter of the next day to her family in the East:

"Last evening we saw a torchlight procession go past on the street from the Capitol. I suppose the Legislature was out and the poor men were so glad of it, for some were hurrahing, and some were swearing, etc. I understand that they went as far as Mr. Durgon's saloon, where they got to throwing chairs, etc., at each other and had a good time generally."

The fourth representative, James Clark Strong, did not die. The legislature split his district between Pacific and Wahkiakum counties, necessitating a new election, and he was not voted back; I do not know whether he even ran.

The fifth representative, John Briscoe, completed the term handily—after all, there was not much of it left—and went on to serve in public life for many years.

Grandpa, one of the only two Republicans in the county, prudently stayed out of politics, but not because he was reluctant to travel. As county sheriff in 1855, he cheerfully hunted down transgressors in scores of isolated settlements, moving about by canoe, horse, and shank's mare. There was no jail to confine prisoners. Grandpa for several weeks boarded a man awaiting trial for murder. They took turns with the cooking and dishwashing, and spent the evenings playing two-handed stud. I do not know who the man was, or whether he was convicted, and if he was, whether grandpa officiated at his hanging; the records show no execution.

Grandpa resigned as sheriff because the county would not pay him the price of a badge. A sheriff in a neighboring county had hammered his badge from a silver dollar, but grandpa refused to demean himself so.

He got about extensively again in 1860, when as census taker of Pacific and Wahkiakum counties he covered every beach shack and wilderness farm in an area of more than twelve hundred square miles.

Oysterville rapidly became a trading center and junction point. It was a convenient stopping-off place between San Francisco and Puget Sound. Even in a dead calm, brigs, barks, and schooners, their sails loosely furled, could drift in and out of the bay according to the flood or ebb of the tide. The overall expanse was shoal, but the central channel was of a respectable depth; lumber schooners drawing eighteen feet could sail up the Willapa River to take on logs.

On the second Monday in May 1855, Pacific County decided at a special election to remove the county seat from Chinook, a fishing village on the north bank of the Columbia River, to Oysterville. On June 4, at seven in the morning, the county officials convened at Oysterville for the first time, in the dining room of the Stevens Hotel. Having no official quarters, they kept the county records in their hats. In 1868, however, Andrew Wirt moved from his cabin to a new, larger home, and sold the cabin to the county for a courthouse, the sales price being $200. It was a single-story frame building measuring thirty-three by twenty-two feet, with a covered front porch, separated from the bay by two hundred yards of salt grass. It remained a courthouse for six years, and then was acquired by the Espys; only a year ago I added a fireplace and some bookshelves, and I am sitting in that old building at this moment, trying to keep my eyes off the bay long enough to do my stint of typing.

In 1874 a larger courthouse was erected for the county. In addition to the courtroom upstairs, it had two rooms on the main floor for offices. 74

Close at hand stood a one-story jail built of two-by-six planks spiked back to back. Steel sheeting lined the single cell, and a stove, frying pan, coffeepot, and dishes were provided for the convenience of the prisoners. The court clerks, alone among Oystervilleans, wore hard-boiled shirts. A laundress delivered these weekly—white, starched, and ironed—for twenty-five cents per shirt.

As county seat, shopping center, and stopping-off place, Oysterville attracted visitors in numbers out of all proportion to its permanent population, which could never have exceeded the five hundred estimated by Mr. Wirt when he first settled there. Some visitors arrived by sailboat, venturing as close to shore as the tide permitted. They were helped overside into a flat-bottomed dinghy and were rowed inshore until the boat grounded. If the tide was high, the oarsman carried female passengers one by one to the narrow sand beach. If the tide was lower, he carried them to the edge of the mud flats, and set them down there to make their way to land as best they could.

Small boys never forgot the first time they were dropped, with their best shoes on, into three or four inches of bay mud. They were given a slap on the rear, and sent toward the beach, while mud clams, like miniature fireboats, squirted tiny welcoming fountains all about them.

A boardwalk five feet wide ran alongside the main street of the town; the man who stepped amiss because of darkness or drunkenness would find himself either floundering in a mud puddle, bogged down in a sand hole, or spraddled across one of the cows, horses, or pigs that used the streets as hostels. Single planks served as sidewalks on the side streets.

In my boyhood I found in the northwest corner of our library, on the lowermost shelf, a mouldering and yellowing set of twenty paperback volumes called *Revised Encyclopaedia Britannica, Adapted from the Ninth Edition, 1891, for the use of American Readers.*

Vol. XIX *(Val–Zym)* caught my attention because it sheltered between pages 6266 and 6267 a foldout map, in colors that had faded to soothing pastels, of Washington, then in its second year as a full-fledged State of the Union. The name

OYSTERVILLE

plowed across the ocean on that map like a frigate under full sail. By contrast, SEATTLE was printed in such trifling type as to be illegible without a magnifying glass.

The editors of that *Encyclopaedia* considered Oysterville a name to reckon with, and they were right.

The birth of Oysterville simplified access to Olympia, at least from the peninsula. A traveler could start at the mouth of the Columbia, walk or ride twenty miles north along the ocean beach (called the "weather beach"), and cross the peninsula to Oysterville on the bay side. He could sail thence across Leadbetter Bar, and tramp the North Cove beach another dozen miles, as grandpa had done in 1854, to the village of Westport, whence reasonably well established trails led east to the capital.

At first, mail was carried to Oysterville from Ilwaco, at the mouth of the Columbia River, once a week by a man on horseback, but by 1855 there was scheduled stagecoach-steamboat service between Olympia and Ilwaco. Stages and freight wagons braved the dunes, as boats did the tides. The *Washington Standard* of Olympia was able to advertise that anyone wishing to see the west part of Washington Territory need only "jump into the wagon which leaves Olympia every Monday morning, carrying the U.S. Mail and Wells, Fargo & Co.'s express, touching at Montesano, Hoquiam and Chehalis point, connecting with the line running via Shoalwater bay to Oysterville and Astoria. Returning, leaves Astoria every Tuesday a.m., and arrives at Olympia by 6 o'clock on Saturday evening."

The stage schedule between Oysterville and Ilwaco varied according to the hours of the tide. The driver sat on a high exposed seat in front; the enclosed center section held mail sacks and seats for five passengers, but occasionally the stage held as many as twenty, extras clinging to the outside. Eight or ten sacks of oysters could be tied on behind. The driver was exposed to salt spray, constant wind, and the vagaries of the elements. Four to eight horses drew the stage, with as many more for the accompanying freight wagon. The mile-long trip along the rutted sand road from Oysterville to the ocean beach was easy for any passenger who hung on tight and did not mind tooth-rattling bumps. To climb the inner dune, however, was a challenge. The dune consisted of soft white sand piled thirty feet high. Four horses were not enough to haul a wagon over

Stage from Ilwaco
to Oysterville · 1875

that obstacle. The driver of the freighter and the passenger stage had to take turns adding each other's team to their own. First the passengers dismounted from the stage and slogged up the dune, shin-deep. Then the four freight horses were joined to the four pulling the stage. Once the process had been repeated for the freighter, the horses returned to their normal roles; the passengers climbed back into the stage; and the two vehicles picked their way through the soft sand, among a litter of logs, roots, and timber, down to the wet sand exposed by the retreating tide. The sand was as solid along the water-line as granite; the wagons zigzagged as fast as their horses could take them, sometimes in and sometimes out of the surf, dodging driftwood and the hulls of wrecked vessels. "Besides handling the ribbons," said an early driver,[*] "a man had to be a first-class navigator. Many a time I have had a big swell lift horses and wagon and toss the whole shooting match up and around like a toy."

A graded road ran from the head of the peninsula to Baker's Bay—really part of the Columbia. The Astoria-bound steamer waited while the stage backed axle-deep into the bay and transferred its passengers by rowboat to the steamer.

Early explorers around the Columbia River bar were puzzled to find remnants of oriental junks, nearly a hundred of them, littered there. These had apparently lost control and drifted east on the Japanese current. They have been cited to explain the oriental features of some Pacific Indians.

---

[*]Raymond J. Feagans, *The Railroad That Ran by the Tides*. Berkeley: Howell-North Books, 1972.

The whites promptly began adding wrecks of their own. Counting only vessels of at least twenty-five tons, more than a hundred and fifty ships ranging downward from more than 5,000 tons burthen were lost in this graveyard of the Pacific between 1800 and 1950—an average of one a year. Many vanished with all hands. Even today it is advisable after a particularly heavy storm to walk cautiously around any bump in the sand at high water mark, lest it conceal a bloated corpse.

Prior to the establishment of regular Coast Guard stations in the 1860s, the citizenry around the mouth of the Columbia trained stallions to swim through the breakers to rescue the crews of wrecked ships. A sailor would catch the stallion's tail; a second sailor would hold to the first; and so as many as six survivors at a time might be towed ashore.

Vessels could not be sure of their safety even after they had managed to cross the bar into the river itself. In the sixties a French ship had to feel her way upstream in a pea-soup fog. The sole English-speaking crewman was sent ahead in a small boat as guide. "Where are we?" he called repeatedly into the surrounding grayness. Finally a voice, perhaps that of some woodchopper, came bellowing from the fog: "Wah-kiakum!" This word being meaningless to the crewman, he kept rowing, calling the same question until another answer came back: "Skamoka-wa!" Still unenlightened, the guide forged forward until his hail was answered by one last disembodied voice: "Cathlamet!" He returned to his captain to report: "Nobody in this country speaks English."

Though wrecks were a regular feature of Oysterville winters, Oystervilleans considered themselves not sailors but farmers; their crop simply happened to be oysters instead of apples or cucumbers. A typical Oysterville farmer was F. C. Davis, who in addition to running oyster beds and a truck farm also was a tanner, and served at need as a customs officer. Mr. Davis was a man of some educational attainments, and his wife introduced the first piano to Oysterville. But his most important

possessions were his two lean, red oxen, Moses and Aaron by name, as gentle as kittens, and broken for riding. He considered them so upright of character that he would not use them to haul whiskey barrels ashore from trading vessels, saying he would not humiliate his noble beasts by associating them with such vile stuff. In his dotage he walked the beaches and marshes calling for his beloved oxen even when he had just locked them safely in the barn.

One day a schooner from foreign parts anchored in the channel of Shoalwater Bay. Mr. Davis waited for the tide to drop, rode Moses to the boat, and left him while he conducted his business aboard. The skipper reported to his owners: "I have been in ports all over the world, and the customs officers have come out in whale boats, canoes, and catamarans. But this man came out on a beef—and tied him to the anchor chain!"

6

Lo the Poor Siwash

The Siwashes were lighter skinned than some Indians – robust, with fine symmetrical forms. Their black hair was parted on top of the head, the men's loose, the squaws in a queue, and the maidens' in braids, decorated with ribbons or twine.

Early white settlers found the first priority of Indian braves in the matter of dress to be an apron over the genitals; the second, a shirt, and, if the weather was cold, a blanket or deerskin robe. The squaws favored skirts made from the inner bark of young cedar, beaten with a stick until nothing remained but the sinews. These were attached to a leather string belt, the cedar ends hanging in a thick fringe to the knees.

The Indians were quick to adopt the attire of the immigrant whites – not only shirts, trousers, and boots, but, for special occasions, business suits, including tail coats. Squaws learned to sew form-fitting calico dresses. This apparel, however, was merely for decoration; when the Indians set about hunting, fishing, and harvesting, they resumed more practical attire. Thus, though they affected boots, shoes, and socks indoors, they stripped to their bare feet when they emerged to hunt, forage, or travel in their great canoes.

In the early 1800s, a chief (or tyee) like Nahcati was presumed to be of royal blood. He was set off from common folk by the flatness of his head, brought about by pressing a board on it while his skull was still malleable in infancy. The result was a head wider than it was long, so that if a tyee wished to show off by wearing a felt hat, he had to put the hat on sidewise. By grandpa's time the status of a tyee had begun to diminish; he was reduced from prince to gentleman, or boss. Indeed, a tyee might be anyone who could afford to buy a slave from the more warlike tribes to the north, or an especially promising papoose from one of his own less prosperous relatives. Purchased papooses were raised as social equals of the tyee's own children; but being fostered rather than adopted, they had no claim to his estate.

Not all the Oysterville pioneers shared grandpa's trust of the Siwashes. The wife of Captain A. T. Stream, an early settler, recalled the chief preceding Nahcati as "hostile to the whites," one who welcomed "runners from other tribes trying to arrange a plan whereby all the Indians on the coast would make war at the same time and massacre the whites." Nahcati, she admitted, was a smart man "who did not dissipate and tried to keep peace." But at his death the rule went to his son Ilwaco:

". . . very different from his father, cruel to his slaves and mistrusted by both Indians and whites. I knew him to sell a slave girl to a chief of another tribe living far away. They took her by force into a canoe to carry her away. When her three-year-old baby ran screaming to go along, Ilwaco whipped the child all the way back to his hut. In those days, when a tyee died it was the custom to shoot a slave and bury the body beside the dead chief so he would have a servant in the happy hunting grounds. It was not long after the slave Dolly went with the stranger chief that his son died, and Dolly was shot and buried at his side.

"After Ilwaco came Chief Chenamus, the greatest friend the whites of this area ever had among the Indians. Well do I remember him stealing to my door in the middle of the night, one night when the Indians from all over the Washington coast, six hundred in all, with four different Chiefs among them, had gathered for a Potlatch and dance. Dear old Chenamus wanted someone to help him stop the men who were selling the Indians whiskey. He said 'Cultus (worthless) white man give whiskey make Indians salux (mad),' and he could not keep peace. Well, a few cultus white men were escorted to a boat and allowed to depart with instructions not to return.

"The whites did not long have their noble Chenamus to stand between them & danger. He was attending a gathering of his tribe near where now stands the town of Chinook, when a cowardly white man, saying 'I want to kill an Indian,' slipped up behind him in the shadows of the campfire & shot him dead. This dastardly deed shocked the community, and no one could see the end, as the cowardly fiend, Dixon by name, ran to the whites for protection behind us women. The Indians demanded the man, & threatened to kill all the settlers if they did not give him up, which they were forced to do.

"The Indians took him, bound him hand and foot, laid him on his back near their beloved chief's body, put a pole across his throat and an Indian got on each end and jumped up & down until he was choked to death . . ."

The Siwashes regarded with equal favor the sweet flesh of quail or pheasant and the fishy meat of such birds as gulls, cormorants, pelicans, and loons. A favorite way of preparing either sort was to build a large fire; pile stones on it; let the fire subside to ashes; lay fern leaves on the hot stones; arrange the birds, disembowelled but still feathered, on the ferns; douse them in buckets of water; cover the steaming pile with mats and blankets; heap sand over the whole; allow a half hour for steaming; take out the birds; strip them of feathers and skin with one quick movement; and settle down to a hearty meal.

If the Indians brought more oysters back to the lodge than they could eat, they dried the leftover oysters for later consumption or strung them together for use as currency.

The Indians were fond also of the flesh of porpoises and seals, while the blubber of the whales that frequently stranded on the ocean beach was as delightful a treat to them as a horehound stick was to me two-thirds of a century later.

Some Indian canoes were high-nosed monsters as much as forty feet long, with four paddles or more to a side. A canoe often contained a score or more of Indians, plus their dogs, who were generally barking. The paddling proceeded by fits and starts. After a burst of furious activity, someone might start telling a story; all paddling would cease, and the canoe would drift until the story was finished. In the event of a breeze, a blanket would be raised as a sail; the entire party thenceforth could devote its time to sleeping or storytelling, with the exception of one steersman charged with making sure the canoe got where it was going.

The squaws were expected to gather edible berries and roots. They also made mats from rushes, and baskets from spruce knots or bark and grass. The Siwashes were nomads, going wherever the plants were ripe and the fish were abundant.

Wicked Indians existed at the outset. There are authentic reports that when white men shot at this immoral type, the Indians shot back. Some even cheated, or lied. At the start of the nineteenth century, Shoalwater Bay Indians sometimes slit the throats of disagreeable visitors, in a gently monitorial way; but by the 1850s they had learned that this was a losing proposition, since the death of one white man seemed always to result in the death of ten Indians.

As recently as 1800, there were about a thousand Indians in the bay area. This estimate may be exaggerated, particularly as their constant peregrinations made their exact numbers hard to estimate. In any event, by the middle of the nineteenth century only a few dozen families remained. Smallpox and measles speeded the rapid decline of the Indian pop⸻tion.

Perh⸻ ⸻elped do them in. One early white visitor, walking into an In⸻ ⸻rted being instantly covered with swarms of fleas so bi⸻ ⸻ned like flaxseed. In m⸻ ⸻n childhood, our

hou⸻ ⸻my father's r⸻ ⸻ediction, as he

kissed each of us children on the cheek at night before blowing out the light, was, "Good night, sleep tight, don't let the fleas bite, and sweet dreams." And they *did* bite; I would wake in the morning covered with red spots, inflamed by my automatic scratching.

Whatever the cause, between 1800 and 1850 the great bulk of the Indian population around Shoalwater Bay perished.

The pioneer whites in the early 1800s were as good-hearted as your next-door neighbor today, and they doubtless felt a twinge or two as the redskins vanished. Indeed, suggestions for ways to protect the Siwashes became more numerous than the Siwashes themselves. The trouble was that nobody took the suggestions very seriously, perhaps not even the people who made them. In 1866, however, W. H. Waterman, superintendent of Indian affairs for Washington Territory, forwarded to President Andrew Johnson this letter from one Giles Ford:

"These Indians, said to consist of some 20 or 40 families, have always lived upon the Beach and subsisted upon fish, clams, oysters, and sea animals. They are unwilling to abandon their former habits of life and turn their attention to agriculture. They desire a place upon the shore where they can fix their homes, without being supplanted and driven off by white men. This tract which they have selected is a sand beach yielding some grass for the pasturage of their horses but of little value for cultivation, and it is my judgment that reserving it for the use of the Indians would work no injury to white men but would have a tendency to promote peace between them and the Indians and would secure the contentment and well being of the latter."

President Andrew Johnson promptly set apart a reservation at Tokeland, across the ocean bar from the peninsula. But it was too late.

When I was a boy in the first quarter of the twentieth century, there were scarcely half a dozen unadulterated Indians left around Oysterville. It would be both boastful and untruthful of me to lay claim to any part of their blood. Still, the Siwashes left their mark on me. My laziness must reflect theirs; I can trace it to no immediate forebear of my own. Though I blame Grandpa Espy for my tendency to grunt instead of speaking, he shared that atrocious habit with the Indians. And it must be they who got me into the habit of lolling around my living room unclothed. In one way or another the Siwashes—branches of the Chehalis and Chinook tribes—are built into me.

Take, to start with, their language, a variety of the Chinook trading jargon. I still use a number of Chinook words automatically, forgetting that they are not English. Skookum, meaning first rate, is one such. I once absentmindedly called my dinner by its Chinook name, muckamuck, confusing the cook. I still require an effort of will not to say potlatch for gift.

Skookum *is* nearly English, at least in the state of Washington. The word Siwash itself is a corruption of French *sauvage*. The Chinook jargon was a verbal pot-au-feu to which every passing trader contributed. 84

The early French trappers left behind them—to name a few—such dollops as laboose, labootai, lahash, lalang, lapool, lapoosheet, lashase, latab, latate, lecoo, leloo, leseezo, lesook. These were corruptions of la bouche, la bouteille, la hache, la langue, la poule, la fourchette, la chaise, la table, la tête, le cou, le loup, les ciseaux, le sucre. English entries included bed, boat, dolla, house, lazy, man, mamma, papa, nose, moon, pusspuss, salt, seed, shoes, smoke, spose (suppose). The Siwashes called Americans Bostons; Englishmen, King Georges. Because of a difficulty in pronouncing f's and medial r's, fish, coffee, and fire became pish, kaupee, and pia; dry, grease, rope, and rum came out dly, gleese, lope, and lum. A handkerchief was a hakachum, a Negro a nigga, an old man an oleman. A crazy person was a pelton, because a demented white named Pelton spent the winter of 1811 in Astoria. There was irony to calling a doctor a keelally, pronounced keel-all-ee. Siah, meaning far off, was an adaptable word; to increase the distance one simply lengthened the second syllable to suit: a one-syllable siah, say, for an interval of a hundred yards; sia-ah for half a mile; sia-a-a-a-ah for ten miles. Totoosh, admirably evocative for breasts, has never caught on in English. Onomatopeia was common in Chinook; heehee, kahkah, kwehkweh, tiktik, and tintin, stood respectively, as scarcely needs saying, for fun (or joke); crow; duck; watch; and bell.

In church next Sunday you might try reciting the Lord's prayer in Chinook. It goes this way:

Nesika Papa klaxta mitlite kopa Sahalee, kloshe kopa nesika tumtum mika nem. Nesika hiuy tikeh chahco mika illahee; Namook mika kloshe tumtum kopa okoke illahee kahkwa kopa Shalee. Potlatch konoway sun nesika muckamuck; pee Mahlee konaway nesika mesahchee, kahkwa nesika mamook, mesahchee kopa nesika. Wake nolo nesika kopa peshak, pee marsh siah kopa nesika konaway mesahchee. Closhe Kahkwa.

Grandpa Espy considered the Siwashes reliable mentors, allies, and friends. He and Chief Nahcati remained comrades as well as business associates until the chief's death in 1864.

I am much less clear about grandpa's relations with the Siwash maidens. If he were leaning over my shoulder right now I could expect a clout on the ear for even mentioning the subject.

It seems unreasonable to assume that, in all those bachelor years at Oysterville, his loins never stirred. But nobody dared refer to the problem or ask how he handled it.

Aunt Dora did once bring up the subject—not to grandpa, you may be sure, but to me, then a boy of thirteen. We were sitting on a blanket in a meadow at the annual Pioneer Picnic. As we were working our way through cold fried chicken, cole slaw, potato salad, and hot coffee, a file of round-shouldered Siwashes, wearing faded cotton shirts and patched overalls, emerged single file from a fortress of gorse at the bottom of the field and shambled into a comparable fortress of evergreen blackberry bushes a hundred yards across the way. Aunt Dora asked through a chicken bone:

"Did you notice the old man at the head of the line?"

I shook my head.

"You should have. He's the chief."

I was not impressed.

"What's more, he is your uncle."

There is no need to repeat his name here. The assertion was thought-provoking, but I found it suspect. Aunt Dora had lived around Indians since the day of her birth in 1872, and they had taught her to draw a long bow.

Still, I did check her claim later with Cecil, indubitably my uncle. Perhaps I should have pondered the implications of his reply more seriously. He did not say, as might have been expected, "Ridiculous!" He only said, "I wasn't there."

A warm soft body to snuggle against must have had attractions for grandpa. Certainly the Oysterville weather in the 1850s was as raw, and the bed coverings as clammy, as they are today. While I have no proof that grandpa rejected cohabitation between whites and Indians, I do know that he objected to wedding sacraments between them. His views paralleled those of an aged squaw he went to comfort after the death of her seventh husband. "With all those marriages, how did you never happen to marry a white man, Mary?" he asked as he was leaving. "Only bad Indian marry white man," she replied; "only bad white man marry Indian. Children all bad."

Grandpa not only liked Siwashes, he may even have preferred them to whites. In the few stories he told about early days in the territory, his sympathies clearly lay with the Indians. One such story was relayed to me by papa one evening as he milked old Rose, the forebear of most of our herd of cows. Papa's account went as follows:

"In Thurston County, during the uprisings of the fifties, most whites took refuge inside a stockade. But four boys your age [I was ten then] considered the stockade more prison than protection, and decided to go personally on the warpath against the Indians. They slipped away from the stockade, and hid beside an Indian trail. Their weapons were man-vine pods, about the shape and size of a baseball, which exploded on impact in a puff of blinding smoke. The expedition was no doubt designed as a fantasy affair, to supply material for boasting when they got back inside the stockade; but all at once thirty hostiles in full war paint actually came riding past. Leschi himself, a famed rebel chief, was in the lead. It was time for prudent boys to drop dreams of glory and fade back into the underbrush; but one of the four, John Metcalf, could not resist a farewell overhand pitch. The pod hit Leschi's horse, blinding it for the moment, and half blinding the chief. His braves were thrown into consternation. No one had seen where the pod had come from; for an instant some of those Indians could have been chased home by a castrated cat. 86

"But not Leschi. As soon as his eyes stopped watering, he pointed sternly toward the huckleberry bushes behind which the terrified boys were crouched, and in an instant thirty Indian rifles were aimed at the spot. The boys had no choice but to reveal themselves; they stood up; but not a one raised his hands over his head. After a frozen moment, the chief laughed heartily, said something in Chinook, and waved his men on.

"Those boys must have been brave little fellows; but father always seemed to feel that the hero of the story was Chief Leschi."

Papa loved to tell stories, and often at odd times. The first time he told me the story of how his father came to be called Major, for instance, he had just finished stripping Rose and was pouring her milk from his bucket into a ten-gallon can.

In the 1850s, reports of Indian uprisings sent spasms of apprehension through Washington Territory. Forts rose in the forests almost as fast as high-rise apartments shoot up today in Manhattan. Even Oysterville, perhaps more to be in fashion than through true worry, organized a militia. Grandpa was elected commander, with the rank of Major.

Finding that the available ordnance was limited to a dozen dubious jager rifles and a few shotguns, grandpa dispatched an urgent plea back east for modern weapons. He also ordered his men to construct a fort north of the village. It did not occur to anyone to set up a picket stockade around the fort, and for the next few weeks, the Siwashes spent much of their time at the edge of the clearing, exchanging ribald comments among themselves while the white men sweated; though for hard cash the reds did occasionally lend a hand with the fitting of one log to another.

By the time the walls were in place, it was generally agreed that the Siwashes had never represented a danger. Besides, an exceptionally good run of oyster tides was due, and not to utilize them would have been criminal negligence. So the militiamen never got around to putting a roof on the fort. Instead, they returned to their oystering.

A few months later, the weapons grandpa had ordered—rifles as good as most fired later in the Civil War—reached Oysterville. The settlers, having enough guns already for their hunting needs, sold the government issue to the Indians.

And that, said papa, patting Rose's haunch, is how grandpa became a Major.

It might be argued that grandpa's fondness for Indians reflected a guilt complex that had been growing in the family for generations. The number of Indians slaughtered by his forebears would have been enough to set up a whole new tribe.

Mama occasionally baited papa with this fact of history. He argued in return that her ancestors had more scalplocks at their belts than his. He had an initial advantage in this argument; most of her people had crossed the Atlantic prior to 1640, which gave them a head start of nearly a hundred years. Besides, they kept better records, so that he could prove against her by the printed word what she could only charge against him through tradition. In all her family accounts, he pointed out, he had found only two examples of whites meeting Indians in friendship. The first of these meetings took place in 1630, when Indians kept one Henry Wolcott from starvation by trading him a bass for a biscuit cake; the second occurred in 1639, when John Parmelee bought land from a squaw. "You won't deny," said papa, "that both Wolcott and Parmelee were your nine-times-great-grandfathers; and I haven't a doubt in the world that on both occasions they cheated the Indians right out of their moccasins. In King Philip's war alone, in 1675, four of your goodness-knows-how-many-times-great-grandfathers that I know of were running around killing Indians—or being killed. Isaac Cummings and Robert Parris both came home with collections of scalps. John Wilson died of an Indian tomahawk. John French caught an arrow in his hip and petitioned the town fathers of Billerica for relief as a 'poor wounded man.' And you have the nerve to call *my* ancestors Indian killers!"

Mama smiled sweetly. "But my people *had* to kill Indians," she said. "Yours did it for fun. Remember, Alexander Hamilton was *your* great-great-grandfather, not mine."

"I admit that Captain Hamilton killed his share of Indians," said papa. "But only to keep from getting killed himself. He was just another poor cuss of a Scotch-Irishman trying to clear a farm in the Pennsylvania woods. Don't talk to me about Alexander Hamilton. Anyhow, even if you leave your New England line out of the picture altogether, think of how many Indians the Virginia side killed!"

"I'd like to see you prove to me," said mama, "that any of my Virginia folks ever killed one single red man. The family Bible makes Colonel John Catlett out to be my eight-times-great-grandfather, I think. But bless you, *he* didn't butcher any savages. In 1670 they butchered *him,* right in front of Fort Royal."

"Yes," said papa triumphantly, "and his widow complained that if they'd had decent respect for the gentry they'd have scalped the sutler and let the colonel go!"

"Well," said mama, "you must admit the colonel *was* gentry. James Madison and Zachary Taylor were both his great-grandsons. If that isn't gentry I don't know what is. What's more, they were also great-grandsons of Colonel James Taylor, and he was an eight-times great-grandpa of mine too."

"I've always told you you were an almost-somebody," said papa. "That's your trouble."

"Is it my fault, Harry, that Colonel Taylor was a member of the House of Burgesses, and surveyor general of Virginia?"

But the only Indian fighter of her family that papa would admit to admiring was James Taylor's wife Martha, born a Thompson. He admired Martha because she found an effective new use for mush, which   88 happened to be papa's favorite food. Martha's kitchen was located in a building separate from the main house. As she was supervising the preparation of dinner there one day in the late seventeenth century, three savages suddenly darted into the kitchen, their voices raised in war whoops and their tomahawks ready for action. But they were not prepared for her defense. She seized a ladle, dipped it into a pot of hot mush, and dashed the boiling liquid over their naked bodies. They panicked; instead of dashing back into the safety of the woods they ran into the house and rolled under a bed, where she held them at bay, threatening them with further applications of the mush, until her husband and sons came rushing in from the fields and captured the Indians.

"Your Alexander Hamilton wouldn't have captured them," said mama. "He'd have scalped them."

"I expect you're right," said papa.

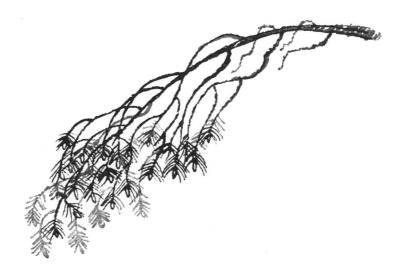

Alexander Hamilton on the Juniata

ALEXANDER HAMILTON begat
ANNA;

Anna married
THOMAS ESPY,
who begat
ROBERT HAMILTON;

Robert Hamilton married
ELIZABETH CARSON
and begat again
ROBERT HAMILTON;

Robert Hamilton married
JULIA ANN JEFFERSON
and begat
HARRY ALBERT;

Harry Albert married
HELEN MEDORA RICHARDSON
and begat

. . .

Alexander Hamilton, Indian killer, was my grandfather's great-grand-father, or my father's great-great-grandfather, or my own great-great-great-grandfather, depending on how you want to put it. His daughter Anna married Tom Espy, who, as you will see by the chart above, begat the first Robert Espy, who begat the second, who begat papa, who begat me.

I cannot leave Alexander out of this account, because he was a mile-stone along one of the main roads to grandpa's village; but I have trouble handling him. Grandpa is a reasonably easy subject; he was alive and expressing himself, albeit tersely, in my boyhood. Papa was expressing himself too, and at inordinate length. Mama's side of the family is even easier to apprehend; they were addicted for generations to preserving their activities and thoughts in diaries, newspaper stories, magazine arti-cles, and doggerel. But Alexander Hamilton is a harder case. The Indi-ans killed him a hundred and thirty years before I was born; and, with one exception,* he seems never to have confided his thoughts to paper at all. All I know about him comes from snatches written by other people. Usually he appears as a name on a muster roll or a land deed. So I have to fill in the empty spaces as an historical novelist might, imagining his looks—long-legged, tousel-headed, eventually bearded—and putting words into his mouth and thoughts into his mind.

He was not the distinguished Alexander Hamilton whose features, looking quizzical and a bit cynical, are familiar on today's ten-dollar bills. My thrice-great-grandfather was, I assume, of humbler clay. But maybe not. He was thirty years senior to our first secretary of the trea-sury, being born in either Ayrshire County, Scotland, or the plantations of Northern Ireland, in 1725. The historic Alexander's grandfather, Alex-ander Hamilton of Grange in Ayreshire, gave his sons the same names my Alexander gave his: John, Robert, Alexander, George, and William. Not that the coincidence implies blood relationship; many a Scottish yeoman not only named his children after those of his laird, but even adopted the laird's surname himself.

In any event, my Alexander Hamilton emigrated to America in the good ship *Dunnegall* at the age of sixteen, in 1741, reaching New Castle, Delaware, in the spring of the year. With him were his father, William; his mother; three younger brothers, John, Robert, and William; and a sis-ter Jane, perhaps four or five.

The elder Hamilton bought two middle-aged horses, a pregnant cow, and a wagon, and the family slogged off for Lancaster County, Pennsylvania, where all good Scotch-Irishmen first settled in America. The cow trudged behind the wagon and Alexander behind the cow, switching flies from its face and body with a maple branch. They fol-lowed a path that not long before had been an Indian trail. Sometimes it was sand, sometimes it was corduroy; finally it disappeared. At this point

---

*See page 108.

they discarded their wagon, loaded their worldly goods onto the horses and the cow, and continued to the nearly uninhabited borders of Marsh Creek, where they set about reproducing an Irish farm on two hundred acres of American wilderness.

Their first home was a one-room affair, with an attached shed to shelter the animals. The walls were formed of unweathered logs; the roof, of bark; the floor, of earth. A hole in the roof allowed smoke to escape from a circular fireplace of rocks in the center of the cabin.

The Hamiltons hacked out a ragged clearing in the close-packed trees. They felled willows, elms, and hemlocks. They hewed straight trunks into logs for cabin walls, split others for firewood, and gradually burned away the stumps in a smouldering fire of branches and limbs. Between these stumps they planted their first seeds, of Indian corn and squash. When winter came, they felt security from hunger as their eyes caught the glint of red corn ears and orange squashes among the sooty rafters. With a rock they crushed surplus kernels of corn into meal, using a burned-out stump as a mortar.

By the second summer, the clearing had grown to four stump-pocked acres. In that year, too, with the help of neighboring settlers, they erected a three-room log house by a spring a hundred yards back from Marsh Creek. They converted their earlier cabin into a barn for their livestock, now comprising four horses, as many sheep, a muley bull, six cows, two female calves, a pair of swine with offspring, and a shifting collection of scruffy chickens.

The eight or ten families within a radius of five miles included the Girtys, the Turners, the McCords, the Elders, the Blairs, and the Reeds, all of whom continued to play a part in Alexander's later life. There were also the Espys and the Carsons, both to become part of my ancestral maze. At the time of the Hamiltons' arrival, John Espy, then twenty-one, was clearing trees on nearby Swatara Creek. Though only twenty-one, John was already a husband of five years' standing (his wife was born Ann Montgomery), and father of a two-year-old son, Tom. This Tom was eventually to marry Alexander's daughter Anna — still not dreamed of in 1741 — and to become father of the first Robert Hamilton Espy, whose son was to found Oysterville.

Upstream from John Espy's farm was that of Adam Carson, an older man. Nearly seventy years after the first meeting of the Hamiltons, Espys, and Carsons, Robert Hamilton Espy, grandson of John Espy and Alexander Hamilton, married Elizabeth Carson, granddaughter of Adam Carson. Even then they could have had no suspicion that they were extending the road toward grandpa's village, still scores of years in the future and nearly three thousand miles away.

The Hamiltons were a close-knit family. In his teens, Alexander stood guard against Indians beside his father and his uncles on the farm. In the French and Indian War, he fought beside his brothers. In the Revolution, he commanded three of his own sons.

93

His mother, with such help as young Jane could provide, carded and spun fleece, pumping the treadle of the big spinning wheel until the wheel hummed like a bumblebee. The food she served her family ranged from blood sausage with greens, to kernels of corn crushed in a bowl and cooked in milk, to apples in maple sugar, to spinach pie and greens, to beef, softened in a kettle and fished out with sticks, to dried squash fried in lard, to pork and green beans. In the early spring, there was salad made of marigold leaves; and every morning there was mush, a favorite dish of grandpa's and later of papa's, but not of mine.

Mrs. Hamilton preserved the physical proof of generational continuity: the family Bible; a bureau that had been carpentered back beyond memory; pewter eating tools brought from Ulster; clay bowls, too, from which Alexander's grandparents had scooped their food.

She was busy out of doors, too. She raked mown hay and forked it into haycocks; dug potatoes; made soft soap; boiled clothes in a big iron kettle. The males of the family meanwhile fed the stock, pitched out the manure, and fired warning shots in the direction of Indians peering from behind trees. They milked, timbered, grubbed out stumps, trudged behind the plow (its nose rooting contentedly, like a hog's, in the rich black bottom land), split logs into firewood or fence rails, and hoed corn.

The savages showed no signs of hostility. The warning shots may have kept them on their good behavior, but did not prevent them from drifting into the clearing and seating themselves in twos or threes on stumps or rail fences, watching silently as the Hamiltons went about their chores. They sometimes sat for hours, until Mrs. Hamilton brought them a snack of blood sausage, or perhaps fried venison; then they grunted and left, gnawing as they went. The Hamiltons could charge them with no offense worse than chicken-stealing.

A greater nuisance than the Indians was the Penn government itself. Like most Scotch-Irish, the Hamiltons had not bothered to take legal possession of their land; they simply cleared it. Authority, they held, resided only in the blade of an axe, the barrel of a gun, and, of course, the pages of the Bible. The Penns, in Alexander's view, were the usurpers; it was an offense against both God and nature to leave thousands of fertile acres untilled when so many good Christians needed the land to raise bread.

Richard Peters, secretary of the Colony of Pennsylvania, took a different view. He recognized that since the Scotch-Irish and Dutch frontiersmen formed a cordon protecting the coastal settlements from Indian incursion, it was impractical to do away with them altogether; but at least, he insisted, they should be forced to recognize that they were living on Penn property and should pay rent accordingly. Since the settlers in Lancaster County ignored the secretary's repeated demands for quitrents, he arrived in the Swatara region one fine spring afternoon in 1744 to throw them out.

It was sugaring time. The Hamilton boys were making the rounds of 94 the trees, emptying the wooden pails of sap into barrels, which their father then hauled on a hand sledge to the house.

Alexander cocked his head, a pail half poured. "There's a horse coming at the run, pa," he said.

A moment later John Espy appeared from the wood trail, his plump bay mare proceeding at a joggling pace a trifle faster than its usual leisurely stroll. John's son Tom, now five, was tucked before his father in the saddle, gripping the pommel with both hands.

Secretary Peters, John Espy reported with no sign of agitation, had arrived at Adam Carson's place an hour or two before with a sheriff, a magistrate, and two surveyors. He was calling on the settlers to gather up their goods and depart for the coastal country, so that he could survey their lands for the Penns.

"But we sort of figured," said John, with a grin that revealed the absence of two front teeth, "that there's more of us around just now than there is of them."

Mr. Hamilton nodded, and dispatched his second son to the house to tell Mrs. Hamilton that her husband and Alexander would be gone a few hours. They caught and bridled two grazing horses, and jogged five miles behind John to Carson's place. There they found Peters and his companions surrounded in the barnyard by a score of Scotch-Irishmen, most loosely holding muskets. The secretary was trying vainly to explain the law of tenancy to men who had no desire to understand it.

Peters was a man with a hawk's beak for a nose, and not much chin beneath; but his glance pierced, and it was clear that he was not accustomed to defiance. Yet now he spoke almost pleadingly. "Please, gentlemen," he said, "understand that this land does not belong to you. It belongs to the Penns. Simply acknowledge their ownership, pay your trifle of rent, and there need be no trouble. Otherwise you will have to go."

There was some shuffling of feet.

"I've been here six years," drawled Adam Carson. "Got nearly two hundred acres cleared. Twenty head of cattle, and as nice a stand of wheat as a man could ask for. Don't hardly figure on turning my place back to the savages now."

Peters, his voice a little shrill, said, "You see the surveyor's chain this man beside me is holding. He is under instructions to use it to obtain an accurate measurement of the land hereabouts. Let him get on with his work; acknowledge the Penn's ownership; and you may stay here forever. Otherwise, you give me no choice but to evict you."

Tom Girty, slightly in his cups as usual, reached out a big, calloused hand and tweaked the chain away from its possessor. He regarded it curiously. "I always wondered what the law looked like," he said. "Never thought it looked like loops of wire. Mr. Peters, we got nothing against you and your friends, but I can't say we care for that chain." He hefted it. "How long is this here chain of yours, little man?"

"Four rods," said the surveyor.

"And just how long would a rod be? You'll excuse my lack of learning."

"Sixteen feet. The whole chain is sixty-six feet long."

"And these here links, they'd be mebbe seven-eight inches?"

"Seven and ninety-two hundredths inches."

"Well now that's a strange figure," said Girty, shaking his red face in wonderment. "Why don't you even it out?"

"That is just what we do. Ten square chains make an even acre."

"So *that's* how you do it!" marveled Girty. He grasped the chain in both huge hands, and twisted; there was a snapping sound; the severed links fell to the floor. He spoke directly to Peters. "Secretary," he said, "I think you better take them pieces of chain to the Penns, and tell them not to try cobbling them back together. Because if they do, and that chain ever shows up here again, there better be a man with a gun for every link in the chain if you expect to drive us offen the Swatara."

Peters returned to Philadelphia, humiliated and raging. He promptly entered an indictment against the intransigent settlers. But an indictment is only a piece of paper. The Scotch-Irish and the Dutch along the borders were the dyke that held back the Indians from the thickly settled coastlands, even from Philadelphia. They were a nuisance, but necessary. Eventually the government decided to call the settlements long-term leases, but to ignore collection of rents. The indictment was dropped.

By 1745, Alexander was going on twenty. He and his next-oldest brother, John, were both taller than their father, and like him walked with the shamble and stooped shoulders of those who have spent much of their lives behind a plow. All the Hamilton boys were also wise in the ways of the woods. Farm chores permitting, Alexander frequently settled a high, squirrel-skin cap on his long, unkempt brown hair, and disappeared into the forest in search of fresh meat. In summer, the meat might manifest itself as a doe bending her head to drink from a stream; in winter, as a whole herd of deer huddling in a snow yard trampled out by their own hooves. The meat might take the form of a mallard duck, its beak pulling at some underwater weed and its body an easy target above surface; or a pair of rabbits copulating; or, in the golden fall, a fat bear standing on its hind legs to reach for berries. Alexander was a good shot; if he could approach within firing distance, the prey was his.

He was known in the area as something of a genius at tinkering. Considering scandalously inefficient the Indian system of crushing corn and wheat into meal with rocks, he developed his own grist mill. It was a small clapboard house at the edge of Marsh Creek, without floor or loft. He cobbled together a three-foot wheel, plus husk, buckets, shaft, hopper, damsil, crank, ribs, arms—the whole elaborate contraption—from wood and stone, without so much iron as a single spike. The hoop was made from a cross section of a hollow buttonwood tree, and the bolting-chest from live-wood puncheons—split logs with the face smoothed.

By his twentieth birthday, Alexander was in demand as a millwright for miles around. And he was married.

I wish I could tell you about his bride. I do not even know her name. If some itinerant artist ever painted the newlyweds on board, the painting has long vanished; and there were no peddlers of tintypes in 1745. I have no idea whether young Mrs. Hamilton's hair was red, flaxen, or black; whether she was stocky or slim, tall or short, quarrelsome or serene, morose or giggly. I only know she was delivered late one night in 1747 of a healthy girl, who was given the name Anna; and the next morning Alexander's wife died.

Alexander took Anna into the woods with him as soon as she could toddle. Sometimes she stood on his shoulders, gripping his long wild hair, or sat on them piggyback. By the time she was four she understood as well as he did the significance of a jay's scream or a squirrel's sudden chattering.

But the valley was changing. The woods were drawing back from the farm; sheep, horses, and cattle grazed on sunlit acres that six years before had been umbrageous forests. Anna was a dear, and Alexander loved her; but he was restless. As his great-grandson Robert was to do a hundred years later, Alexander began to listen to siren songs of a Beulah Land, this one west of the Susquehanna. It was the Juniata Valley, sacred hunting ground of the Delawares, where white men were forbidden to set boot or moccasin. But inevitably one white man and then another did. In 1750 the Six Nations issued a stern warning against the trickle of immigration:

The [white] people will be put off now, and next year come again, and if so, the Six Nations will not bear it.

For the Scotch-Irish to ignore their rental obligations to the Penns was bad enough; but now they were throwing the colony's whole fragile live-and-let-live arrangement with the redskins into jeopardy. James Peters, still secretary of the colony, led an official force of the Pennsylvania militia to the Juniata River, and on the twenty-second of May, 1750, his soldiers drove out every white family they could locate in the wilderness. In the process they burned thirty homes; Peters, reporting to Philadelphia, explained that these "were of no considerable value; being such as the country people erect in a day or two, and cost only the charge of an entertainment." He was referring to the fact that the nearest settlers generally cooperated to throw together each new cabin, and celebrated at the end of the day.

But Peters's decisiveness was to no avail. Scotch-Irish families continued to drift into the Juniata Valley. And the Six Nations, despite their warning, at first did "bear it." In 1755 they agreed for the sum of £400 to allow white settlements all the way to the western borders of Pennsylvania.

97

Why should Alexander remain behind? His parents no longer needed him; they were well settled; they could afford hired hands; by some accounts, they even had a black cook in the kitchen. When Simon Girty, sober for a change, drifted by to announce that he and his family were selling their Marsh Creek land and heading west, Alexander and his brothers decided to go too. Anna, only eight, was not yet ready for wilderness life; but her grandparents assured him they would care for her as their own.

Other neighbors joined in: the Girtys; John Turner and his two sons; the McCords; the Blairs; the Elders and their twelve-year-old Barbara; the Reeds and their ten-year-old Amanda. The Carsons were too well along in years to be interested. The Espys, too, stayed behind. "When pa brought me here in the twenties," said John, "all he wanted was a farm big enough to stretch out in; but he had to spend half his time fighting off the Penns and the other half fighting off the hostiles. I've been doing the same for thirty years. Now Ann and me have got us a nice place—crops to go around, cattle to go around, no Penns bothering us, no savages bothering us. We reckon we'll stay."

The move west began in late January. Flatboats were poled up the Susquehanna. At Duncannon, they swung into the Juniata itself. No Indians showed; in fact the most memorable part of the trip, apart from the cold, was a brief blowup between Simon Girty and his old friend John Turner.

Poling the flatboats against the current was a hard job, and when the emigrants bivouacked each night the men were generally bone-tired. Simon's way of relieving weariness was to drink. In his cups he liked to fight, and on this particular night he took umbrage at the sight of Turner sitting close to Mrs. Girty before the campfire. The two men exchanged epithets; the epithets grew to blows; and, before a porcupine could have shot its quills, Girty and Turner were in grunting combat, fists swinging and boots kicking, until one seized the other about the waist and flung him to the frozen earth. There they rolled and bit and roared, the men cheering them on and the women watching with critical appraisal—all, that is, except Mrs. Girty, who, no fragile blossom, leaped and shook her fists and shouted, "Kill the bug-tit, Simon! Knee his balls, you fool!" along with injunctions of like tenor, until the two men, wrapped in each other's arms, rolled into the fire. As they leaped away, Turner stooped, seized a blazing knot, and brought it down on Girty's head so hard as to stretch him unconscious to the ground. Mrs. Girty was on the victor in a trice, screeching, cursing, her nails raking his bearded cheeks, her fingers thrusting at his nostrils. To no avail; he was a big man, and when he seized her wrists she was helpless.

"Call me bug-tit, will you?" asked Turner, glaring down past a split lip at her enraged countenance half a foot below his. "Well, I'll bug-tit *you!*" He threw her, still screeching and kicking, over his shoulder, and stamped off into the woods. That was the last anyone saw of them until

98

the following morning, when they reappeared, apparently on the best of terms, just as the emigrants began to stir. Girty by then was hale as ever, sober, and amiable. His wife washed the cut on his head; the two men shook horny hands; and their friendship continued unabated.*

The emigrants' journey ended, at the flat place where Lewistown now stands. They scattered about the countryside, making and reconciling claims. Alexander, with the help of his three brothers, constructed a cabin uphill from the river. He annexed two hundred and eighty acres — the first land on the Juniata, as far as I know, ever to be surveyed, much less legally recorded.

That spring the immigrants cleared and planted, undisturbed. The axes chunked, the trees toppled, the smoke from burning branches dimmed the sky, but the Indians gave no sign. Only Arthur Buchanan, an early settler who had managed to avoid the Peters dispersal, voiced concern. Buchanan had bought his land from Captain Jacobs, an Indian so called because of his resemblance to a man of that name back in Cumberland County. "Captain Jacobs," said Buchanan, "he's mighty upset that so many palefaces are coming in, and I expect he ain't the only one. We got to have us a fort, or we're dead men."

The government agreed. In December of 1755, it established Fort Granville at a fork on Buchanan's property. The following spring and summer passed without incident. To be sure, there was word from the west in July that the English General Braddock had been defeated and killed at Fort Duquesne; but the settlers could not have cared less about General Braddock. Their only worry was that the Indians had accepted French leadership—and who knew what the French might have in mind?

They found out the following January. Alexander first got the bad news from Jim Kelty, who pounded up, his horse a-lather, to report that the hostiles had overrun McCord's place. They had passed the Blair cabin on the way:

"They brung along Jim Blair's head," said Kelty, "and throwed it in Liz McCord's lap. They told her it was her husband, but they couldn't fool her—she knowed it was Blair."

Alexander had danced with Mrs. McCord at a haying bee the summer before. In his childhood, Jim Blair had taught him how to tamp powder into a musket. He nodded. "The boys and me will keep a watch out," he said. Next day, he leaned a target the size of a six-foot man against a sycamore tree, and took turns with his brothers blazing at it. Hostiles watching from the woods would know that any Hamilton could shoot straighter than an Indian.

Alexander understood the grievances of the redskins. What puzzled him was the whites who assumed Indian innocence was close to the

*John B. B. Trussell, associate historian of the Commonwealth of Pennsylvania, insists that by 1755 Girty was already dead, and Turner had married his widow. If Mr. Trussell is right, the dates of some ensuing events will have to be juggled around.

Garden of Eden. When a Quaker wool comber living downstream was slaughtered, Alexander thought he had only got what was coming to him, because he had refused to believe the Indians were really on the warpath. Only madmen like the Scotch-Irish, the Quaker insisted, would kill human beings without reason. So when three Indians of his acquaintance dropped by at suppertime, he invited them to share the meal. "Nope," replied one of his visitors; "tonight we want scalps, not jerkin." At this point the wool comber's fifteen-year-old son began sidling judiciously toward the back door; he looked back just in time to see an Indian cleave his father's head with a tomahawk. As the boy ran for the shelter of Fort Granville, he could hear behind him the last screams of his mother, sister, and brother.

Soon afterward Simon Girty was shot and killed in his field by an Indian whom Mrs. Girty recognized as a mendicant called Fish. When John Turner learned of the killing, he trailed Fish for two days, killed him, lifted his scalp, and brought it back for Mrs. Girty to hang over her fireplace.

With French officers in the lead, the Indian irruption now blazed across the Juniata Valley like a grass fire. The Scotch-Irish fled downstream to settled, safe country, poling and rowing as urgently as if the red devil himself were in the next flatboat back. In their eyes, Fort Granville had provided no support; the provincial government, as they saw it, had purposely left them unprotected from the savages. so they brought with them grim reminders — the corpses of butchered men, women, and children. These they sent to Philadelphia, where the bodies were hauled about the streets in carts to arouse the indignation of the citizens. A tract of the day reads:

When a Waggon load of the scalped and mangled bodies of their Countrymen were brought to Philadelphia and laid at the State House door, and another Waggon load brought into the town of Lancaster, did they rouse to Arms to avenge the Cause of their murder'd Friends? Did we hear any of those Lamentations that are now so plentifully poured for the Connestoga Indians? O my dear friends! Must I answer — No?

Actually the provincial government reacted with celerity. On April 9 they issued a bounty schedule:

For every Male Indian prisoner above ten years old, that shall be delivered at any of the government's Forts, or Towns $150

For every Female Indian Prisoner or Male Prisoner of Ten years old and under, delivered as above $130

For the Scalp of every Male Indian of above Ten Years old $130

For the Scalp of every Indian Woman . . . . $ 50

These prices seem generous, considering that only two years earlier, the Six Nations had accepted £400 in full payment for several million acres of virgin land.

The government also rushed to the forts in the wilderness as many troops as could be spared from the defense of the inner settlements. In June, a detachment came from Cumberland County to the aid of Fort Granville, where the dozen Juniata families who had refused to abandon their fields still huddled.

Of all the whites in the area, only the Hamilton brothers refused to take refuge. They farmed as usual, pausing at intervals to ram powder into their rifles and take another shot at the target against the tree.

In July, half of the Fort Granville soldiers were detached a few miles eastward to the Tuscarora Valley to guard farmers harvesting grain. The French and Indians at once attacked the weakened fort. A hundred of them crept up a deep ravine to one of the walls, piled brush against it, and started a fire, which they nursed with pine knots until they managed to burn a hole all the way through the logs. Through this opening they discharged their guns, killing the commanding officer and wounding several men who were trying to put out the blaze.

John Turner then made the fatal mistake of accepting the shouted assurances of the attackers that all who surrendered would be safe. He swung open the fort gates; twenty-two men, three women, and a number of children were seized.

Meanwhile, hearing the firing, the Hamilton boys had made their way to the fort along forest trails. When they reached the edge of the clearing, the Indians were already lining up their prisoners. One man, limping, was apparently not considered in marching condition; an Indian cleaved his skull and scalped him as the Hamiltons watched.

Since four men cannot fight a hundred, they followed the raiders, always at a discreet distance, to the Indian base at Kittanning, three days' march away. Here the Hamiltons, concealed behind sumac bushes, watched the torture of John Turner. Avenging the death of Fish, the savages painted a post black, tied Turner to it and danced around him. They heated gun barrels cherry red in a roaring fire, and ran the metal through his body. After tormenting him for three hours, they scalped him alive, and at last held up an eight-year-old boy with hatchet in hand for the finishing stroke.

The Hamiltons retreated undiscovered. But this time they did not stop at their farm. Instead they paddled down the Juniata and up the Susquehanna to join the garrison at Fort Augusta, a defense center just built where the west and east branches of the Susquehanna join.

Alexander had liked John Turner. It was time, he thought, to do something about those Indians.

Alexander Hamilton on the West Branch

Year after year, decade after decade, the Indians continued to sign solemn treaties with the whites, each treaty assuring the red men that their remaining lands were inviolable. Before the smoke from the peace pipe had faded, each new treaty was swept away, helpless as a pine chip, on the foaming current of white invasion. The Indians could scarcely be expected to treat as moral paragons an alien race out to exterminate them like rats in a corn crib. Alexander Hamilton felt no more compunction about dispatching an Indian than the Israelite Gideon felt about striking off the heads of Oreb and Zeeb. Alexander's children later estimated that during his tour of duty with Captain James Patterson's company at Fort Augusta, he dispatched personally, on one-man scouting expeditions, more than two score savages.

The first few months of his enlistment, however, were bloodless. The Hamilton boys were put to work building bateaux. These were flat-bottomed riverboats, tapered at the ends. The bateaux carried militiamen on harassing raids up the Susquehanna, enabling Alexander to prove to his own satisfaction, and that of Captain Patterson, that he could outmaneuver and outfight any red man, or Frenchman either. Patterson used him increasingly to locate Indians and forecast their movements. As a side benefit, Alexander ambushed unwary strays, either leaping out from the underbrush to dispose of them with a stroke of his hatchet, or picking them off with a rifle shot.

The West Branch of the Susquehanna River enraptured him. He returned from each expedition there, rhapsodizing like an oldtime preacher describing the fields of the Lord:

"Game — my Jesus! I've heard the quail whistling and the pheasants rustling and the grouse booming like a fife and drum corps, all at once! Boys, if a man was to grub out a clearing this afternoon from that forest, he'd find a deer cropping in the clearing tomorrow morning, just begging to be shot and gutted and hung up. Why, I've run into elk as high as elephants. In the spring, the shad climb the West Branch so thick you can catch your supper with one dip of a coonskin cap — and in the fall the eels wiggle downstream so close together they look like a net of willow boughs."

The schools of pike, catfish, bass, roach, and perch, he said, were enormous. Trout jumped so high from quick water that they would fall into a man's cupped hands. Hills and mountains, dark with forests of black walnut, elm, shellbark, and sycamore, stood back to back like the ribs of a washboard. Alexander told of a vine he had seen so heavy with purple grapes that it groaned aloud under its burden; the vine clasped in turn a tree weighed down by ripe butternuts; the largest butternut limb clung for support to the limb of a tree loaded with red, juicy plums; and in the shade of all this abundance, hazelnuts were ripening.

In 1757, the Penns ceded the land lying north and west of the Alleghenies back to the Six Nations, and the Indian war paused for breath. For the

Hamiltons the significance of this pause was that the white settlement along the Juniata was now legitimized, in theory at least, by the Indians themselves. At the end of the year Alexander, William, and John Hamilton collected their wages in scrip from Captain Patterson and paddled back home; their brother Robert preferred to continue building bateaux at Fort Augusta. As they paddled upriver they could hear axes ringing on either bank; their neighbors were back, and log houses were rising again from the ashes around still-standing chimneys. William and John stayed with Alexander long enough to help him put up a new log house, with a bedroom-living room for himself, and extra rooms for the housekeeper and hired man he expected to take on. Then William wandered east to settle in the Tuscarora Valley, and John wandered west to scout from Fort Bedford.

Alexander was a farmer again; but memories of the West Branch still whispered in his mind.

He was now in his prime, thirty-three years old—and ten years a widower. He did not believe celibacy was God's notion of the way a man should live. Certainly it was not Alexander's. He may have been an Indian killer in the woods, but at home he was a domestic man. He missed his daughter Anna, whom he had not seen for four years. He wanted more children, and not just to help around the place.

He made one unsuccessful mating gesture toward Barbara Blair, a high-stepping, rawboned filly who took his fancy because she could match him shot for shot at a target. Her choice, however, fell on one of the Elder boys ("Elder," she is said to have told Alexander, "but younger.") He turned next, and more successfully, to fifteen-year-old Amanda Reed, a girl who prided herself on her ability to read, write, and cipher. Amanda wore her dress short enough to show a pair of neat ankles, but only because a longer skirt would have been impractical for farm work. Her calico bonnet shaded a pair of cool gray eyes that saw the world without illusion. She brushed her straw-colored hair with a whisk of twigs. Alexander, who cleaned his teeth as best he could with ashes, found it magical that she kept hers snowy white with a twig of chewed birch.

Alexander may have smelled of grease from skinned deer, or manure from the barn, but he was a respected man, a man of growing property—a man to call mister. Amanda valued these qualities, and appreciated his valuing in turn her schooling, her blooming health, and her willingness to work.

They were married in 1760, and over the next dozen years she bore him children as fast as nature could arrange it. The eldest, Alexander, Jr., was born in 1761; John, in 1762; Robert, the year after that.

In the summer of 1763, the Indians once more took to the warpath— suddenly and, at first, with dismaying success. Unified by the powerful personality of the Ottawa chief Pontiac, they raged through white settlements like fire through dry corn. Eight frontier forts fell before the whites could rally.

After a second cup of hot buttered rum, Alexander's brother Robert, down from Fort Augusta on leave, yarned about what was going on. He said, for instance, that a couple of Delawares had trailed a Yankee in a forest of the Wyoming. The Yankee had a head start, but the Delawares lessened the gap without difficulty, proceeding at a half trot, until the spoor of their prey vanished at a hollow log. The Indians seated themselves on the log to discuss which way he might have gone, unaware that for the past hour and a half he had been fitted as tightly as a rifle-held bullet inside the log itself. He could hear their voices clearly; he could even hear the bullets rattle in Indian pouches. At length it occurred to one of the Delawares to check inside the log; as he bent down, the fugitive could see his scalp lock silhouetted against the opening. Meanwhile, however, a spider had been industriously weaving a web over the entrance. The completed web, in the midst of which the spider sat munching a fly, was evidence enough for the Indians that the log had lain long undisturbed, and they padded away. After another hour, the Yankee wriggled out, apologized to the spider for breaking its web, and made his way to the nearest fort.

Alexander considered the spider the hero of that story; like any Scotch-Irishman, he had no use for the Yanks.

Indians began to raid the Juniata seriously in the spring. Once more, locals took refuge in Fort Granville, or retreated to more settled country. Once more they were betrayed by a fatal compulsion to get in their crops.

One Sunday evening in July, Alexander's brother William rode up from the Tuscarora to tell him that a handful of hostiles had shot and killed Bill White through his open doorway, as he was holding a prayer service with his family. Bill Anderson was similarly slain an hour later as he sat reading his Bible; his son and adopted daughter were slaughtered and scalped. The Indians, said William, were at that moment ranging up and down the Tuscarora Valley, setting fire to cabins, barns, and haycocks; William was to be one of a posse setting off at sunup next day to catch and exterminate them. He wanted Alexander to have his farm if anything went wrong.

As it happened, something did go wrong. Guns roared from a presumably empty barn; savages bounded out, whooping, each with his target picked. One white man escaped; four, including William Hamilton, were slain and scalped.

Word of William's death was followed in August by a report from Fort Bedford that John Hamilton had failed to return from a scouting assignment. Of the Hamilton brothers, only Alexander and Robert remained.

Pontiac's uprising, fortunately, blew out as fast as it had blown in. The French withdrew their support, and Pontiac had to pull back his braves. By 1764 the Juniata was so serene that Anna could come west to help her father around the house. For a while the years passed like flocks of geese flying south, too high to see, unnoticed save for the sad honking of their passage.

Alexander's farm prospered. His retinue increased. Swinging his scythe one day, naked to the waist and sweating, he noticed the beginning of a sag where his belly met his trousers. He raised his eyes to the riddled target still leaning against the sycamore tree, and could not remember when he had last bothered to test his aim on it.

In the spring of 1767 young Tom Espy dropped in. It was his third visit since Anna's coming. No, not so young at that, thought Alexander; he must be all of twenty-eight now. He was beetle-browed, thick in the shoulders, comfortable with a grubbing hoe or a plow. Alexander hoped he would speak his mind this time. Anna must have wished the same thing. A strapping girl, straight of back, but too sharp-nosed for conventional prettiness and over-given to unvarnished opinions, she would soon be twenty, old to be single in the wilderness. So when Tom did blurt out his request for Anna's hand, Alexander was relieved. Yet he replied with a question of his own:

"Tom," he asked, "have you ever thought of trying the rich soil out yonder in Indian country, all waiting to be cleared and put to feeding Christians?"

"Well, sir," said Tom, "pa and ma moved from Derry to Newville when I was a boy, and I was kind of sorry to have to change even then. But they have a nice place, and it will be mine some day."

"You're a good boy, Tom," said Alexander, "and Annie could do a lot worse." (But you'll never be anything more than a farmer, he thought.)

The next morning he looked at the buds red against the blue of the maples, and the green nimbus on the trees lining the river, and wondered if he too was anything more than a farmer. He could not complain; he was doing well. But something was missing.

Maybe the sound of a war whoop.

The following year, a new treaty between the Penns and the Six Nations opened the West Branch of the Susquehanna to the whites, and Alexander at last knew what he had been waiting for. He began making canoe trips upriver, seeking out by name Indians whom he had encountered before only along the sights of a rifle. He wanted land at the farthermost limits of the Indian cession; and he was determined to make his deal with the savages themselves, not with the Penn government. The palavering was picked up each year where it was suspended the year before; the Indians and Alexander were equally patient. After four years he acquired, for a payment of which nothing is known save that it included three pairs of long red underwear and a keg of whiskey, two hundred and sixteen acres on Bald Eagle Creek, these to belong to Alexander and his issue as long as the rain should fall and the rivers flow. In 1772, after making a bow to mortality by arranging for the solemn baptism in the Presbyterian faith of his eight children by Amanda, he installed his family and their possessions on flatboats and brought them to their new home.

Curiously, Alexander did not keep those two hundred and sixteen acres more than a few months. This may have been just as well; the land appears to have lain beyond the area opened to white settlement by the new treaty. He sold his property to a bold fellow named McManus (of whom no further word has come down) and retreated to Pine Creek, whither a few hardy families had preceded him. Here he bought a square mile of barrens—land easy to tame because its coverage was mostly underbrush, uninterrupted by stubbornly rooted trees.

Samuel Horn's house, a mile upstream, was the last outpost of the whites. John Henry Antes was farming the bank opposite Alexander; William Reed, Amanda's father, took up a claim nearby. In 1773 a numerous family of Jacksons arrived from Orange County, New York, and Alexander, deciding a square mile was too much for one family to work, though his three oldest boys were becoming of some use, turned half his holdings over to John Jackson.

Amanda Hamilton tended to look down on the Jacksons, on the grounds that they could barely read or write. Elcy Jackson, John's wife, on the other hand, considered the Hamiltons her inferiors, because her father was a brigadier general and a member of the Continental Congress, while her brother John Armstrong was a promising young officer who as it happened went on to become a member of the United States Senate, a minister to France, and finally, under President Madison, Secretary of War.* Alexander Hamilton and John Jackson paid no attention to this female backbiting, though if John could have known the future, he might well have lorded it over all the rest: down in the Carolinas a young cousin of his, name of Andrew, was growing up to become President of the United States.

On the West Branch, Alexander Hamilton had to peel his eyes for not just one set of enemies, but three.

First, the Indians. At the start these, having accepted his red underwear in trade, were the least of his concerns.

Second, the representatives of the Penns. The Pennsylvania government, holding that the Pine Creek settlers were occupying land prohibited to them by the treaty of 1768, enacted a law declaring that any settler refusing to leave such land was "to be punished by death without benefit

---

*"In spite of Armstrong's services, abilities and experience," wrote Henry Adams, "something in his character always created distrust. He had every advantage of education, social and political connection, ability and self-confidence; . . . but he suffered from the reputation of indolence and intrigue."

of clergy." The sanction appears to have been all bark and no bite; no such execution ever took place. How could the government command obedience in areas where, according to its own admission, its writ did not run? Once in a while, a sheriff would paddle up Pine Creek with orders to evict the settlers; but he never found anyone at home. The Indians would send runners ahead to warn the whites that the law was coming. The womenfolk and small children would then disappear into the underbrush like quail. The men, if in a playful mood, would canoe upstream just ahead of the sheriff, shouting back to him to paddle a little faster.

Finally, the Connecticut Yanks, who for years had been trying to take over the Wyoming Valley, in eastern Pennsylvania, for their home colony, were now casting covetous eyes on the West Branch as well.

Much as the Pine Creek settlers hated the Indians, the Penns, or the Yanks, they hated King George and his surrogates more. This hatred led to one of the more bizarre and less reported incidents of the Revolution. On July 4, 1776, at which time Alexander Hamilton was a Fair Play man,* a member of the Committee of Safety, and a second lieutenant under Captain John Henry Antes in the Eighth Company of the Northumberland Militia, several score settlers foregathered in the shade of the huge Tiadaghton Elm, on the bank of Pine Creek. They broached kegs of rye whiskey and rum, and began an afternoon of carousal and declamation that ended only when the kegs were empty and the Fair Play men full. In the midst of their jollification a number of them managed to scrawl their signatures to a remarkable affirmation—the Pine Creek Declaration of Independence.**

This document proclaimed that King George had trampled persistently on the Fair Play men in their exercise of their rights, particularly through outrageous taxation and failure to protect their persons and property from the Indians. Therefore, said the Fair Play men, they would

hereby dissolve any political bonds which may have heretofore connected us with the Old Country, or its provinces in America, and finally absolve ourselves of all allegiance to the Crown family of Great Britain

and

hereby accept and adopt as rules of life, all the Constitution of the Congress, as superseding in government the rules of conduct of the Fair Play Men's Association, to which we have remained loyal . . .

---

*Some historians consider the Fair Play administration of the Pennsylvania wilderness settlements to be the simplest and most effective governments in history. In each district the ultimate authority consisted of three Fair Play commissioners, each elected for a one-year term. They were prosecutors, legislators, and judges rolled into one; they accused, tried, and sentenced. Their customary punishment was to set a miscreant adrift in a canoe without a paddle, knowing that if he ever reached shore it would be far outside their jurisdiction.

**The Pine Creek Declaration is reprinted on page 296.

The signers of this forthright declaration had no idea that on that very day representataives of the thirteen colonies were affixing their signatures to the Declaration of Independence in Philadelphia.

Alexander is by tradition author of the Pine Creek manifesto. This makes the Alexander Hamilton of Pine Creek also the Thomas Jefferson of Pine Creek—and, as first man to sign the declaration, the John Hancock of Pine Creek as well.

For the truth of what went on along the West Branch during the Revolutionary War I rely on John Jackson's daughter Anna, who married Alexander Hamilton's son Robert and is hence a distant cousin of the Espys. Since Anna's account was not put on paper until 1855, at which time she was ninety-two years old and arguing her right to a pension from the Pennsylvania government, some may carp at either her memory or her reliability. Not I; her account is coherent; and no matter how loudly Mandy Hamilton may once have sneered at the illiteracy of the Jackson tribe, Anna's writing was to the point. "I am old now," she admitted, "but was onct young, came into this world in the Reign of George III, in Orange Co., state of New York, in January 1766, learned to read young, took delight in reading History, till I became acquainted with the governments, their changes, and ruleing families of Urope, & the true settlement of America. *I had a mother abel to instruct.*"

Prior to the outbreak of the Revolution, the Indians on the West Bank had lived on a basis of mutual toleration with the white settlers. When the crunch came, however, they sided with the British, and vanished into the forests. "Some of them had told particular white friends," wrote Anna, "to move away if the English got to Phila., the Indians would be back with tomahawks and there would be war here."

By the time the British did indeed capture Philadelphia, in September of 1777, there was scarcely an Indian visible on the West Bank. All that was left was a foreboding stillness.

Sure enough, in late 1777, invisible sharpshooters picked off Robert Fleming, Robert Donaldson, and James McMichael, as they unsuspectingly planted in their separate fields. The community took quick precautions: "I spent much of my time," recalled Anna, "running to warn others, hiding in thickets for fear of the tomahawk and knife of the Indians, melting pewter to make bullets, learning to shoot, very good at a mark, hearing constantly of murder being done around us of our nabors and friends."

General Washington dispatched one Captain John Brady to direct the defense of the West Branch. He had scarcely arrived when, with one of his sons, he was ambushed, scalped, and butchered. A younger son escaped; recognizing Chief Bald Eagle among the murderers, he tracked the Indian for years, and long after the Revolution killed him finally in a dark ravine hundreds of miles from the Susquehanna.

In July 1778—by which time the Colonials had already recaptured Philadelphia, so that massacre had lost all military value for the British— the Tories and Indians nonetheless struck with overwhelming force in the Wyoming Valley to the east. They slaughtered hundreds; the survivors reeled into the mountains to perish or make their way downstream toward safer territory. The West Branch was clearly next in line for destruction, and the government sent a scout to order its instant evacuation. He was barely in time; women and children were still piling their possessions into flatboats and canoes when the first contingent of hostiles whooped from the surrounding forests. This was the beginning of what history calls the Great Runaway.

"A man by the names of Jones would not believe there was danger," Cousin Anna reported. "Him and his man were killed, his wife made her escape. A short time after a Mr. Culbertson and his son went a short distance to their farm, they were both killed."

She might have added that Alexander Hamilton's sister-in-law, wife of the elder Robert, made the astonishing gaffe of running back to her cabin for an old silver pitcher. The Indians intercepted her, split her skull with a tomahawk, scalped her, and left her for dead. Yet she recovered consciousness and staggered and crawled to the river, where a passing boatload of refugees picked her up and took her to Fort Augusta. There the skin of her face was hoisted up and sewn fast, while a silver plate was affixed in her skull. The plate was still there when she died quietly in her bed at the age of ninety-five.

A few hours' warning made the difference between the annihilation in the Wyoming Valley and the comparatively small mortality on the West Bank two days later. The Hamiltons were able to fight off the hostiles for a full night in their own home and then to pack forty bushels of ground meal into a walnut chest and transport it to the river, where it was loaded into a flatboat waiting for Amanda and those of her children still too young to bear arms. As the family started downriver, their home was already in flames. In all, says Anna, the Hamiltons lost "houses, barns, stables, sheeps, hogs, three hundred bushels of corn in the crib, twenty acres of corn in ground, oats and spring wheat in ground."

Alexander Hamilton and his three eldest sons, with every other man or boy of the community old enough to aim and fire a rifle, formed a protective cordon on either side of the bank of Pine Creek as the women paddled their broods downstream. Some women, however, marched with their men, either because they were too late to catch a canoe, or to preserve the family livestock. Among these were the Jacksons.

"I recall an aged female," said Anna, "carrying the infant of her daughter, who had a bealed breast and was remarkable swelled. In passing a spring the daughter was unable to lie down and drink but the mother laid down the child and dipped up in her hands and gave her. My own mother had four cows to drive, and, having no other food, lived two days by milking in her hand and drinking, at the same time carrying gold in her pockets the weight of which had beat her legs until they were black and blue. I could not guess the number of refugees on their way down the river; one might as well attempt to guess the number of drops of water falling from a cloud."

Prior to the Great Runaway, the Hamiltons, father and sons, served in the Northumberland County Militia, first at Horn's Fort, not far from their own home, and then at Fort Augusta. The Great Runaway took them back down the West Branch to the town of Northumberland, where, according to Alexander's son Robert, "they were met by 18 men who, with the most pressing entreaties, urged them to halt at that place and make a stand for its defense until other help could be obtained." Alexander was put in command of those he had led down the Susquehanna.

Alexander was by now a full-fledged militia captain, though there is some question as to whether he was promoted at Northumberland or before. It is clear that he was elected to his rank in a contest with his friend Sam Horn; Horn supporters complained that Hamilton took unfair advantage of the frailty of human nature by offering whiskey *ad libitum* for votes. In any event, he remained a captain for the brief span left to him. His company at full strength included, besides himself, two lieutenants, one ensign, four sergeants, and thirty-three drums, rank and file.

Three of the rank and file were his own sons. Anna said the eldest, John, was "very tall, slender, fully six feet"; the youngest, Alexander, was "a very large boy . . . a handsome young man of 21 when they returned to their home place in 1783"; while the middle son, Robert, Anna's own husband-to-be, was only fifteen and "a short but fully developed young man or boy."

The Wyoming Massacre and the Big Runaway marked the highwater line of British and Indian belligerency along the Susquehanna. Within a year, settlers began drifting back to the West Branch. Alexander and his sons, though they remained subject to military orders, could take time off from their duties at Fort Augusta to rebuild their house and outbuildings.

It was a day of premature summer in 1779. The birds were silent on account of the heat, and the insects were loud. Alexander had removed his boots, and was sitting outside his quarters at Fort Augusta, leaning back to feel the untimely warmth of the sun on his face. When his son-in-law, Tom Espy, briefly on leave from the Lancaster militia, came up to speak to him, Alexander opened only one eye.

Tom was a seasoned family man now; his fifth child, the first Robert Hamilton Espy, was already a year old. Tom had a proposition to make. He wanted to buy Alexander's old place on the Juniata.

"I figure there ain't no more reason to worry about hostiles," he said. "They've had a bellyful. And it's a sizable place, enough to keep a big family busy."

Alexander regarded him out of his one open eye. "Tom," he said, "the Indians are still there, and they still ain't good until they're dead. You told me yourself you had no hankering to fight redskins, Tom; you're a farmer born."

"I calculate it's a chance worth taking," said Tom.

"Well, you're too late, son," said Alexander. "I sold the place to Jim Bratten just a month ago."

He closed the other eye as soon as Tom had gone. Farmer, he thought. By God, he'd soon be back to farming himself. It was a depressing prospect. Why, Amanda might expect him to go back to sleeping in a *bed*. He had grown accustomed to earth as a mattress; even when visiting his Pine Creek home, he customarily spread a blanket on a table to sleep.

He was only in his middle fifties, but he felt something inside him running down. He could no longer run easily for hours in the woods. Looking back seemed to offer more rewards than looking ahead. Somewhere, he thought, he must have made a wrong turn. Not in choosing Mandy—she had been a good wife, he couldn't fault her . . . yet perhaps . . . His mind drifted back to Barbara Blair, who used to match him shot for shot at a target, the same Barbara who had taken one of the Elder boys instead of him. Maybe he had become too old too soon . . .

A few days afterward he heard once more of Barbara Blair Elder, and felt as proud of her as if she had indeed been his own wife. Felix Skelly, just in from the Juniata, still barely eighteen but towering over most grown men, told him the story:

"Miz Elder was visiting ma one Sunday last May," said Skelly, "and I thought I'd better walk her part way home. Well, she claimed she saw an Indian behind a bush, and before I could decide whether she was imagining things a whole passel of hostiles jumped out. They got Mrs. Elder by the hair, and locked my arms behind my waist, and what could we do? They didn't kill us, I expect because they needed someone to carry wood they'd found in the Alleghenies that looked good for bows and arrows. So they loaded me up, and they made Mrs. Elder tote a long-handled frying pan, one of them monstrous heavy things the Dunkards use. Wouldn't surprise me if it was a hundred years old. That evening we came to a town where the hostiles were drawn up in two lines, maybe six feet apart, everyone waving a club or paddle. The load was lifted off my back, and I had to run the gauntlet. So I strolled easy up to the line, like I had nothing on my mind except what would be for supper, and then I took off. I tell you, captain, I expect there has never been such a bust of speed before and I expect there never will be again. I went through that whole gauntlet with only a couple of raps on the shoulder blades, and they couldn't make me run twice, them's the rules.

"But I was worried about Mrs. Elder—she's put on a few pounds since you knew her, and she couldn't be expected to run like no deer.   112

But I should have known better. She started marching along slow, and the first savage that stooped to give her a hit, he leaned over so far his arse was out, and Mrs. Elder she hit him there with that frying pan so hard he went sprawling on all fours. The chiefs who were looking on like to died laughing, and the next few braves in line were so taken aback they didn't even get around to raising their clubs. When one did, she swung that frying pan down on his head, and he must have seen more stars than ever lit the welkin dome. From then on nobody raised a hand to her, and she got through the line unscratched. But she said afterwards, she 'did it in a hurry.'"

Soon after running the gauntlet, Skelly escaped his captives by jumping from the top floor of a mill to the water sixty feet below. He did not know what had become of Mrs. Elder. Alexander never learned that she was taken first to Detroit, where she served the British garrison as a cook, and thence to Montreal, where she was exchanged.

Still, the thought of her courage somehow made him feel better. He was still feeling better in September of 1781, when he set out from Fort Augusta on a routine scouting expedition, and never returned. Nobody knows how he was killed, or even whether his body was buried. All we can be sure of is that his corpse had no scalp.

A year later, Amanda, a practical woman, married again. "Do you think," she inquired, the first child by her new mate at her breast, "that a woman of thirty-eight should remain without a husband?"

Vale, Alexander Hamilton. You made grist mills, beat back the wilderness, traded in spirits, loved your family, and killed Indians. I suspect that in your own way you even loved the Indians you killed. All I am sure of, though, is that there is no record of one of my forebears ever killing an Indian again.

9

Grandpa Takes a Wife

JEFFERY ESTY begat
ISAAC;

Isaac married
MARY TOWNE (THE WITCH)
and begat again
ISAAC;

Isaac married
ABIGAIL KIMBALL
and begat
MEHITABLE;

Mehitable married
JOSEPH JEPHERSON,
who begat
ICHABOD;

Ichabod, who spelled the name Jefferson, married
BETSEY CLAFLIN
and begat
WILLARD JAY;

Willard Jay married
SUSANNA BURT
and begat
DELOS;

Delos married
MATILDA JANE APPERSON
and begat
JULIA ANN;

Julia Ann married
ROBERT HAMILTON ESPY,
who begat
HARRY ALBERT;

Harry Albert married
HELEN MEDORA RICHARDSON
and begat

. . .

One aspect of Oysterville did divert the John Marshall who in 1860 found the village so hard a habitat: "The men in this country," he wrote, "get married and then have to send their wifes to school. I think that it is so funny to see married ladys go to school."

At first there were no married ladys, and there was no school either. Grandpa, I suspect, did not miss the one or the other. He was busy making money from oysters (although, apparently skeptical about the long-term future of the business, he invested his profits in timberland and city real estate, particularly in Portland and San Francisco).

Twice he took a vacation. Once it was to prospect for gold in the Blue Mountains, whence he returned with a single nugget and a chronic gold fever which was eventually to waste much of his substance. Again, after a scarlet fever attack in 1859, he entrusted his oyster interests to hired hands and holed up for almost a year in the North Cove lighthouse, across from Leadbetter Bar, to recover his strength. Here he went through an experience that seems to have solidified, perhaps rigidified, his religious beliefs.

It was his custom to row once a week to Oysterville and back for supplies. Returning one night in a storm, he ran aground a hundred yards offshore. Assuming he had reached the mainland, he left his boat and started wading, testing the depth of the water ahead of him with an oar. But whichever way he turned, the water deepened; he was trapped on a sandspit, with a channel between him and land, and the tide on the rise. When he slogged back to where he had left his boat, it was gone; he had failed to throw out the anchor. He began to call for help, and was heard; but no one could figure out from which direction he was calling.

The tide reached his hips; it reached his chest. Finally he had to cling to his floating oar (since he could not swim), giving an occasional kick to keep his lower extremities from sinking, and hoping the current would carry him to the beach. He insisted later that he at no time despaired. This may have been true, since as a devout Baptist he could not afford to doubt that God would look out for him. Still, he must have felt relief when an object darker than the darkness loomed up beside him. It was his boat, returning like a dog—or perhaps a dogfish—to its master. Grandpa scrabbled over the gunwale and rowed ashore, offering up thanks. The spit was known thereafter as Espy Spit.

Baptist faith had proved itself. If he had placed his reliance in the Methodist proposition of salvation through works—at least such works as leaving a boat unanchored in a rising tide—he would have drowned.

I can report one other incident about grandpa's bachelor days in Oysterville—not because he ever told it, but because others saw it happen. One day in the late 1850s, a winter tide lifted the Stout home from its location on the bay bank (the house must have been about the size of a two-car garage) and carried it seaward in the midst of a driving rain, with Mrs. Stout and their three small children trapped inside. A neighbor rushed to grandpa with the news. Grandpa set aside the accounts on which he was working, unlaced and removed his shoes, pulled on wool socks and gum boots, donned slicker and sou'wester, and waded down the flooded lane to his dinghy. He upped the anchor, settled the oars in their locks, and began to row, using short, even strokes. The wind was intense, the rain was heavy, and the house had been bearing toward the bar for nearly an hour. Grandpa, however, followed without hesitation the path of the now retreating tide, glancing over his shoulder at intervals to see where he was going. At last the Stout house hove dimly into view, already listing to starboard, and well down in the water. Overtaking it, he snubbed his boat to a porch post, waded over the porch, and forced the front door open against the pressure of the water inside. In the living room he found Mrs. Stout in water up to her balloonlike breasts, which she appeared to be using as water wings. She was holding the head of her one-year-old above the surface with one hand and that of her two-year-old with the other. Her three-year-old sat on her shoulders, his hands rooted in her hair.*

The building had sunk too deep to be towed back home against the tide. Grandpa used the painter and anchor from his dinghy to moor the house for future salvage, and rowed the Stouts back to Oysterville. He could not swim, but he knew how to row.

In 1869 grandpa was elected head of the school board. By this time he felt himself financially secure enough to marry, and the school post seemed an ideal vantage point from which to scrutinize prospective wives. He was determined to find one who in education and background was a cut above the average pioneer. Any wife at all would have been a good investment economically; the territory of Washington gave a married man a section of land free, whereas a bachelor was eligible for only half as much. This had led several of grandpa's companions to marry the first female who would have them, often a Siwash; but grandpa preferred to bide his time until he could pick and choose.

That spring he and Lewis Loomis, a fellow board member, traveled by boat and buggy to the University of Salem (now Willamette University) at Salem, Oregon, to seek a teacher for the Oysterville school — whose students, as in the days of John Marshall, still included "married ladys" and hulking young oystermen.

Grandpa and Loomis settled on Julia Ann Jefferson, the prettiest girl in the graduating class. ("Girl" is misleading; Julia Ann was eighteen, and in those days any female of eighteen was a woman grown.) She was the eldest of eight living children, and for seven years had run her father's home; her mother Matilda had been shuttling in and out of a mental hos-

---

*Miss Faye Beaver, now eighty-five, points out that at the time of the floataway the Stouts were a newly married couple with but one child, Miss Beaver's mother-to-be. She is right, but I tell the story as it was told me throughout my childhood; I am too old and stiff-necked to change my memories now.

pital since 1863, addled by the shock of losing two daughters on two successive days to diphtheria.

Matilda, born Matilda Jane Apperson in Tennessee in 1830, had sat proudly beside her own mother Jane in 1847 as their ox team plodded into Oregon City. They had lost Jane's husband Beverly to cholera at Hamsfork on the Oregon Trail. Delos Jefferson took the same trail a year later from Ohio, and married Matilda in 1850. Delos, though he lived by farming, was considered a cut above his neighbors, because he had an ear for music, and at one time even taught singing in Portland. My only photograph of him shows an aging man, clean-shaven except for throat-whiskers. He wears rimless glasses, and a wide-brimmed fedora hat; he looks resigned to the worst.

Grandpa took a boat with Julia up the Willamette River from Salem to Oregon City, holding her firmly by the elbow until, the gangplank being raised, it was too late for her to change her mind and run back home. A second boat carried them from Oregon City to Portland, and a third down the Columbia to Astoria, where Julia, hearing someone called Major, turned her head to see who was addressed, and found that the Major was her own new employer. The title impressed her; his scraggly beard suddenly looked more luxuriant.

An Oysterville teacher held a position of honor in 1869. Oysterville was District No. 1, the educational showplace of the county. Julia taught up to fifty pupils in her one classroom. Her only serious problem was the bull that occasionally broke from its nearby pasture to paw and snort at the school steps, daring anyone to emerge. If the pupils were not home by suppertime, their parents knew the bull was loose, and formed a posse to recapture it.

Julia Ann was paid twenty-five dollars for teaching a school year. In the Willapa school that had been recently formed across the bay, by contrast, pay was not yet in cash but in kind; one teacher's compensation in 1868 had consisted of a sow, which was devoured by a bear before the teacher could either sell or eat it.

The roof of the Willapa school was made of shakes—shingles split from logs three or four feet long. The walls were vertical one-by-sixes. The floors were one-by-twelves, which shrank as they dried, leaving cracks wide enough for a rat to squeeze through. In rainy weather, the pupils sat all day in their wet clothes. The need to keep a window partly open to let out the stove pipe canceled much of the heat thrown off by the stove. There was no clock; when the sun struck a line drawn across the teacher's desk, school was out. Sunlight being a rarity, the length of the school day depended on the teacher's state of mind. At recess the children played hide-and-seek among the trees pressing in on the school-house yard. The lack of privies was no problem; as one of the pupils recalled in later years, the surrounding forest lay "deep and boundless."

Julia could afford to look down on the amenities of the Willapa school. Her school, by contrast, sported a privy for each sex. Built in   118

1863 of California redwood, it had but one room and measured only eighteen by thirty, but was at least rainproof, unlike its counterpart across the bay. Julia's desk and chair stood hard by a recitation table. But the pupils' desks, like those in Willapa, consisted only of two wide boards extending the length of the room, nailed to opposite walls. Pupils sat with their backs to the teacher, the boys facing one wall and the girls the other.

Julia "boarded around" according to the custom of the day. There were two hotels in Oysterville in 1869—the Swan and the Stevens. Julia lived at each in turn, but mostly at the Stevens place, partly because the Stevenses had four daughters near her own age. She appears to have been more pleased with them than they with her. According to family tradition, they resented the fact that her clothing, though homemade, was of better cloth than theirs. Their resentment grew when it became evident that grandpa had honorable designs on her. He would be a poor match, they warned her; he was in his forties, and set in his ways.

Her father, Delos, was dubious, too, about acquiring a son-in-law only two years younger than himself.

But Julia very reasonably shrugged off the caveats of the local girls as manifestations of self-interest; why should they encourage an eligible bachelor to pass, with all his worldly goods, into the hands of an outsider? As to her father's objections, she paid about as much attention to them as any normal, self-supporting daughter would today. Besides, Grandpa Espy was a determined man, who did not take kindly to "No." It pleased him, he told her, that she "had a mind of her own, that she was serious, but neither morose nor proud, that she was not flippant nor giddy." Wooing couched in such romantic terms must have been difficult to resist. And financially grandpa was the best catch around.

Julia taught for one nine-month term. On a showery August 7, 1870, at her father's home near Salem, Oregon, Julia Ann Jefferson, eighteen, hardcore Methodist, and Robert Hamilton Espy, forty-four, landmark Baptist, became one flesh.

By selecting a mate from outside the Shoalwater Bay community, grandpa set a pattern which has plagued his descendants to this day. So far it has been broken only once, in 1941, when Barbara, youngest daughter of Uncle Cecil, married Brongwyn, son of the D. Walter Williamses of Ilwaco. Her marriage knot tied the Espys, for better or worse, richer or poorer, to most of the other early families of the area, the Williamses being related to everybody.

Though grandpa initiated the Espy policy that the males should marry above themselves, it is doubtful whether the Jefferson breed was basically superior to his. Grandpa, however, had never finished grammar school, and it impressed him that his wife was a graduate of a teachers' college, while Delos actually had a parchment from Ohio's Oberlin College—or at least from the Academy; I have a notion that the Academy was only a preparatory school.

The Jeffersons, like the Espys, were of farming stock. The immigrant ancestor, Thomas, settled in Massachusetts before 1714. Thomas's son Joseph served in his middle age as a private in the Revolutionary Army; and Joseph's grandson Willard marched about a bit in the War of 1812 before finally settling in Huron County, Ohio.

Just as I took for granted in my boyhood that I was a direct descendant of *the* Alexander Hamilton, I assumed also a close family connection with our third President, Thomas Jefferson, partly because my great-grandfather, Delos Jefferson, commonly referred to the President as "cousin." Unfortunately, as far as I have been able to trace the matter, the two Jefferson branches had nothing in common but their name and possibly their place of origin in England. Yet my childhood feeling of identification with towering figures of American history certainly helped to form my own sense of self.

My grandmother had wanted to postpone the wedding until she could complete the business of 'sewing up the family,' which meant making dresses for four girls, and suits for three boys. She had previously shared this responsibility with her sister Jane, her junior by eighteen months; but the preceding spring Jane had married a Willamette steamboat captain, so that the entire chore now devolved on Julia and entailed several weeks of sewing at a minimum. Grandpa, unwilling to wait so long, resolved the problem by harnessing the Jefferson gelding and driving with the boys into Salem, where he bought them the first store clothes they had ever owned.

Julia's wedding photograph shows a self-possessed, slender young lady with a determined lower lip, a high, broad forehead, and a straight hairline. Corkscrew curls hung to her shoulders, exposing her ears. She wore a high-collared, pinch-waisted crinoline dress, with a checked panniered skirt, doubtless of her own sewing, that reached the floor. She was lovely.

The photographer posed grandpa in the same position as his bride, his right hand resting on a fake railing backed by a tasseled curtain. His hair was still full and black; his beard was short, the hair not yet filling all the space beneath his lower lip despite his forty-four years; he wore a frock coat, and held, in the hand resting on the railing, what I take to be white gloves. His face, broad-browed like his bride's, is unexpectedly even and elegant, with a thin, rather long nose.

The couple honeymooned in grandpa's alder-shake cabin, where they were still living when their first child was stillborn the following year. Soon afterward they removed to a new, larger house, which grew room by room as the family expanded. It is now the retirement home of their youngest son Cecil, who sleeps in the bed where he and all his siblings were born.

As a married woman grandma was above schoolteaching, and grandpa and Mr. Loomis had to revisit Salem the following year to find a re- 120 placement. They again chose the prettiest candidate, perhaps inspired by a motto over the school door: *Mens Sana in Corpore Sano*. Their translation was, "The best-looking girl is likely to be the best teacher." This was sharp thinking, which papa emulated when his turn came to run the school board thirty-five years later.

If the unattached young ladies of Oysterville were upset when grandpa slipped through their fingers, they must have been even more exasperated when the new teacher fulfilled her one-term contract and

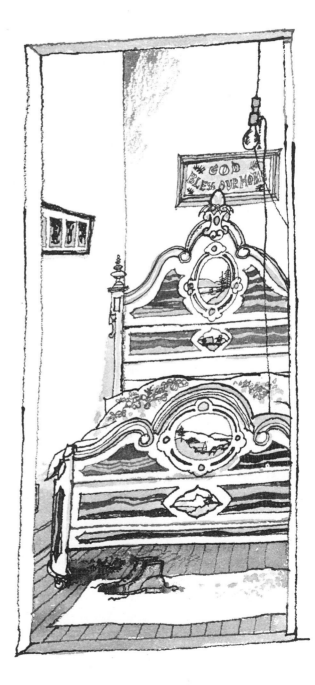

uncle Cecil's bed

then married Mr. Loomis, who, save for grandpa himself, was the most prosperous pioneer to live out his life on the peninsula.

Grandma taught her own children through the first four grades, and she never ceased trying to teach grandpa the niceties of civilized existence. To break to double harness a middle-aged man, more accustomed to Indian lodges than to drawing rooms, was an exercise in both willpower and frustration. Grandpa had dwelt in common-law marriage with whiskey and tobacco since before his wife was born. He saw no reason to desert these agreeable companions now, simply because he was a married man, up in the world. He was a sparing drinker, but for fifteen years it had been his custom to down a tot of whiskey before breakfast and to sip a glass of port before supper. He continued to keep a pipe in his mouth most of the day, and to stock his humidor with the finest Havana cigars that San Francisco could supply.

Though he did respect grandma's refusal to allow alcoholic beverages inside their home, he circumvented the spirit of the prohibition: he kept a barrel of whiskey and another of port in the toolshed, one of a series of outbuildings connected to the main house by a roofed-over cement walk. The roof enabled the Espys, alone among Oysterville residents, to gain the succor of their privy in a downpour and still remain dry.

Grandma's abhorrence of alcohol and nicotine stemmed from her strict Methodist upbringing. Prior to her marriage she went through total immersion as a concession to grandpa, but her heart remained Methodist. She knew that salvation depended on works, and that the inevitable result of even moderate sinfulness was damnation. Grandpa, on the other hand, had a pact with the Almighty: in return for his agreement to believe in God, God agreed to keep His itching fingers out of grandpa's affairs.

On June 4, 1871, grandpa organized four local Baptists into a church he was to operate at his home for twenty-one years, with the help of an occasional visiting pastor. When no professional man of God was available, each communicant in turn led the service, reading his favorite from a standard collection of Baptist sermons.

Whenever grandpa and grandma argued the relative merits of faith and works, he reverted to the miracle of his rescue from drowning on Espy Spit. It was a difficult point to counter.

"I remember only once," papa used to say, "when your grandfather raised his voice against your grandmother. When he was earnest, he tended to roar, and this time he was very earnest. 'Woman,' he exclaimed, 'I take good care of you, but I won't have you interfering with what I think is right.' And he stalked off, pausing only to grit through his teeth, 'Julia, never let me have to tell you again: I am *saved!*"

My grandmother did improve my grandfather's morals in one respect. She made him give up poker.

But if he who lusts after a woman in his heart is guilty of adultery, then grandpa remained guilty of poker to the last. Though he never touched a card after his wedding day, he repaired repeatedly to one or another of the Oysterville saloons, to stand silently behind a poker table, evaluating the skill of the contestants.

As Oysterville boomed, poker became a major industry. "It was nothing unusual," said one old-timer, "to see a five-dollar ante and nothing but gold on the table, several thousand dollars' worth. If the owners seen the big-money people come in, they pushed the silver aside and used only gold."

In the summer of 1880, grandpa, by then a co-owner of the Morgan Oyster Company, watched a game in which his former factor in San Francisco, John Hunter, was one of four participants.* Hunter's partners had bought him out of the oyster business, apparently because they feared he might lose company money at cards; and he had returned north to farm on Wallicutt Creek.

The other players were Isaac Lane, a timber cruiser; Wallace Stuart, later a member of the Washington State legislature; and a third man whose name I never learned. The play ended after five hours, when Hunter, having lost $20,000 in cash and IOUs, finally threw a deed to his farm into the pot and lost again. Suddenly sober and remorseful, he begged for the loan of a revolver; he said he would retire to the front stoop of the saloon — which stood on stilts above the mud flats — and shoot himself in such a fashion that his body would fall into the bay and drift away on the tide, never to offend the eyes of decent citizens again. It was a quixotic project, the drop from the stoop to the mud flats being less than four feet, and the tide being out anyhow; Hunter, dead or alive, would have wound up stuck among the quahogs. But Stuart, who had won $3,000 and the farm, consented — out of consideration, he said, for Hunter's "nice wife and family" — to return the deed, and Hunter decided not to kill himself after all.

Once the matter was settled, grandpa shrugged into his slicker, fastened his sou'wester under his chin, said, "Good night, gentlemen," and splashed home through the rain puddles. The only comment he was ever heard to make on that poker game was, "Mr. Hunter has not been my factor for some time."

Like other husbands, grandpa deferred to his wife's wishes in some respects and ignored them in others. He might have walked more carefully had he known that she was descended from a witch.

---

*"In 1867," said Hawthorne's account, "[Espy] formed a partnership with J. F. Warren, W. C. Doane, H. S. Gile, John Hunter, and I. Y. Doane, under the name of Espy and Co. at Oysterville, and Warren & Co. at San Francisco. Mr. Warren soon withdrew from the firm, and a few years later Mr. Hunter retired. The remaining four members of the firm, after continuing their operations for several years, united their interests with the Morgan and Swarching Oyster Companies and formed the Morgan Oyster Company of San Francisco."

10

The Blessed Witches

If you will look back to the chart at the beginning of the preceding chapter, you will see that one of Grandma Espy's eighteenth-century progenitors, Mary Towne, married an Isaac Esty. (The similarity of the name to Espy is a coincidence.) Their granddaughter married a Jepherson, and the great-grandson of that Jepherson, by then spelled Jefferson, was the great-grandfather of my great-grandfather Delos.

When papa looked back down the roads that led his forebears to Oysterville, there was no other ancestor along the way in whom he took such pride as he did in Mary Towne Esty, who was hanged as a witch at Salem in 1792. He was proud not because she was a witch, but because, by his lights, she was a saint.

He spoke of her often with admiration as we sat about the nursery stove or before the library fireplace, and when particularly moved would even read aloud her communications to her judges. Nonetheless it took me years to fit Mary's story into some sort of reasonable sequence. The best way I can describe her to you is to pretend for a minute that you, my reader, are yourself Mary Esty.

You are a housewife approaching sixty, low-voiced, vigorous, a little below the middle height, gray-eyed, tending to corpulence. If acquaintances were asked to name a distinguishing feature about you, they would be hard put; some, though, might remember a wen, looking like a small, wrinkled walnut, on your right cheekbone.

It is May 18, 1692, and you are snugly pillioned aboard your sway-backed bay nag, your arms clasping the waist of your goodman. You are returning, praising God in your heart, to your farm in the village of Salem (the part that is now Danvers), Massachusetts. It is a sunlit day, and a trace of breeze ruffles the bonnet protecting your graying hair. The boulders along the trail are green with mosses and tendrils. Grapevines festoon the roadside trees. The creeks your horse splashes through are lined with pink-flowered marshmallows, and foxgloves shine purple along the sandy hillocks.

These are reasons enough for praising God. But in addition, you have just been cleared of anathema—the charge that you, Mary Esty, blameless for fifty-eight years before the world, had signed your name in the Red Book—had sold yourself body and soul to the devil—had become the word none must speak—a witch.

Innocent you are, of course; but also, now, *declared* innocent! So you nod and smile at the good folk you pass, and some, though not all, nod and smile back; Goody Putnam, feeding her chickens, deliberately turns her wide rear quarters, and a seventeen-year-old girl named Mary Herrick makes a sign against the evil eye. And warm as the sun is, a tiny chill lingers at your nape; for you know that your sisters Rebecca and Sarah, jailed before you, still await vindication. But surely that, too, will be only a momentary tribulation, for two more pious, God-fearing women never lived; any day now, their innocence will become manifest.

I pray that joy will overflow every crack and cranny of the three days of freedom that lie ahead of you; for from then on you will live in irons, and four months and four days from this very May 18, you will be hanged as high as Haman, and a good Christian clergyman, viewing your corpse and seven more dangling beside it, will say, shaking his reverend head, "What a sad thing it is to see eight firebrands of hell hanging there!"

Fortunately, you cannot look four months or even four hours ahead; you can only know that before a court of inquiry you have maintained your innocence with such meekness, candor, and conviction that your very accusers retracted their charges. You know too that you are again with your man, Isaac — cooper, selectman, juryman — Isaac, who bears you a loyal love as rare in the seventeenth century as in the twentieth — Isaac, who (though this you are not to know) will pursue the Massachusetts courts for twenty years after your murder, until finally the dreadful verdict against you is expunged.

The farm is just ahead. Bossy the cow will let down her milk more willingly now that your familiar fingers are again urging her teats; and Squat, the old, purblind mongrel, will scramble into your lap, and lick your face, and wag his tail like a fan; and for all you can say, or I can say, even the chickens will peck and the pigs will grunt more contentedly, knowing their mistress is back home.

Three precious days. After that, the girls who retracted their charges will go into fits again, and report that Goody Esty is choking them; and then, Goody Esty, you will be rushed to Boston jail. The instant the great door clangs behind you the afflicted children will recover, and you will be doomed.

Goody Esty, sometimes spelled Easty, was my eight-times-great-grandmother. Her seventy-year-old sister Rebecca, Mrs. Francis Nurse, and her forty-four-year-old sister Sarah, Mrs. Peter Cloyse, were also condemned as witches, and the first two were hanged.

I do not propose to retell the story of the witch trials, or to speculate again on the motivations of the accusers, the judges, the clergy, or even the victims themselves. My concern is only with the three sisters whose blood I share. Other accused witches bore their persecutions as nobly, and many less so, but let them be. They were not the ones we talked about when I was a boy sitting around a red-hot stove in the nursery at Oysterville.

Salem Village consisted of a few mean streets, with wharves sticking like the tines of pitchforks into Massachusetts Bay, and marshes and creeks and farms crowding in from the back — a typical God-fearing New England village of the late seventeenth century.

Not only was the puritan God a jealous God; through His appointed agents, He regulated not just the public deportment but the private lives of His creatures, down to the shape of the buckle of their oldest shoe. These agents were, by and large, ministers, merchants, lawyers, and their peers, and it is their professed standard of conduct that the word

Puritan has come to connote. But they were the respectable cover for a heaving, squirming mass of yeomen, servants, mechanics, storekeepers, swineherds, beggars, and ne'er-do-wells.

Now these yeomen, servants, ne'er-do-wells, and so forth cared very little about presenting themselves as shining lights before the Lord. Their overriding desire, apart from survival, was to be let alone. In one sense, they were alone indeed; the world outside existed only in letters from England, and the bulk of the population could not read or write. This saved them a great deal of trouble. It also saved trouble for the ruling powers because it enabled those powers to shape history in their own image. Who cared if an Irishman was imported as a slave, as long as he couldn't write anybody to tell about it?

The villages created schools, but were reluctant to pay the teachers. They refused flatly to tithe themselves for the education of girls, which in the eyes of the early Puritans would have been a waste of village money and the girls' time.

The general populace lied, stole, cheated, and whored at the rate customary since Adam. They were the most creative cursers this side of Pandemonium. They fought Indians when the authorities so ordered; if by good luck they overran a village containing maidens of tolerable attraction, they raped the maidens, because it was the natural and reasonable thing to do.

Their common enemy was the Law. In New England the Law, a hard enough master in any event, was also God's surrogate. The New England Law hanged Quakers in the 1660s and witches at random throughout the century. Not long before the Salem witchcraft trials, a court ordered that one Philip Ratcliff "shall be whipped, have his eares cutt off, fyned £40, & banished out of ye lymitts of this jurisdiction for uttering malicious & scandalous speeches against the govmnt & the church of Salem." Faced with such a sanction most of us would become good churchgoers.

Even after the witchcraft madness, Massachusetts imposed on any able-bodied person who failed to show up for church for the space of a month a fine of twenty shillings. If the sinner was unable to pay the fine, he was "to be set in the cage or stocks not exceeding three hours according to the discretion of the justices." Stocks, whipping post, and pillory stood near every parish church.

It would be pleasant to say that the meetinghouses were at least comfortable. They were not. They had no stoves, these costing money; they were so cold in winter that Samuel Sewall reports seeing sacrament bread frozen as hard as pebbles, and hearing pieces of it rattle as they fell into the pewter plates.

Under such circumstances, discomfort in church must have been shared by rich and poor. The people of substance, however, could always be sustained by the dignity of the seats allotted them. Reports one town record:

127

✛ Impr. it is agreed that mr william Browne & mr. Georg Corwin shall be seated with Maiorhathorn in that wch is Called the magistrate seate.

✛ that the seate of mrs. Endicot being enlargd we agree that mrs. hathorne & mrs. Corwin shallbe there seated.

✛ that mrs Price sister Elizabeth Browne the wife of John Browne & sister Grafton & the wife of Sergent Porter, we agree they shalbe seated in the second seate where Mrs. hathorne & Mrs. Corwin latelie sate.

✛ that Sargent hale his wife & ffrances Skerie his wife are to sitt in the seates of mrs Price & sister Grafton.

✛ That mrs. Norris shall be seated with mrs. Browne.

✛ that sister Prince to be seated where Sergent Porter his wife latelie sate.

✛ that Sergent Porter shall sit in the seate with Capt Trask.

The rest of the congregation sat — or stood — where they could.

So much for the background of the strange events of 1692. Whether the witchcraft delusions were brought to a head by class antagonisms, judicial arrogance, ministerial vindictiveness, or some sudden contagious plague of the soul I know not. But this much is on the record:

In early 1692 a forty-year-old minister named Samuel Parris assumed the pulpit at Salem Village. Six months later, nineteen women had been hanged as witches; one hundred fifty had been thrown into prison, where several had died; and an aged man had been pressed to death for refusing to plead.

The first sign of the horror to come was the sickening of several young girls. The earliest were Elizabeth, the minister's own nine-year-old daughter; Abigail Williams, his eleven-year-old niece; and Ann Putnam, the twelve-year-old daughter of the parish clerk. These became possessed, it appeared, by the devil, as evidenced by fits which were called "preternatural, both as to the manner, which is so strange as a well person could not screw their body into; and as to the violence also it is preternatural, being much beyond the ordinary force of the same person when they are in their right mind."

The accusers, all girls, finally totaled ten. Whether they began as fraudulent imposters, or were hysterics all along, the special subject of their attacks appears to have been the middle-class families of the village. One's chances of being accused as a witch rose in proportion to one's ability to read and write.

On March 1, 1692, the girls accused threee local women, including the Reverend Parris's West Indian slave Tituba, of witchery, and the great hunt was on.

Rebecca Towne Nurse

The girls reported molestations by the spirit of Rebecca Towne Nurse — seventy-year-old sister of my ancestor Mary — whose piety and devotion to good works had hitherto been unquestioned. On March 24, a committee was sent to examine the deaf old lady, with the results described below:

We whose names are underwritten being desired to go to Goodman Nurse his house, to speak with his wife, and to tell her that several of the afflicted persons mentioned her; and accordingly we went, and we found her in a weak and low condition in body as she told us, and had been sick almost a week. And we asked her how it was otherwise with her; and she said she blessed God for it, she had more of his presence in this sickness than sometime she have had, but not so much as she desired; but she would, with the apostle, press forward to the mark; and many other pieces of Scripture to the like purpose. And then, of her own accord, she began to speak of the affliction that was amongst them. And in particular of Mr. Parris his family and how she was grieved for them, though she had not been to see them, by reason of fits that she formerly used to have; for people said it was awful to behold; but she pitied them with all her heart, and went to God for them. But she said she heard that there was persons spoke of that were as innocent as she was, she believed; and, after much to this purpose, we told her that she was spoken of also. "Well," she said, "if it be so, the will of the Lord be done." She sat still a while, being as it were amazed; and then she said, "Well, as to this thing I am as innocent as the child unborn; but surely," she said, "what sin hath God found out in me unrepented of, that he should lay such an affliction upon me in my old age?" And, according to our best observation, we could not discern that she knew what we came for before we told her.

Israel Porter
Elizabeth Porter

The verdict of "innocent" would normally have been inescapable; but there was no resisting the outcry of the afflicted girls. Rebecca was arrested. A witchcraft court, appointed by Governor William Phips, found her so hard of hearing and so full of grief that she could not understand all that was said against her, and no pains were taken that she should hear. The court brought in a verdict of not guilty; but the afflicted children thereupon created such turmoil that William Stoughton (Phips's lieutenant governor, acting as chief justice) ordered them to go back and change their verdict. This they did on June 30. Stoughton condemned her to death, and she was hanged on July 19.

Sarah Cloyse

On April 3, 1692, when Rebecca Nurse had been jailed but not yet condemned, the Reverend Parris chose as the text for his sermon John 6, 70: "Have not I chosen you twelve, and one of you is a devil." The implication that Rebecca had been proven guilty even before being tried so outraged her forty-four-year-old sister, Sarah, that she rose from her seat, left the meetinghouse, and slammed the door behind her "to the amazement of the congregation."

Within days the afflicted girls began to see the apparition of Sarah Cloyse in their fits, taking the devil's sacrament of "red bread and drink." A warrant was issued against Sarah on the eighth day of the month, and an examination conducted on the eleventh. John, another Carib Indian slave of Parris, was a witness for the prosecution. Goody Cloyse, he said, or her spirit, had hurt him—choked him, and brought him the devil's book to sign.

"Oh," exclaimed Sarah, "you are a grievous liar!"

But emotions had reached a pitch where charge alone assured conviction. The following day Sarah Cloyse and Rebecca Nurse were sent off with other accused witches to Boston jail.

Now, here is a curious circumstance, for which I have no explanation: though Sarah Cloyse, like her sisters Rebecca Nurse and Mary Esty, was convicted of witchcraft, she, alone of the three, was not executed, and was eventually released.

Mary Esty

The last of the three Towne sisters to be charged by the ailing girls, my own ancestress Mary Esty, continued to milk her cow and feed her chickens in freedom for one month less four days after the incarceration of her elder sister Rebecca, and twelve days after that of her younger sister Sarah. But then the afflicted girls found her too choking them nightly, and she was rearrested.

Mary was at first less frightened than baffled by the charges against her. Witches were real enough—everybody knew that. But how could she and her sisters, respected God-fearing members of the community, be singled out for such a hellish molestation? She could not understand. And being Christian to the core, she could not even blame the accusing girls. Their courtroom fits, she was convinced, were no frauds. She could only shake her head: "It is an evil spirit," she said at her trial, "but whether it be witchcraft I do not know."

By this point in my researches, my idea of the reality of a Salem witch had been considerably changed. A few were obviously wicked or mad, but taken by and large they were certainly a superior lot to their accusers and their judges.

Just as I arrived at this decision, I found in a drawer of my father's rolltop desk two documents by Mary Esty. Papa had read them to us time and again, but I had forgotten. And suddenly I realized that all this while I had not been witch-hunting at all; I had been entertaining an angel unawares.

Mary was still languishing in Boston jail on the dreadful day of July 19 when her sister Rebecca was hanged by the neck until dead. The 130 shock of that happening led Mary to address the following communication to the Court:

The Humble Request of Mary Esty and Sarah Cloyse to the Honoured Court humbly showeth, that whereas we two sisters, Mary Esty and Sarah Cloyse, stand now before the Honoured Court charged with the suspicion of witchcraft, our humble request is — First, that seeing we are neither able to plead our own cause, nor is counsel allowed to those in our condition, that you who are our judges would please to be of counsel to us, to direct us wherein we may stand in need. Secondly, that whereas we are not conscious to ourselves of any guilt in the least degree of that crime whereof we are now accused (in the presence of the living God we speak it, before whose awful tribunal we know we shall ere long appear), nor of any other scandalous evil or miscarriage inconsistent with Christianity, those who have had the longest and best knowledge of us, being persons of good report, may be suffered to testify upon oath what they know concerning each of us; viz. Mr. Capen, the pastor, and those of the town and church of Topsfield, who are ready to say something which we hope may be looked upon as very considerable in this matter, with seven children of one of us; viz. Mary Esty; and it may be produced of like nature in reference to the wife of Peter Cloyse, her sister. Thirdly, that the testimony of witches, or such as are afflicted as is supposed by witches, may not be improved to condemn us without other legal evidence concurring. We hope the Honoured Court and Jury will be so tender of the lives of such as we are, who have for many years lived under the unblemished reputation of Christianity, as not to condemn them without a fair and equal hearing of what may be said for us as well as against us. And your poor suppliants shall be bound always to pray, etc.

As may be imagined, her judges paid no attention to this moving missive. The trial took place as scheduled, and the sisters were condemned. Mary made one more unavailing protest:

The humble petition of Mary Esty unto his Excellency, Sir William Phips, and to the Honoured Judge and Bench now sitting in Judicature in Salem, and the Reverend Ministers, hereby showeth that, whereas your poor and humble petitioner, being condemned to die, do humbly beg of you to take it in your judicious and pious consideration, that your poor and humble petitioner, knowing my own innocency, blessed be the Lord for it! and seeing plainly the wiles and subtility of my accusers by myself, cannot but judge charitably of others that are going the same way of myself, if the Lord steps not mightily in. I was confined a whole month upon the same account as I am now condemned for, and then cleared by the afflicted persons, as some of your Honours know. And in two days' time I was cried out upon by them, and have been confined, and am now condemned to die. The Lord above knows my innocency then, and likewise does now, as at the great day will be known to men and angels. I petition not to Your Honours for my life, for I know I must die, and my appointed time is set; but the Lord he knows it that if it be possible, no more innocent blood may be shed, which undoubtedly cannot be avoided in the ways and course you go in. I question not but Your Honours do the utmost of your powers in the discovery and detecting of witchcraft and witches, and would not be guilty of innocent blood for the world. But, by my own innocency, I know you are in the wrong way. The Lord in his infinite mercy direct you in this great work, if it be his blessed will that no more innocent blood be shed! I would humbly beg of you, that Your Honours would be pleased to examine these afflicted persons strictly, and keep them apart for some time, and likewise to try some of these confessing witches; I being confident there is several of them has belied themselves and others, as will appear; if not in this world, I am sure in the world to come, whither I am now a-going. I question not but you will see an alteration of these things. They say myself and others having made a league with the Devil, we cannot confess. I know, and the Lord knows, as will shortly appear, they belie me, and so I question not but they do others. The Lord above, who is the Searcher of all hearts, knows, as I shall answer for it at the tribunal seat, that I know not the least thing of witchcraft; therefore I cannot, I dare not belie my own soul. I beg Your Honours not to deny this my humble petition from a poor, dying, innocent person. And I question not but the Lord will give a blessing to your endeavours.

Again, her judges paid no attention. As James D. Phillips, editor of *Salem in the Seventeenth Century,* says: "That [the judges] could remain unaffected by a petition like Mary Esty's can be explained only by realizing that they had long ceased to pay attention to anything said by a suspect. Their minds and hearts were so filled with the hideous torments of the afflicted and the frightful tales of the confessors that they were quite unable to absorb anything else."

To this day, no one can point with certain finger at the devil or devils behind the Salem witchcraft horrors. Was it Cotton Mather, the fire-breathing Calvinist? Or courts with closed minds? Or the whole ministry? Or the afflicted girls? We know only that as suddenly as the persecutions had sprung up, they vanished.

There were no other executions for witchcraft in Salem after the day that Mary Esty and her seven companions swung from their gibbets. Within a month, a proposition was made in Salem for a day of repentant fasting. One after another, the accusers of the unrecallable dead recanted. The town woke from its nightmare.

Why? Perhaps from sheer surfeit of bloodletting. Perhaps from the leveling of charges higher and higher into the ranks of power, until even the wives of the governor and of Cotton Mather himself were accused. This, the authorities may have thought, was going too far. Thoughtful men like Samuel Sewall publicly repented their part in the persecutions. 132

Yet surely the letters of Mary Esty, coming at a moment when people were beginning to come to their senses, played no small part in the revulsion. If she was one of the last victims of the witchcraft delusions, her shade can claim a full share of credit for finally putting them down.

I think often of the Towne sisters. I find myself again and again checking the fates of one against the other. I wish I could have known them. I wish I had been able to sit beside them as they sat tranquilly rocking after the hard work of the day was over. I even wish I might have lent a hand at milking old Bossy, and learned if she would let down for me.

The reason for these idle thoughts is only partly that Goody Nurse and Goody Esty and Goody Cloyse were my kin. Principally I think of them so often because these three women have convinced me that despite all argument, all outrage, true goodness and mercy do exist in this wicked and merciless world. At home or at church, in irons, in obloquy, they remained faithful to themselves, to one another, to their families, their church, their God. They did not revile false accusers and deaf judges; they forgave. They did not curse the God who held this cup to their lips; they accepted.

Among my forebears there are some of whom I am proud, and others whom I could do without; but my only genes with halos spring from the loins of Mary Esty, the blessed witch of Salem.

Gorse
in
bloom

11

The Saved and the Damned

In 1870, Oysterville boasted two hotels, two stores, one church building, seven saloons, and a post office. The postmaster was paid twenty-five dollars a year. This was not munificent when compared with the nine-hundred-dollar salary at Olympia, but must have looked good from Fort Willapa, where the going wage was five dollars. A few more commercial establishments were added during the years when my father was growing up: another two stores; the Davis tannery; the Holman smithy; a sail-maker's shop; and a weekly newspaper, the *Pacific Journal*. John W. Phillips, arriving in 1885 to become the new editor of the *Journal*, reported his welcome as follows:

The wind blew us into the printing plant, and slammed the door behind us. The printer's devil was waiting, his lamp lit; he was trying to remove the insignia of his office from face and hands. In a short while he informed us that it was grubbing time and that we were to adjourn to his boardinghouse for refreshments. We reached the house after stumbling along a side street in the dark, sometimes on the single twelve-inch plank that formed the sidewalk, sometimes up to our knees in mud and water, and arrived to find frogs by the hundreds loose in the lobby, evidence of a practical experiment in human and frog psychology by two small boys, Gilbert and Harry Tinker.

Most of my information about the period between 1870 and 1890 comes from papa and Aunt Dora, who was a more frequent visitor to Oysterville during my childhood than papa's other siblings. Papa and Aunt Dora had much in common: they were the oldest surviving children, she born in 1872 and he in 1876; they liked to reminisce; they had big noses; they had loud voices; and they were both very sure of the correctness of their memories, even when they remembered the same event entirely differently. If I had seen more of Aunt Sue or Uncle Will or Aunt Verona or Uncle Cecil in my childhood, some of my impressions of early Oysterville might be quite different.

The village was divided between the saved and the damned, with the damned, I am afraid, frequently in the majority. Indeed, the county seat in the seventies and eighties was a magnet for the lawless element up and down the coast, particularly the drinkers, the gamblers, and the type of young lady who favored their company. Oysters fed them all. When the oyster business collapsed and the county seat was kidnapped a few years later, not only the business establishments but the saloons and dance halls vanished overnight from Oysterville, as if the Lord had rubbed them off his blackboard with an eraser. By the time my own parents made their permanent home there in 1902, the village, or what was left of it, was as stuffed with piety as a dying atheist.

There was one major difference between papa's and Aunt Dora's reflections: his principal interest lay in the saved, and hers in the damned.

He would tell ruefully how, up until the age of seven or eight, he and Dora had to accompany their mother twice a week in formal calls on their neighbors.

"Mother made sure," papa said, "that I looked her — not my — best on these occasions. Dora would be ready, elegantly turned out, I suppose, according to her own lights, while my mother was still trying to entice me into what she called kilts but what I think of as a smock, built like a double-breasted coat and coming to my knees. Generally it was an affair of blue checked gingham, with trousers of the same material well hidden underneath. Once mother had decided I looked passable, she would spend an interminable time deciding which of her black gloves to wear, the kid or the silk. Sometimes she chose mitts, with a fourth to two-thirds of her fingers exposed."

Grandma alternated her calling schedule, covering the north end of town on one round and the south end on the next. "In the center, where our own home was," pop explained, "mother followed a less rigid calling routine, knowing that before the next visiting day she was bound to see her neighbors repeatedly across the fence or at the kitchen door."

"But don't imagine," he would add, especially when mama was listening, "that we lived like yokels. Why, there were times when it neither rained nor blew; there were even times when the sun came out. And remember, we had merchandise pouring in to pay for our oysters — the best that San Francisco, Portland, and Seattle could provide. The better homes may not have been palaces, but they were not hovels. They were solidly constructed of redwood. By the middle seventies the board and lathe construction of the first houses had given way to plaster. I admit, Helen, that the furniture was mostly from Grand Rapids, but there is nothing prettier for the upper half of a front door than a Grand Rapids imitation stained-glass panel. Ours used to have a picture of a six-pronged buck, his head raised to sniff the air. When the sun shone through the glass the colors of that buck could have come straight from Heaven. I'd give a good deal if we had him here right now."

Oysterville had two levels of licit social life. First, there was the continuing sort that went on outside the Methodist church after the sermon each Sunday, when the men discussed oysters and the weather while the wives exchanged reports on their flower gardens. The flowers lined sparkling paths of crushed oyster shells. These were kept sprinkled with bay water, which by its salinity not only held down weeds and pests but made the shells glisten in the sun.

Favorite flowers included blue forget-me-nots; wallflowers, equally fragrant whether their tint was yellow, orange, or brown; cornflowers — blue, purple, pink or white; blush-pink moss roses; red climbing roses; white York roses.

Garden-variety socializing was supplemented on another level by the more elaborate entertainment in which the entire community took part. The height of the year's social excitement was reached in the summer, during the annual court term. Territorial judges sometimes came from as far away as Spokane, attorneys from Astoria and Portland, and jurors, witnesses, and spectators from all over the country. In the 1870s Court Week was climaxed by the Fourth of July regatta of the Shoalwater Bay Yacht Club.

The crowning event of the regatta was a plunger race, which covered a triangular thirty-mile course. Grandpa (a poor sailor himself) donned special black broadcloth pants, a maroon and black brocaded vest, a light linen duster, a stiff shirt with boiled bosom, a stiff collar, a bow tie, and a beaver hat, to act as commodore of the day. He would discharge the cannon that started the boats on their run, and would award the prize to the winning crews—a silver cup for first prize; a silver watch for second; a gold-headed cane for third. Captain Wes Whitcomb's *Occidental* made the best time in the first race, but was disqualified for not turning the stakes on the correct side, allegedly because he thought port meant starboard. The quality of boat design and seamanship varied widely; in one race the winning crew had time to get tipsy before the second boat crossed the line.

"Everybody dressed up afterward," recalled Aunt Dora sixty years later, "and ate oysters and drank lemonade. Lemonade was much more precious then than champagne is now."

The regatta banquet and ball were held the same evening in the dance hall above the post office and saloon.

Besides the dances, which my grandparents did not attend, there were lawn parties lighted by Japanese lanterns; baseball games; sack races; three-legged races; and potato races. But there were no swimming parties. Even at high tide, anyone trying to swim in the bay would have had to wade or row out hundreds of yards to be more than waist deep. There was some unorganized ocean swimming, though the water was always cold. The swimmers, aware of the lethal undertow, had sense enough to remain connected to a lifeline, a custom that their descendants might usefully resume today.

Oysterville was not the only bay settlement that looked forward to community festivities. In Bay Center, ten miles away as the salmon swims, the great event of the year occurred at Thanksgiving. A few days beforehand, the villagers set up two competing teams of hunters to bag fowl for the ceremonial feast. The winning captain got the biggest pie; the loser had to make a speech. The winners were awarded the wishbones; the losers had to clear off the tables. For scoring purposes, birds were assigned point values as follows:

Crane or coot	5
Teal, butterball, jacksnipe	10
Widgeon, redhead, spoonbill, bluebill	30
Mallard, canvasback, sprig	40

Brant	60
Honker goose	100
Swan	300

Salads, crisp pickles, spicy relishes, cranberries, celery, and fluffy mashed potatoes framed the fowl on four rows of tables that ran the length of the community hall. Only the gradual decline of the duck population brought the famous Bay Center Duck Dinner to an end.

Parties aside, there was not much excitement around the bay for the saved in the seventies and eighties. Once in a while, to be sure, the treeing of a bear set Oysterville aflutter, or a ship broke up in the breakers. In the latter event, oystering was suspended while the villagers beachcombed.

Aunt Dora, as reported, was more interested in the damned than in the saved. At the age of ten, when she went calling on neighbors with her mother, her apparel was more sedate than her thoughts. Her ambition was to dress as colorfully as the birds of passage who at irregular intervals came twittering into Oysterville. They slept late at the hotels and preened their feathers far into the night at the dance hall, until all at once they took flight and vanished as suddenly as they had arrived.

Their arrival generally coincided with that of certain reputed shanghaiers from Astoria, across the Columbia River. Astoria, being in the state of Oregon, had difficulty extraditing accused criminals from Oysterville in the territory of Washington. It was, therefore, convenient for one who found Astoria temporarily a little hot to relax in Oysterville until Astoria cooled down. The birds of passage contributed to this relaxation.

Aunt Dora explained that when these outlaws arrived, their first move was to hire the dance hall, where "a one-legged Indian would saw out the tunes on an old fiddle."

Grandpa Espy happened to be the owner of that dance hall, which was located above his store. Neither of my grandparents would have dreamed of cutting a rug or doing a buck and wing themselves, nor would they have permitted their children to do so. Still, dancing was a respectable diversion in the village, which was well supplied with young people. There were dances once a week—twice a week when court was in session. Business was business, and a Christian could even own a dance hall if, like grandpa, he knew he was square with the Lord. I find it somewhat surprising, though, that grandpa allowed Dora, prepubescent by little more than a hair, to help sweep out the hall, and then to stay long enough to watch the first Virginia reels, in which the feet of the dancers pounded so hard that the coal oil lanterns swayed and smoked overhead.

When the birds of gay plumage were aflutter in town, grandma was reluctant to have her daughter walk alone even to the post office. If Dora   138 crossed paths with those colorful creatures, she was under no circumstances to acknowledge their existence; above all, she was not to accept the pennies and nickels that they offered local children in a rather pathetic effort to win a smile and a kind word. Aunt Dora recalled with some satisfaction that she did accept peppermint candy.

She considered the visitors exquisite. "Particularly," she used to say, "I loved the bright ribbons they wore. Once mother bought me some turkey-red calico for a dress. I tore strips off and made bows and tied them in my hair so I would look like those beautiful ladies. When I walked the street the grown-ups would say, 'Hello, little girl, where did you get your bows?'"

It was Aunt Dora—not papa, you may be sure—who told me about the rivalry between an out-of-towner, reportedly a Spaniard, and a local Siwash for the favors of an Indian maiden of pleasing prominences. The Spaniard owned a stiletto of the finest steel, its ebony handle inlaid with silver. In a dispute over proprietorship of the maiden, the Siwash wrestled this weapon from his adversary, tossed it away, and proceeded to thrash him soundly. A few days later the Siwash was found stabbed to death on the ocean beach, the stiletto lying the sand nearby. The Spaniard was never seen again.

Aunt Dora justified the bawdiest story she ever told me as proof that even the most unregenerate sinner can be saved. A certain Oysterville blade, she said, for years had been exceptional in his amorous successes, even against seemingly insuperable obstacles; if his current fancy was wife of the local Methodist minister, that only made the challenge more exciting. His lack of fastidiousness gave him a head start; it mattered not a whit to him whether the female he was stalking was thin or stout, pocked or clear, red or white, young or old, wanton or virtuous. The pleasure of the chase was all, and his percentage of successes was acknowledgedly phenomenal. To commemorate each new conquest he was in the habit of clipping off and binding with a thread a snippet of his love's pubic hair. These he kept in a brown paper sack, which on request he would produce for his friends, identifying the source of each snippet by its straightness, kinkiness, coarseness, fineness, or color. The snippets ran the spectrum; some were golden, some brown, black, red, grizzled, or gray, and a surprising number white. One youth was incensed to find a sorrel-colored specimen attributed to his own fiancée, whose hair happened to be mouse brown; he charged that the hair had been clipped from a local horse, and a stallion at that. But on his wedding night he found that her lower growth was as handsomely sorrel as the stallion's.

When the brown paper sack was finally full, the young blade, by then less young, buried it in a secret place, married a fourteen-year-old virgin, and became a deacon.

With a few such exceptions, the decent element of Oysterville was in at least nominal charge. Its visible symbol, from 1872 on, was the Methodist Church. The Crellin family, though they were Catholics, gave the bell, and George H. Brown, a Catholic from Tokeland, presented a gold-gilded cross—the only cross I have ever seen surmounting a Methodist Church. The principal room measured forty by twenty-eight feet, and the anteroom ten by twelve feet. The presiding elder was the Reverend John F. Devore, who had dedicated the first Protestant church north of the Columbia in 1853, and continued fighting the devil without intermission for the next thirty-six years.

As Baptists, the Espys refused to worship in the Methodist Church. Baptist circuit riders used the Espy home as their headquarters; one of them, the Reverend Huff, whose white beard fell below his waist, lived there for eight years, in a room that became known as the Prophet's Chamber. In the 1870s an exemplary Christian, Kate Hulbert, crossed the continent from Pennsylvania to fulfill a mail-order betrothal, and stayed several weeks with the Espys while awaiting the arrival of her fiancé, the Reverend J. Wichser, who was off in the wilderness saving souls. Fellow church workers described Wichser as "a dwarf in stature, but a little giant in mind and a great giant in heart."

1870 Methodist Church
Oysterville, Washington

The marriage took place; and the newlyweds set out after more souls. According to a Baptist history of the time, "They journeyed on foot, blazing their way through the uninhabited forests a distance of nearly one hundred and fifty miles. . . . They established preaching stations, prayer meetings, and Sunday schools. They carried a church basket and knapsack with them, in which they gathered eggs, butter, and vegetables, bringing them into the market and turning their proceeds over to the church buildings. Finally, his health broken, they removed to Southern Oregon, where the dear Lord had need of him and called him up higher."

I record these events because Kate Hulbert, while waiting in Oysterville for her fiancé, struck up a warm friendship with grandma. They corresponded for the next quarter of a century, and a few years after grandma's death, Kate married grandpa.

Grandpa ceaselessly pushed the Baptist sect. A characteristic letter from him appeared in the *Baptist Beacon:*

There are Baptist ministers who are idle. Here is a large vineyard. Enter it and labor, and whatsoever is right the Lord of the vineyard promised to pay, and we will go bail that he will fulfill his promise.

Grandpa was the one who went bail.

The part of the Oysterville population that was damned spent much of its time directly across the street from the church, in the saloon that occupied a wing of the Pacific Hotel. This structure, built at about the same time as the church, was for years the largest hotel in the county; during Court Week it served as many as 250 customers a day. When the Methodist Church was formally opened, Richard Carruthers, owner of the Pacific Hotel, closed his doors for the duration of the ceremonies, so that his parishioners could pay their respects to the Lord. When the blessings were over, the Methodists and the tosspots alike repaired to the saloon, the Methodists presumably to toast the Father and the Son, while the tosspots, I suppose, toasted the Holy Spirit.

Thereafter, according to Aunt Dora, "Carruthers was always slipping across to the services and getting converted. The townspeople went around saying how nice it was that Carruthers was saved, but then he would backslide again. I used to wonder what God would do with him after he got him finally saved."

Rodway's saloon, just across the way from the Pacific Hotel, did not close even briefly out of respect for the new church. But then, Rodway was not one of your come-again-gone-again sinners; he was a sinner all the way through. It is said that no woman ever pushed open his swinging door except to wield a hatchet on the bottles, or to drag home an errant husband.

Grandfather refused to sell liquor to the Indians. Other storekeepers had a barrel of homemade whiskey in the back room of their stores for

Indians' special use. This tanglefoot could be bought by the thimble or the pencil. The Indian who bought it soon found himself eager to defend any point of view against all comers.

If you had asked grandpa whether the Indians were saved or damned he probably would have replied that with a little help from the Lord they *could* be saved. But grandma was less sanguine. Her father had taught on a reservation school in western Oregon, showing the Indians such peaceful arts as saddle-making. He had considered them his friends. Yet in a sudden uprising the Jeffersons barely escaped with their scalps.

So grandma could not bring herself to trust even the most harmless appearing Siwash. When they brought berries to her kitchen door, she welcomed them politely, and provided them with ritual food; but she hid her children away in back rooms. Once a squaw asked, "Hiya sic?" ("Are you my friend?"). Grandma replied firmly, "Certainly not," meaning she was not sick at all. The squaw stalked away scowling.

When one particularly high tide covered the streets and meadows, grandpa caught a drifting buoy and towed it into a field near the house as a plaything for his children. A few nights later the village was aroused by an iron clangor; grandma crawled into bed with Dora for reassurance. It developed that the Indians were hammering on the buoy to drive the devils out of a sick child. "Mother thought we were about to be slaughtered in our beds," said Aunt Dora, "but father, who was downstairs by the fire smoking his last pipe of the day, called up that there was nothing to worry about. He spoke with the Indians, and soon quieted them down. They always minded father."

When it came to major crime, the whites were more likely to break bounds than the Indians. In 1891 certain nameless citizens of Oysterville, outraged that a pair of convicted murderers remained in their cell unhanged, donned stocking masks one night and forgathered at the jail. Unable to persuade the jailer to surrender the keys—he spiritedly flung them into the fastness of a gorse bush—the vigilantes took turns firing rifles and shotguns through the barred window of the cell. The prisoners, crouching in a corner, were safe from direct hits, but ricocheting bullets eventually disposed of them. Next day grandpa, over grandma's anguished protests, led Uncle Cecil, then five, to view the bodies lying in their blood. "My boy," said grandpa solemnly, "this is what you get for breaking the law."

The only death sentence ever legally carried out in Pacific County was that of a Chinese, Lum You, one of the laborers who arrived near the turn of the century to cook, log, wash dirty clothes, and, as some sort of compensation, gamble. Lum You, under admittedly severe provocation, had shot and killed one Oscar Bloom. Sympathy for the convicted man was so intense that county officials connived at his escape from jail. It was understood, however, that the fugitive would have to return to China, where as a convicted murderer he could expect to be beheaded.   142

Since Lum You believed he could not enter eternal bliss without his head, he gave himself up and the hanging proceeded on schedule. The sheriff sent favored citizens invitations to attend. An example has survived:

M *Chris Sarris*

You are respectfully invited to be present
at the execution of

LUM YOU

Friday, January 31, 1902, at the Pacific County Court
House at 9:00 o'clock a. m.

Present this Card
Not Transferable

Thos Rouey Sheriff

12

They Had to Use "Distressing Methods"

Papa, very young then, sat in the living room where his father was giving instructions to Pete, the company foreman. "Father sat in his usual rocking chair in the corner," Papa recalled; "Pete sat on the opposite side of the fireplace in an armchair, and I squatting on a mat, square in front of the middle of the fire. There was some talk about putting out cull beds for the fall, and arrangements for the winter shipping season. Father told Pete he was laying down full instructions because he would not be on the beds so much the following winter. 'I'm glad,' Pete said. 'You know, Major, work as hard as that is too much for so old a man as you.' Father replied, 'Yes, Pete, if I live till the tenth of next February, I will be fifty-four years of age.' That would have made me, listening, less than three years and eleven months old, for it could not have been later than early 1879."

Grandpa no longer considered himself a working oysterman, but an executive. He was becoming a victim of what grandma would have called False Pride.

It was her contempt for False Pride that put grandma on the losing side during the Great Name Debate of the 1880s. Grandpa's prosperity peaked in that decade, leading several of his children, with Uncle Ed as ringleader, to contend that the spelling of the Espy name was too stark. The name smacked, they said, of peasants feeding swill to swine. Such chores no doubt had been common among previous generations of Espys, and indeed, as Ed had personal reason to know, were common still; perhaps he thought that with a more impressive name to live up to, his father might hire a man to feed the pigs. Ed proposed that E S P Y become E S P E Y, which, he felt, had a Norman gloss to it. Grandma, with my father's backing, dissented vigorously; the change, she declared, was an act of hubris (though I doubt whether she used that word), a thumbing of the nose (I doubt whether that was the expression she used, either) at the Almighty, certain to bring down divine wrath.

Grandpa decided in favor of the change (though Ed had to go on feeding the pigs.) New calling cards, with the name spelled E S P E Y, were ordered all around. But grandma was right; within a few years, much of the fortune grandpa had accumulated from oysters washed away with the tailings of gold mines bought in Northern California. Grandpa knew oysters, but he did not know when a gold mine was salted.

Grandpa, abiding by the logic he had accepted earlier, returned to the original spelling of his name. If you ever find me signing myself E S P E Y, you will know I have struck oil in my oyster beds.

In her heart, grandma as well as grandpa probably believed that being in more comfortable circumstances than most of their neighbors did make the Espys superior; but she regularly warned her children, "Don't flaunt your money" (without giving them any to flaunt), or "Don't let your friends feel you think you are better than anybody else."

She also fought the sin of pride in her own home. Most of the time she ran the house without the help of a hired girl. She sewed the family clothes, repaired the furniture (and even built tables and chairs herself from scratch), and hooked the rugs. She fed the chickens and cultivated the vegetable garden. She had learned early that pennies were made for pinching, and she pinched.

Grandpa took a different view. He did not flaunt his wealth, but he had proved he was a better man than his competitors, and figured his family was automatically better too.

Since it was convenient to pay wages and bills in hard money, grandpa kept a supply of twenty-dollar gold pieces in his rolltop desk. They filled one drawer almost to the top. In the presence of a visitor, grandpa was likely to open this drawer in an absentminded fashion, scoop up a handful of coins, and let them dribble through his fingers; no one could be sure whether he was listening to what the visitor was saying or to the clinks as coin after coin landed back in the drawer.

During my father's childhood, dinner (the Espys were among the few local families who considered their evening meal dinner, not supper) ended promptly at half-past seven. Grandpa would then settle himself by the living room fireplace in his platform rocker, whose deerhide covering was worn hairless by the years his back had rubbed against it. For an hour he would read the newspaper or a religious tract. At exactly eight-thirty o'clock he would rise and cross to the closet; choose a Bellflower apple from a barrel of them waiting there; return to his chair; pry his jackknife open; and pare and eat the apple. At eight forty-five grandma would read aloud one or more Bible chapters, after which grandpa would pray, all the family kneeling. He would then shuck his jacket, hang it in the closet above the apples, remove his gold watch from his vest pocket and the watch chain from his fob, place the two in a slipper-shaped holder on the wall (grandma had knitted it for him early in their marriage), bend down to unlace his shoes, pull them off, set them beside the chain, and announce, "Time to go to bed." This was the signal for retirement for everyone except grandma, who might sit up and write letters or go over accounts. Grandpa, in the master bedroom, would hang his trousers and vest over the back of a chair and climb into bed still wearing his underwear and socks. If his wife did not follow him immediately, he would summon her within half an hour.

Grandma laundered the socks, underwear, and shirt once a week. Her husband bathed every two weeks, on Saturday evening, sitting in a wash tub in the kitchen.

When grandpa traveled to San Francisco on business, he returned with prime cuts of beef, veal, lamb, and pork, ignoring the meat products of his own ranch. Although seafood was to be had simply by opening a window and whistling the fish in, few fish appeared on the Espy table. Oysters were served fresh once a year, at Christmas. A keg of salted salmon bellies stood in the storeroom, but even they were rarely eaten. Grandpa had had his fill of seafood as a bachelor; in marriage, he was a meat and potato man.

Grandma did, however, develop a recipe for baking oysters so delicious that the family never wearied of eating them. Indeed, we are still eating baked oysters from that recipe to this day. (The other members of the family, that is; during my childhood I was so sated with oysters on the half shell, oyster soup, oyster stew, baked oysters, and, if memory serves, even oyster pie, that I have not been able to swallow one of the odious bivalves since.) In any event, for you who love baked oysters, here is the recipe as created by grandma, refined by mama, and perfected by my sister Dale:

Use oyster shell or other individual container.
Place one or two oysters in container.
Pour 1 tbs hot-sauce over oyster.
Lay 1 strip bacon over hot sauce.
Lay one slice cheddar cheese over bacon.
Bake 1½ hours in 325° oven.

The paths of grandpa and his bother Tom parted in 1852. Thereafter neither heard of the other, directly or indirectly, for more than thirty years. This was not unusual; there was no official postal service in the third quarter of the nineteenth century, so that the delivery of letters was scarcely more reliable than it is today.

But blood draws to blood. In 1884, grandpa, sitting in an Astoria hotel lobby waiting to take a steamer to San Francisco, heard a registrant at the front desk say, "I see you have an Espy here." "Yes." "Major Espy?" "Yes." "From Oysterville?" "Yes." The clerk pointed out grandpa, and the man approached him doubtfully. "Haven't seen you for some time," he said, "but you look smaller than you did. Are you big Tom Espy?" "No." "Well, we called the Espy I knew big Tom. Looked like you, though." "Where was he from?" "Pennsylvania." "That would be my younger brother."

Grandpa's brother Tom was also known as Major; I have no idea why. And his address was Oysterville—but Oysterville, Oregon, not Oysterville, Washington. (The place was later called Winona.) Tom had wandered north from the California gold fields in the late fifties, and for more than a quarter of a century had lived less than a hundred miles from his elder brother. Each was unaware that the other was even alive. On his return from that trip to San Francisco, grandpa made his way to Oysterville, Oregon, and found Tom, an arthritic, childless widower, sawing wood in the yard.

Aunt Dora was then in her early twenties. She recalled her Uncle Tom as an earthy type. "Uncle Tom swore quite a bit," she said. "He used to say he was glad he lived in Oregon instead of Washington, because Washington had Indian names that nobody could pronounce, but Oregon had names a man could understand, like Bull Shit Springs, and Whorehouse Meadows, called after some local women who offered personal services to sheepherders in a field after dark. That kind of name, Uncle Tom said, warned a man in advance what he could expect."

The Federal Bureau of Land Management has now euphemized Whore-house Meadows to Naughty Girl Meadows, and Bull Shit Springs to Bull Shirt Springs. This shows that time does not always bring progress.

Grandpa and Uncle Tom got together barely in time. They visited once or twice, and then, in 1885, Uncle Tom died.

Sometimes grandma's detestation of false pride bumped against grandpa's contempt for poor-mouthing. One evening, bringing guests home for supper (as he was prone to do without forewarning), grandpa found his wife and his two eldest daughters in the sitting room cutting cloth for a quilt. The pieces were scattered in disorder over the floor. "Throw that mess away," ordered grandpa, "and send to Sears Roebuck for blankets!"

I suspect that grandma's rug-weaving and furniture-making expressed feelings she could not put into words. The neighbors called her "creative." This meant that she might scrape moss of varying colors from rotting logs, and arrange it into primitive pictures of mountains, woods, meadows, and seas, framed in pine cones or human hair. She made a mourning frame for a steel engraving of Abraham Lincoln from the rippings of black kid gloves. She made a playhouse for her daughters from a wooden packing box; carved tables, chairs, and bureaus to fit; and peopled the residence with neatly gowned dolls, all carved by butcher knife.

Since she was by all accounts a severe woman, unbending, suspicious of laughter, it is not surprising that this passion for creation, if that is what it was, went virtually unremarked by her own family. My mother, I think, was one of the few people who sensed this frustrated side of grandma. Mama became engaged to papa in Oakland, California, in the summer of 1897, and Grandma Espy promptly came calling from Oysterville.

Papa was nervous about the impending confrontation. "Helen," he asked, "would you mind wearing your plainest dress when you meet mother?" Helen, puzzled but acquiescent, donned a black serge with a wide black satin girdle. Her own mother saw her in it, and was appalled. "Why," she said, "Mrs. Espy will think you are the scullery maid!" Mom compromised on a somewhat brighter costume, and her future mother-in-law was charmed by both dress and girl.

Several years later, when mama and papa came to Oysterville to live, my father again warned Helen to bring only her plainest clothes. She managed, however, to smuggle in a handsome pink brocade, heavy with a pattern of maidenhair fern in satin, and trimmed with panne velvet. (This is my mother's language, not mine.) Grandma Espy, investigating a closet, came across the frivolous creation. "Helen," she said, "would you mind wearing this pretty dress to church?" She even picked a handful of pink roses for my mother's dark hair.

Severe, however, grandma certainly was. Her young offspring frequently provided testimony to that by the redness of their bottoms —

redness imposed by the strap for such venial sins as unscrubbed finger-nails or unfilled woodbins.

A portion of her severity was the product of her own strict upbringing. The rest, however, was imposed by the special rigors of married life. That is, by grandpa.

Grandpa was a meticulously honest and religious man. He was also, however, arrogant, self-centered, and insensitive toward any problems that lay outside his own immediate interests.

Even before he married grandma, her physician had warned him that she had a "pregnancy problem"—that is, an abnormally narrow pelvis, so that childbearing would be dangerous. Grandpa considered such risks to be simply the nature of things. He was determined to sire a dynasty, and would brook no prohibition from wife, physician, or nature itself.

Of all her miserable pregnancies, the first, initiated within days after her marriage, was probably the worst. Living in the most primitive of surroundings, repeatedly threatened with miscarriage, she had to spend long hours flat on her back to save the unborn child—knowing that each reprieve was only postponing the ultimate confrontation with the Grim Reaper.

Grandpa was not the most empathetic of husbands for a pregnant eighteen-year-old. He considered that the bearing and rearing of children was woman's work; he did his own job, and he expected her to do hers.

But as her pregnancy advanced, even he became worried. It was a winter of violent storms. Ice floes drifted up and down the bay. All the wood he could pile into the fireplace failed to keep the cabin warm. The effort required for grandma simply to clean and straighten one room, cook and serve the meals, and wash the dishes—all these were women's jobs, and it would not have occurred to grandpa to share them—made it clear that her strength was failing. If the pregnancy had come a few years later, grandpa would have been able to enlist the services of Mrs. Smith, a midwife whose reputation was to grow so great that she took applications "no less than a year in advance." In 1871, however, Mrs. Smith had not yet appeared on the scene. Grandpa was forced to think the unthinkable: he had to summon a doctor.

Such a pandering to human frailty went against every grain in his being. Espys had been having babies without doctors at least since 1610. In childbirth, as in any other form of physical difficulty, home treatment had always been the order of the day. The victim of a broken leg, for instance, was expected to swig down copious drafts of whiskey, and to bite on a bullet—no figure of speech—while the mightiest men of the community pulled the bones into place and splinted the leg.

One raw March morning, Andrew Wirt asked grandpa, "Did you hear about Anderson?"

149   "Can't say I did."

"Well, he crossed all the way from Long Island to Sealand yesterday, hopping along on the ice floes."

"Seems like a durn fool thing to do," said grandpa. "What did he do that for?"

"His baby was due, and he wanted to get there in time."

"Durn fool," repeated grandpa thoughtfully. That afternoon he called in Jim Johnson, owner of the fastest plunger on the bay.

"Jim," he said, "I want you to do me a favor."

"Anything you say, Major."

"Take that sailboat of yours and fetch me Dr. Balch. I don't think Mrs. Espy is well."

"Might take a little time, Major. There's the floes to watch out for; that'll slow me up some. And the doc might be hard to find; I hear there's a heap of smallpox around the Willapa."

"Well, you just fetch him for me, Jim, fast as you can, and maybe I can do a favor for you some day."

Jim upped sail forthwith. Two weeks passed. On April 7, 1871, grandma was delivered of Delos Jefferson Espy, born dead after long labor. The neighbors were compelled to use what they called "distressing methods" to deliver her of the tiny corpse. Dr. Balch did not arrive for another three days.

That was the first of eight dangerous deliveries.

> Delos, stillborn, 1871;
> Dora Jane, 1872;
> Robert Hamilton Edwin, 1875;
> Harry Albert (my father), 1876;
> Susan May, 1878;
> Thomas Willard, 1883;
> Cecil Jefferson, 1887;
> Laura Ida Verona, 1889;

Before the birth of Uncle Will in '83, Grandma was so convinced she would not survive that she spent weeks drilling Dora, then eleven, in running the household. Make sure, she urged, that all the children finish college; they must become educated men and women, capable of making the Espy name one to conjure with in the world.*

---

*Uncle Will, once Water Engineer of San Francisco, currently holds court over innumerable grandchildren and great-grandchildren in Oakland. Uncle Cecil, retired from banking in Portland, maintains the old family home at Oysterville. By day he tends the yard and the flower and vegetable gardens, as well as the graveyard. By night he sleeps in the bed where he and his brothers and sisters were born.

Grandma died of a stroke in 1901, at fifty, and grandpa of old age in 1918, at ninety-two. Their differing views of life and death are reflected on their tombstones.

R. H. ESPY
Justified by the Faith of Christ
Gal. 2:16

JULIA ANN JEFFERSON ESPY
Safe in the Arms of Jesus
Safe from Corroding Care
Safe from the World's Temptations,
Sin Cannot harm Me There.

Uncle Cecil's wheelbarrow

The Train That Never Pulled In

Oysterville's surge to prosperity, reaching its peak in scarcely a year, continued into the early 1870s, paralleling that of gold rush towns mushrooming in California and the Rockies. Most of these have long since vanished. Oysterville is still around, but barely.

Ancillary settlements sprang up around the edges of Shoalwater Bay. Bruceport, earliest of all, reached a peak population of twenty-five families; Cougarville and Bay Center arose next, farther south and smaller; on the west side of Long Island, Diamond City, seventy-five strong, received its name because anyone looking east from the peninsula saw the windows of the settlement blaze like jewels when the afternoon sun struck them.

In the fifties, sixties, and early seventies, Oysterville was one of the wealthiest communities per capita known to pioneer history. It was common to see men tossing twenty-dollar gold pieces at a line scratched in the sand, the best throw winning the pot. The careless carryings-on of the itinerant population were the envy of raffish elements up and down the coast.

Yet there were warnings of trouble from the start. Freezing temperatures killed millions of oysters in the winter of 1853–54, even before Oysterville was founded. An even colder winter in 1861–62 seemed for a while to have destroyed the entire oyster population. Soon afterward a red tide swept into the bay, rendering the oysters inedible for most of a season. Cougarville and Diamond City, living off shallow beds, lost their crop in the record freezes of 1876 and 1878. Bruceport washed away. Starfish and drills—the latter a marine snail that bores through oyster shells to suck out the sweet meat inside—destroyed oysters by the millions. Inedible shrimp took over acres of beds, burrowing beneath the sand so that the surface grew soft and the oysters sank underground and smothered. Dredgers poached at night without lights; no man's oysters were safe from his neighbor. Besides facilitating poaching, the dredges picked up indiscriminately with each scoopload layers of silt, indispensable to the survival of future generations of oysters. The oyster reefs of the fifties dwindled into legend; seeing the end of the business looming, even conservative oyster owners overharvested, sacrificing future security for present profit.

At the same time, technological revolution put an end to Oysterville's primacy as both an oyster supplier and a stopover for shipping. Rail lines, cutting through from the east to San Francisco and Puget Sound, transported eastern oysters and eastern spat* to the West Coast in a few days. Oysterville eked out its diminishing supply of oysters by importing Chesapeake and Long Island seed; but the newcomers neither matched the imperiled natives in taste nor thrived in Shoalwater Bay.

---

*An oyster begins life as a free-swimming, microscopic fish. Soon, though, it develops a carapace, and settles on the handiest object around—a pebble, say, or a tin can. These young, affixed oysters, still scarcely visible to the naked eye, are called spat.

Vessels using windpower between Seattle and San Francisco had found Oysterville a convenient layover, tying up at the end of the wharf that ran on pilings a quarter of a mile into the bay. The first steamboats stopped there too; but after a tempest and high tide in 1888 combined to lift the wharf from its supports and float it away (it came ashore a mile or so to the north, and a farmer used the wood to make a barn), steamboats and sailing vessels alike went right on by.

I have indicated that grandpa, foreseeing an early demise of the oyster business, invested most of his profits off the peninsula. But he made one major, and curious, exception, and late in the day at that. In the 1880s he sank capital into a narrow-gauge railway called the Oregon-Washington Railroad and Navigation Company, designed to connect Oysterville with Cape Disappointment, at the mouth of the Columbia River. There may have been some local chauvinism involved in this odd blind spot in his usually twenty-twenty business judgment, but I suspect the reason was more personal. My guess is that his decision to put cold cash into the Oregon-Washington Railroad and Navigation Company was born of a stomachache, which hit him one morning at least a decade before the railroad was dreamed of.

Stomachache is a feeble word. He woke up with arrows lancing through his innards; he had a raging fever, and a headache so intense that he did not dare open his eyes. He could not lift himself from his bed. With no medical diagnosis to refer to, there is no telling what the trouble was; appendicitis seems as good a guess as any. In any event, his condition rapidly worsened. He wasted like an eclipsing moon. The Indians pounded their bell buoy, and the neighbors whispered that he was dying. Once more, Jim Johnson was sent posthaste for Dr. Balch.

As it turned out, the trip was unnecessary. Whatever had struck grandpa, his constitution pulled him through. When the doctor finally dropped anchor five days later and rowed his dinghy ashore, he found his patient, completely recovered, waiting for him on the beach.

This experience had a traumatic effect on both Dr. Balch and grandpa. It convinced the doctor that he had to find some faster and more reliable way of making his rounds. He therefore bought a small steamboat (which he called the Pill Box) and turned his son into a qualified marine engineer. There was just one trouble with the Pill Box: however extreme the emergency, a half hour was required to heat the water in the boiler enough to make steam.

Dr. Balch's bag, papa recalled, contained a selection of vials filled with varicolored pellets the size of peas. He would combine medical fluids in various proportions, depending on his diagnosis of the ailment; soak a pill in the solution; and push it down the throat of his patients. They all recovered.

As for grandpa, his narrow escape did not set him to thinking about steamboats; it set him to thinking about steam trains. He had looked death in the face, and had not liked what he had seen. He resolved to   154 assure himself of more immediate medical aid in emergencies. To make such aid available for himself, he had to make it available also for the rest of Oysterville. The fastest, most reliable way to get hold of a doctor was by train. And that, in my judgment, is why grandpa invested in the Oregon-Washington Railroad and Navigation Company; it was a form of personal protection.

The investment was by no means disastrous. The line continued in existence, after all, for more than forty years. But the service left something to be desired. It was a narrow-gauge road; the cars were only seven feet wide, and the first right-of-way was but three feet wider. Like the stage that preceded it, the train's schedule trailed the tide, since it had to meet the steamer at Ilwaco, and the steamer could dock only at mid-flood. So the train schedule moved back fifty minutes a day for seven days, and on the eighth day jumped six hours ahead. To fuel the two locomotives, residents stacked wood along the track and sold it to the engineer at two dollars a cord.

But from grandpa's viewpoint the calamity was that the northern terminus of the line was finally set at a location four miles to the south of Oysterville. There the channel swung in close to shore, so that the train needed only a short wharf to connect with steamboats and the other side of the bay. The terminus was named Nahcotta after grandpa's old friend.*

So if grandpa was seeking quick attention for his bodily ailments, he was only partly successful. And if he was seeking to restore the economy of his village, he was not successful at all. Far from reviving as a center of commerce, Oysterville became a stagnant backwater once and for all.

Not only did the train fail to bring business to Oysterville; even worse, the mainland was outgrowing the peninsula. The Willapa Valley had long seemed as primitive to Oystervilleans as early Rome to the ancient Greeks. Long after Oysterville was a bustling community, letter mail in the Willapa backwoods was still delivered only once in two or three months, while newspapers and magazines were not delivered at all. Oysterville could boast incandescent gas lanterns (when air was forced under pressure into the lantern's base, two small cloth sacks inside the globe gave off an intense white light) at a time when the only illumination of most Willapa farmhouses was still a saucer of tallow with a twisted piece of cotton cloth placed in it for a wick. In the valley, families with fireplaces (which were rare for lack of either brick factories or natural stone), "contented themselves," said an early inhabitant, "by

---

* "It must have been quite an affair," says *The Railroad That Ran by the Tide* (Raymond J. Feagans. Berkeley, Calif., Howell-North Books, 1972), "when the first train from Ilwaco arrived in Nahcotta on May 29, 1889. Charles Nelson and Willard Espy, both six years old at the time, remember going to see it. Charlie went with his folks, but Will [my uncle Will, that is] was forbidden to go. Will escaped, 'requisitioned' someone's horse, and galloped off to the celebration. He says his mother made him stay upstairs in bed for two days for running away, but that it was well worth it."

watching the flames go up the chimney of an evening, and often this was the only light in the room."

But in 1868, three men set up a sawmill on the Willapa River. The hunger for wood for building material had become as insatiable as the earlier demand for oysters, and with the passing of the years, larger lumber companies converged on the area.

One effect of the burgeoning lumber industry was the emergence of two fast-growing villages, Raymond and South Bend, South Bend at the mouth of the Willapa and Raymond a few miles upstream. By 1890 the Northern Pacific was laying down a roadbed to extend its line to South Bend. Why, asked the imperial citizens of this new Rome, should they leave as county seat the isolated hamlet of Oysterville, at the end of nowhere across the bay?

In 1892 — helped, so indignant Oystervilleans averred, by the illegal votes of temporary railroad crews — South Bend won an election making her the new county seat. When a court battle delayed the transfer, South Benders took direct action.

On February 5, 1893, a stormy Sunday, eighty-five South Benders, reputedly fortified by alternate swallows of rum and whiskey, crossed from the mainland on two small steamers, the *Cruiser* and the *Edgar*. The *Cruiser* dropped anchor off Oysterville and passengers and crew rowed ashore. The *Edgar* continued south to Sealand, contiguous to Nahcotta. Though a saloonkeeper there at first waved a shotgun to keep the passengers from debarking, he relented when they agreed to buy drinks all around. He even provided wagons to carry them along the soft sand road to Oysterville, where their comrades were already congregated about the courthouse. On signal, a burly tailor and taxidermist named John Hudson kicked in the door.

Phil Barney, the county auditor, happened to be working that Sunday morning. He wanted no trouble, and at first ignored the rampaging intruders; but when they tried to break into the locked drawers of his desk, he charged them, swinging a leg wrenched from his chair. Sheer numbers overcame him, but Mr. Barney almost saved the county seat for Oysterville single-handed.

John Hudson later went on display in a sideshow at the Chicago World's Fair billed as "The Man Who Kidnapped the County Seat."

One after another, from then on, the saloons, the hotels, the tannery, the slaughterhouse, the printing shop, closed. One after another, the buildings collapsed in winter storms.

That is all there is to the decline and fall of Oysterville, except that the whilom courthouse, after a respite of a year or two in which it housed a private secondary school, was abandoned until 1903, when my father turned it into two buildings, using one as a cow barn and the other as a ranch house. The barn crumpled in a winter gale in 1933, but the ranch house is still standing. The jail too became a barn. But it proved hard to throw manure through the bars, so the owner, Mr. Wachsmuth, gave up and made it a chicken house.

14

The Reverend Crouch Preached
Two Good Sermons

On December 23, 1892, en route from Centralia, Washington, where he was a boarding school student, to Oysterville, where he was planning to spend the Christmas holidays, Grandpa Espy's second son Harry, just turned seventeen, bought a diary. It measured a bare three inches by five inches by a quarter of an inch, thus confining the effusions of the diarist as rigidly as the sonnet form confines the effusions of a poet. In this diary, during the first nine months of 1893, he recorded in a microscopic hand such occurrences as he considered noteworthy.

The diary first came to my attention seventy years later. I confess disappointment at how few events, or rather categories of events, it contained. Harry was to become my father, and it would have been a source of pride to me if even a few long, long thoughts of youth had wound their way through his journal; if even a few wisps had remained from the clouds of glory that, according to Wordsworthian science, trail all infants into the prison house of human existence.

A few pithy apothegms, a few outbursts of rage at an indifferent world, a few plaintive calf bellows for love weaned away — any of these would have made me rub my hands together and say to myself, "Like father, like son."

The remark would have been a lie; actually, papa wrote exactly the kind of journal I probably would have written at his age, or at my present age, for that matter. He revealed nothing about himself at all, except that his principal, if not only, interests, were the weather, church, and girls, in that order. I must accept this fact, or resort to the untenable assumption that he was a deep, deep fellow who deliberately eliminated from the record everything he truly felt, so that in later years he could know exactly what happened each day by recalling what he had left out.

Even girls were a minor interest compared with the other two. I fear the essence of my father at seventeen is caught in his very first journal entry, written at Oysterville:

Sunday, January 1. Rather stormy; cold
rain. I went to church both morning and
evening at the Baptist church. Rev. Crouch
preached two good sermons.

It takes no Nero Wolfe or Sherlock Homes to deduce from these two sentences, first, that papa had a farm boy's preoccupation with weather, and second, that he accepted churchgoing as an inevitable human condition, like fleas.

One may infer from the phrase "Rev. Crouch preached two good sermons" either that the sermons truly were of a high standard; or that papa admired Reverend Crouch so extravagantly that he also admired whatever the preacher said; or that in fact he paid no attention to the sermons at all, his attention perhaps being on pulling the braids of the Goulter girl in the adjoining pew, or throwing spitballs at young Dewitt Stoner, two pews ahead.

The cumulative tenor of the diary forced me to conclude, to my surprise, that the second of these speculations contains the most truth. It became clear that papa did admire the Reverend Crouch—admired him, perhaps, not wisely but too well.

By way of background, you should understand that Grandpa Espy had given the church to the Baptist community just the year before, paying fifteen hundred dollars for its construction. It was a rectangular building, thirty-eight feet long and thirty-five feet wide, with a lobby opening off the front door, a belfry overhead with a bell rope hanging from it, a room on the right-hand side for Sunday school classes, and the principal area taken up by pews, for a hundred worshippers. There was a large wood stove off the lobby; an organ, powered by foot, forward and to the left of the pews (this is retained now in the Espy home for safekeeping); and a platform for the pulpit. Behind the pulpit was a trapdoor. Opened, this ordinarily revealed an empty, zinc-lined tank. In the event of a baptism, however, the tank turned out to be full of water—I have no idea where the water came from; perhaps its presence was a local miracle, or perhaps it was carried to the tank at midnight in buckets. Here new converts were immersed, lying back in the preacher's arms. He

The Baptist Church

wore hip boots, and received them into the water one by one, lowering them gently and briefly beneath the surface.

Two coal-oil lamps, one near the front of the church, the other near the back, hung on pulleys suspended from the ceiling. The lamps were connected by a rope running from one pulley to the other. If you pulled the near lamp down, the far one would rise.

The windows of the church were of the ordinary frame variety, but those back of the platform were covered with translucent, colored paper, picturing biblical scenes and intended, I suppose, to look like stained glass.

Grandpa also presented the Baptists with the house across the street as a parsonage. This house had been constructed in 1869 by a member of the Crellin family — the only Oysterville pioneers, it is said, who both arrived and left with money in their pockets. The Crellins, natives of the Isle of Man, are credited with importing the first daffodils and evergreen blackberries in the Northwest. They are anathematized, however, correctly or not, for also introducing gorse, a thorny pest that grows in brown-orange clumps of monstrous size, covering as much as an acre at a time. The Baptist parsonage, constructed from redwood carried up from San Francisco in schooners as ballast, was considered the most elegant house in town; it even had plastered walls.

The first pastor to occupy the parsonage was the Reverend Josiah Crouch commended by my father in his earliest diary entry. Papa approved each of the Reverend Crouch's sermons uncritically in his diary, though out of the dozens he mentions I find only four of defined subject matter:

✛ "The preacher came down pretty hard on spiritualists . . ."
✛ "He asked 'Where are the dead' and explained that
    they were in the heart of the earth."
✛ "The sermon was on the second coming of Christ."
✛ "The sermon tonight was about our being asleep & for us to waken. It was very good."

Papa's idealization of the Reverend Crouch was not shared by Tommy Nelson, a neighboring teen-ager, who years later summed up the minister's stay in Oysterville as follows:

He was a tall, handsome fellow — had an alpaca overcoat. He could sway the women. He baptized one woman who'd been a Catholic all her life. I've heard Crouch's wife singing when she was alone, and she could sing like a mockingbird. But when a stranger was around she had nothing to say. My sister went there once. She said she was kind of embarrassed, how Crouch would talk to her and turn his back on his wife. One day he took his wife and baby on a church call up the Willapa River and their sailboat tipped over. Well, Crouch swum ashore with the baby, but his wife drownded. Well, he was interested in another woman at the time. Well, the sheriff found marks on Mrs. Crouch's neck. Crouch was exonerated, but it got too hot for him and he left town.

Papa's diary indicates that he was well aware of Crouch's difficulties, but he appeared to pass no moral judgment on the matter at all:

Monday, July 10. I took Mr. and Mrs. Crouch to Sealand. They are bound for South Bend.
Sunday, July 16. Quite a pleasant day, indeed the sun shone all day. About noon Will Turner came down from Sealand with the news that Mrs. Crouch was drowned in the Willapa yesterday.
Thursday, July 27. Still the fine weather continues. Papa went to Sealand where he heard there was a rumor to the effect that Mr. Crouch was suspected of having killed his wife.

I've never been able to understand my father's apparent indifference to the serious charges leveled against Reverend Crouch. His reports continue as before: *Wednesday, August 2,* "I went up to Sealand and got Mr. Crouch, his mother, brother, & daughter." *Sunday, August 6,* "Osborne met Mr. Crouch, who came in on the late train from Ilwaco alright. There was no cause for uneasiness. He preached two good sermons here but none in Sealand today." *Sunday, August 13,* "Mr. Crouch, Mr. Huff, Jim & I went to Sealand. Mr. Crouch intended to preach but did not." *Sunday, September 2,* "I took Mr. Crouch, Charley and Cecil to Sealand in the carriage. There was no preaching because of the ballgame."

I am in no position to judge the guilt or innocence of Josiah Crouch. Applying a previously quoted remark of Uncle Cecil's, I was not there. Obviously, the evidence against the minister was inconclusive; not only was he not arrested, but years later he was reported as practicing law in San Francisco. But the likelihood is that his guilt would never have been admitted by papa, however overwhelming the evidence against him. The Reverend Crouch, having preached from the Espy pulpit and shared the Espy bounty, was incapable of sin. And papa, having rendered his loyalty, was incapable of taking it back. Once, a man papa trusted put him into debt for most of his life; but I never heard papa utter a harsh word about that man.

Once grandpa became sire of a strapping brood, he had to find something for them to do; so he bought the Douglas land claim, a square mile of salt meadows, huckleberry bushes, alder trees, and marsh abutting his

162

property. This he turned into a farm, or, as the family euphemistically called it—because they raised cattle for meat as well as milk—a ranch.

I doubt whether grandpa himself ever lifted a hand to nail barbed wire onto a fence or to castrate a bull calf. He operated his ranch by interposing tenants, hired hands, and, eventually, his own sons. His oystering and his real estate dealing up and down the coast were his real interests.

Not that he intended his sons to be farmers. On the contrary, he was resolved that all his children, boys and girls alike, should receive the education he had missed, and that each boy should master some respected profession. Curiously, he seems never to have urged any of them to take up the profession he honored most of all—that of the ministry. Instead, Uncle Ed became a lawyer, papa a mining engineer and teacher (though events were to turn him into a farmer), Uncle Will a water engineer, Uncle Cecil a banker. As a first step toward these careers, as soon as each boy finished the eighth grade he was shipped off to Centralia Academy, a Baptist boarding school lying about halfway between Oysterville and Seattle. The girls—Dora, Sue, and Verona—were sent to finishing schools in Portland.

During the period covered by papa's diary, Ed was in his final year at Centralia; Harry was a year behind him; and Will was a freshman. They wore jackets and school ties; but at heart they remained farmers. At least, papa did.

Not only did the opening entry in his diary start with a description of the weather, but so did nearly every entry that followed:

> Nice, although some heat; cloudy in the
> afternoon . . . Quite fine, but rained a very
> little this evening from a clear sky . . . A
> beautiful day, but cloudy, and indeed it
> rained some . . . A pleasant day excepting
> it misted all morning . . . A very good day
> but was foggy all morning and part of the
> afternoon . . . A pretty fine day, but there
> was a thick fog & a very cold wind this
> evening.

As far as weather goes, papa was easily satisfied.

In the summer of 1893, for the first time, papa, not his elder brother Ed, was in charge of the ranch, his father being away on business and Ed having started clerking for a lawyer in Portland. Papa was exultant at being out from under the thumb of his brother, who took his two years of seniority seriously. Papa's feeling that he stood in Ed's shadow went back to one morning in his fourth year when, as he was being primped to accompany his mother on her weekly round of social calls, he discovered that Ed had taken a notion to come along. Recalled papa: "I felt despoiled of my place in the sun. Whenever Ed was around, he took, as a matter of right, the platform and the limelight."

A joint sheepherding venture in their early teens illustrated the problem. Most of the rams had to be gelded, and the geldings had eventually to be slaughtered; Ed assigned these disagreeable chores to papa, for whom the hurting or killing of an animal remained a traumatic experience all his life.

Once papa came close to obtaining a bit of revenge. At a community baseball game, Ed was in danger of being thrashed by a bigger boy. "I should have stood up for him," papa recalled, with no visible signs of regret; "but I figured the argument was his own fault, so I just sloped off into the crowd." Ed, as usual, talked his way out of trouble.

By and large, however, the two boys seem to have gotten along together as well as most brothers, and better than some. Moreover, in certain contests papa had the upper hand. Among these was stick-war, a game played in the woods. The contestants gathered rotted sticks from the ground, then hit them against tree trunks in such a fashion that the ends, snapping off, spun away in the general direction of the enemy. Stick-warfare is an art not easily mastered, and papa always swore he was a better shot than Uncle Ed.

Ed, however, had an instinct for self-aggrandizement and the jugular; papa had not. In 1900, for instance, when Ed, then working toward his law degree in Oakland, California, was home visiting, his friend Dewitt Stoner set a bear trap on the ocean beach. Next morning a sound of squalling, so loud that it reached all the way from the ocean to Oysterville, informed Dewitt that his trap had sprung. He rode out in his wagon to investigate, and Ed asked to go along. When it turned out that a rather mangy bear was caught in the trap, Ed requested the privilege of dispatching it. "I didn't care, I'd killed lots of them," Stoner recalled. "Bear was just a-threshin' and a-hollerin'. I walked around and closed in and kind of got him watchin' me steady. Then Ed shot him right in the ear. Ed took that bear and had it put in his law office in Frisco. He said he wasn't going to tell anyone he shot it in a trap."*

Papa would never have shot a bear in a trap, except to put the creature out of its pain. And in that event he would not only have acknowledged the circumstances, he would have described them in endless detail.

During this first summer in charge of the ranch, papa had two full-time helpers, Jim and Dye. He was responsible also for four horses — Charley, Kate, Fly, and Tom. Backed by men and beasts as needed, he

---

*Uncle Ed presented the stuffed bear to California College. This, in 1910, was incorporated with the University of Redlands, where later my brother Ed, my sister Dale, and I all took our undergraduate degrees. The trophy was prominently displayed in the school museum above a legend saying "Ed Espy and his trusty gun bagged this." In my college generation it was assumed that the bear fell not to my uncle but to my own elder brother Ed, who, unlike me, was a big man on campus.

plowed, harrowed, mowed, raked, windrowed, and cocked. He hauled oats and tideland hay; cleared land; dug potatoes, set out rutabagas; fixed fence; logged; transported manure; broke up clods; fertilized; fired undergrowth in the marsh and on the hill; brought in fence rails for wood; rimmed the horses' hooves; milked the cows; cleaned the barns; tagged the lambs; separated the ewes from the wethers; picked berries; and burned trash. "We found Greenman's cow in the pasture," says one diary entry, "and drove her out. The bottom wire was not down & her bag being very full one of her teats caught in going over, and took quite a strip of skin off."

Papa also drove either the buggy, the carriage, or the wagon almost every day to Nahcotta to pick up visitors or deliver parting guests to the train. Frequently he returned to Oysterville along the ocean beach, so as to show off the pungent carcass of a ninety-foot whale that had recently stranded there. The great skeleton of this beast is presumably still tucked away in some museum of natural history.

During summer vacation, papa received and answered letters from several girls, among them Alma Fangestrom and Flossie Ammerman. He also reports that only six days after meeting one "Honey" Stratton, "Honey & I cut up most terribly in the front seat." There are signs of life here.

The summer of 1893 eventually ended, as all summers must, and papa returned to Centralia, where not only the church but the Baptist Young People's Union and the Temperance Hall proved themselves socially acceptable and effective places for meeting girls.

If the inferences in the diary are to be credited, girls seemed willing to battle with God for papa's soul. Occasionally the girls won. On January 18, 1893, when a powerful speaker had almost persuaded him to abandon worldly temptations to become a missionary, he instead walked one Caroline McNitt to her home. Five days later he actually skipped the Baptist Young People's Union to walk home with Evaline McNitt, Caroline's sister. "I enjoyed myself," says the diary with some ambiguity, "but am sorry that I did not do better."

After reporting on the weather papa had very little room left in his diary. The most breath-stopping drama evoked but a stroke of his pen: "The stove-pipe fell in Mrs. Trimble's classroom. While putting it in, a joint fell and would have struck Mrs. T. had I not caught it. It cut my little finger on the right hand quite badly." (Was papa putting in the joint, and so responsible for its falling?) Personal triumph is shrugged off: "The Society had the election of officers Saturday. I was elected President." Anger is smothered: "Last night I got pretty mad at Will and let him know it but we both asked forgiveness before we went to bed."

Fires were second only to girls in distracting him from God: "There was a fire last night about 10 P.M. I went. One at 5 this morning. I did not go."

But girls were behind most of his indiscretions: "Professor would not let me go to the Prohibition meeting last night because he thought

Sam Gaches and I came up the fire escape from the social Thursday night."

After papa was graduated from Centralia Academy, in 1894, he followed Ed to Oakland to attend college. There his road and another road to grandpa's village were to join.

Mama's Road

Around the Horn

THOMAS RICHARDSON married
KATHERINE DUXFORD,
and begat
EZEKIEL and SAMUEL;

Ezekiel married
SUSANNA,
and begat
JOSIAH;

Samuel married
JOANNA,
and begat
STEPHEN;

Josiah married
REMEMBRANCE UNDERWOOD,
and begat again
JOSIAH;

Stephen married
ABIGAIL WYMAN
and begat again
STEPHEN;

Josiah married
MERCY PARRIS,
and begat again
MERCY;

Stephen married
SUSANNA WILSON,
and begat
AMOS;

Mercy married
EPHRAIM HILDRETH,
who begat
JOSIAH;

Amos married
SARAH FROST,
and begat
JOSEPH;

Josiah married
REBECCA WRIGHT,
and begat
MIRIAM;

Miriam married
the aforementioned JOSEPH RICHARDSON,
her third cousin once removed,
who begat
DAVID;

David married
SARAH GOODWIN FORD,
and begat
HORACE;

Horace married
SARAH HALL RAND,
and begat
DANIEL SIDNEY;

Daniel Sidney married
ANNIE MEDORA TAYLOR,
and begat
HELEN MEDORA;

Helen Medora married
HARRY ALBERT ESPY,
who begat . . .

On her paternal side, mama's road to Oysterville is more clearly marked than papa's, because early New England villages recorded the vital statistics of their inhabitants in every church and courthouse; nor did any of these latter suffer extinction by hostile burning, as often happened in the South during the War Between the States. It is on record, therefore, that Ezekiel Richardson arrived in Massachusetts in 1630, and his brothers Samuel and Thomas either then or six years later. Both Ezekiel and Samuel were mama's direct forebears. They settled at Charleston, Massachusetts, and were founding members of the church at Woburn. Both were selectmen, and in 1636 Samuel was on a committee to lay out lots of hay. This is all I know about him, except that in 1645 he paid the highest tax of any man in Woburn. His descendants have been complaining about taxes ever since.

The Richardsons were a litigious lot—one sure way to immortalize one's name. The Higby branch of the Richardson line was particularly apt at this. For hundreds of years before they reached America, they sued each other and any available neighbors in England. Edward Higby, my seven-times-great-grandfather, reached Connecticut in the 1640s and within weeks filed a suit against one Tom Scudder, on the somewhat convoluted grounds that he, Higby, had been charged by him, Scudder, with "houlding of him [meaning Scudder, I assume, not Higby] by the throt hallf an our, and all most throttled him." Edward won the suit.

This same forebear was tried with friends for stealing and killing a pig. Says the court record:

They say they was in want of provision and did it to supply their neede; though that appeared not, because they had Indian corne aboard their boat and some cheese. The court considered that they could not judge it any less than plaine theft, and therefore ordered the defendants to pay Thomas Whitway double for the Hogg.

On May 12, 1660, Edward, long overdue from a trading voyage to the West Indies, was declared legally dead. Soon afterward he arrived home, only to find that all his family had removed to the establishment of his wife's brother. Edward hopped on his nag and galloped to his brother-in-law's farm; he leaped from his horse into his wife's arms; and his brother-in-law promptly arrested him for kissing his wife on a Sabbath.

Blue blood is also useful in the tracing of ancestry. Unfortunately, it is hard to find any blue blood in the Richardson line, with the possible exception of the Brown connection. One Christopher Brown, sheriff of Rutlandshire in the early sixteenth century, reportedly "assisted Henry VII so valiantly against Richard III that his eldest son and all first-born sons were henceforth authorized to appear with their heads covered in the presence of the king." It pleased papa to think that any of his offspring who saw someone standing around wearing a hat in the presence

of the king could march up and say, "Hello, cousin!"

But the principal characteristic that has run like a burning fuse down the Richardson generations, perhaps sputtering a bit in Grandpa Richardson and his descendants, but never quite going out, is hatred for the devil and all his works.* Though the Richardsons produced farmers, doctors, storekeepers, even the owner of a sawmill, their specialty was ministers. Early Richardsons fought the Indians; later generations fought the British; but their continuing enemy was the devil himself.

No Richardson ever shook the world. The newspapers say that a member of the family (according to the Richardson book he must be my eighth cousin three times removed) has recently been playing "Hail to the Chief" on his audio system. He would be well advised to bear in mind that though several descendants of the immigrant Richardson brothers did reach the White House—Garfield, Pierce, Hayes, Coolidge among them—none of these occupants even warmed the Potomac, much less set it afire.

Mama's road to Oysterville is also easier to retrace than papa's because the Richardsons were a scribacious lot. I think their propensity to commit to paper any vagary that entered their heads stemmed from mama's great-grandfather, Deacon Elisha Rand. The Deacon's mother was first cousin to the novelist Helen Hunt Jackson's grandmother. At first glance this connection between the Richardsons, the Rands, and the literary muse may seem a bit remote, but ever since I saw a musical version of Helen Hunt Jackson's *Ramona* in an uninhabited California canyon years ago, I have realized that genius can actually go back through time, cross quietly into the genes of some poor preacher or simple farmer, and manifest itself again generations later, perhaps in a third cousin five times removed. The hidalgos and Indians and señoritas with mantillas and high-back combs in that outdoor musical were a sight to see. They would emerge on the top of a distant rock—sometimes a crowd of them, sometimes only one—strike a pose against the blue sky, and sing at the top of their lungs:

Ramona
Da-da-da-di I hear you call
Ramona
We'll meet beside the waterfall
I'll bless you
Caress you
And da-da-di you taught me to care
I'll always remember
The rambling rose you wore in your hair . . .

Or something like that. Whether or not the nebulous Jackson connection had anything to do with it, Deacon Elisha Rand combined his

*My brother Ed, for years general secretary of the National Council of Churches, currently nurses the flame in the fuse.

love for the Almighty with a compulsion to moralize in rhyme. The following stanza from a verse called "Life's Western Window" reflects the talent that raged in him:

We stand at life's west windows
    And turn not sadly away,
To watch on our children's faces
    The noontide of sparkling day;
But our sun must set, our lips grow dumb,
    And to look from *our* windows our children
        come.

Since Elisha's time the Richardson-Rands have carried the writing sickness dormant in their blood as blacks carry the risk of sickle cell anemia or Eastern European Jews the risk of the Tay-Sachs disease. Two of Elisha's sons were correspondents in the war between North and South; both later established their own New England newspapers. When their sister Sarah, my great-grandmother Richardson, moved west along with their other sister Cornelia, the two women had a guaranteed market back home for anything they chose to write. Cornelia especially scribbled countless dispatches on citrus fairs, Chinese New Year celebrations, sequoia trees, silk culture, and the like. Sarah confined herself to rhymed lamentations on the death of small babies.

It was in the children of Sarah and Cornelia, though, that the scribbling disease was to run rampant. These wrote first for their uncles, then for other New England newspapers, then for magazines like *The Youth's Companion, The Atlantic Monthly,* and *The Overland Monthly.*

Whether or not they enriched the American literary heritage, at least they left behind them guideposts along the Richardson road to Oysterville.

For convenience, I am assuming that the Richardson road begins with her grandfather, the Reverend Horace. Horace, though innocent of Rand genes, tended to attack the devil and the devil's instruments through rhyme, the devil's own specialty. Here is an example of how he battled the Great Adversary:

TOBACCO

Tobacco is the foulest weed
That e're in nature grew
One worm alone will on it feed,
But man the thing will *chew.*

Not only so, the same will *snuff*
And *smoke* it *day* and *night,*
As tho' he could not get enough
Of what's his chief delight.

Though poison this narcotic be
To *body, mind,* and *soul,*
And bad alone in tendency,
He won't himself control.

No matter that his *beard* he fills
With *spittle* flowing down
No matter though *himself* he *kills*
And all about him drown,

No matter tho' he may create
Miasma fouler far
Than ever rose from *marsh* or *lake*
To putrefy the air,

Yet still he'll *smoke* and *chew* and *snuff*
In spite of *manner's laws*
For they are not to him a *puff*
Or twisting of his jaws.

Vain man on your tobacco bent
O, let it now alone,
And hereafter, be *content*
To leave it to the *worm.*

Don't rob the *reptile* of the *weed*
Made for *himself alone*
Let *him alone* upon it *feed,*
"But no one *human born.*"

Horace received his undergraduate degree from Dartmouth College in 1841. Three years later he was graduated from the Baptist Theological Seminary in Newton, Massachusetts, and for the next ten years he preached Christ risen in Iowa, New Hampshire, and Massachusetts. During this interval he married Sarah Hall Rand and sired four children: Helen Louisa; Martha Elmira; my grandfather, Daniel Sidney Ford Richardson, born in West Acton, Massachusetts, on March 19, 1851; finally, Horatia Cornelia. In 1853 Horace followed God's call to save the multifarious sinners of California, and on November 28, 1854, his family left Boston in his wake aboard the good ship *Reindeer,* Obed Bunker, skipper. With them was Sarah's aforementioned sister Cornelia, twenty-three and still a spinster.

Cornelia kept a log of her trip around the Horn, much as papa forty years later was to report the outstanding events of his life at Centralia Academy. I still have the log — a lined copybook filled with neat faded entries in girlish script. It gives the latitude and longitude for every day, the state of the weather, and at the end of the voyage, as a sort of valedictory, several later verses written by her and members of her family. One of these, her own creation, throws some light on why she made the trip:

CALIFORNIA

Where do men all wish to go,
When credit's gone and purse is low?
                    To California.

Where does the thief find safe retreat?
Where does the rogue oft bend his feet?
                    To California.

Where are the *idle* and the *rich*,
Oftenest found within the *ditch?*
                    In California.

Where should the girls the quickest hie
Who fear in maiden-hood to die?
                    To California.

It may be pushing fantasy too far to sense a quirk of the lip, a suppressed sense of the ridiculous, in such lines as *"Where are the idle and the rich / Oftenest found within the ditch? / In California."* No such whimsy brightens Cornelia's account of her trip around the Horn. "I never read anything more barren," complained my mother. "Can you imagine taking a six-months' journey and never expressing a single reaction, or any sign of interest in a fellow passenger?"

Yet with death simpering daily over one's shoulder, numbness may have seemed a precondition for survival.

Cornelia did record anniversaries: "Horace's birthday—40" . . . "Father's birthday—60" . . . Helen's birthday—17" . . . "Sarah's wedding day, 8 years ago" . . . "Father and mother were married this day in 1820" . . . "Daniel's birthday, 4 years old" . . . "George's birthday—30. This is also the day that mother died 4 years ago."

And though she may have lacked interest in her fellow passengers, she made up for it by interest in food: "Sarah eats onions" . . . "Had shark for supper" . . . "Whortleberry pie today" . . . "Gooseberry and peach pie for dinner" . . . "Pancakes" . . . "We ate bonita" . . . "This is Washington's birthday, so we tried to celebrate it by eating nuts, candy, and raisins" . . . "today we had our last potatoes."

Cornelia reported more dramatic events as skeletonically. A sailor fell overboard and could not be rescued. The second mate caught a flying fish. A wave soaked Cornelia's berth. She hooked a hundred-pound shark, and found that its heart continued beating several hours after its death. She caught her first sight of such novelties as stormy petrels, the Magellan clouds, and the Southern Cross. She sailed imperviously past the coast of Patagonia, where the natives were supposed to be man-eaters. The mate signaled what he thought was an island; it was, in fact, an iceberg and "heeded him not." They sailed close to Juan Fernandez, where "a man [presumably Alexander Selkirk, prototype of Robin-

175

son Crusoe] lived alone for 5 years." Finally, on the fourteenth of April, 1855, they entered the Golden Gate:

Came into San Francisco Bay and anchored about noon. We were soon thronged with reporters, butchers, merchants, land sharks, and many other inquisitive looking bodies. The scenery here is grand beyond description. Green hills surround us on every side, many vessels are anchored not far from us, and here and there we see a steamboat crossing the bay, while all around us little rowboats are passing from vessel to vessel. When coming into the bay we came very near a rock, which the tide was carrying us on to, and which we only just escaped. It seemed to be covered with birds; but they flew away when seeing us so near.*

The Richardsons had completed the first leg of their journey from Massachusetts to Oysterville.

---

*The birds were pelicans, *alcatrazes* in Spanish. The island, which bore their name, later became a notorious prison site.

Dunes near Oysterville

16

The Preacher Is My Papa Dear

In California the Richardsons found that the Golden Rule did not pay off so well in creature comforts as the Rule of Gold. Horace preached vigorously around San Francisco Bay, but dozing parishioners probably dreamed less of the Golden Streets of Heaven than of the San Franciscan who had died insolvent, only to have the value of the land he left skyrocket so fast that before his administrators could settle his estate they had $40,000 a year to distribute among his heirs. A poor soldier bought a plot of San Francisco land for a few hundred dollars and within weeks was renting it for $50,000 a month.

Horace did not share such dreams, and could not grasp their hold on his parishioners. They did not want carefully reasoned sermons about the evils of nicotine; they preferred to be either exhilarated by the promise of a rich lode in heaven, or terrified by the threat of a salted seam in hell.

Most of them, barely literate, preferred their peers as preachers. Appalled by the execrable speech of the average California minister, Cornelia consoled herself: "They do as much good anyway, as the Californians do not know the difference."

Poverty was a near, if not dear, companion of the Richardsons. Years later, Sarah wrote in one of her rare admissions of despair: "Horace has agreed to stay one month longer as pastor here in Petaluma—without pasture, I expect, as heretofore. What will become of us then? Perhaps the grapes will be ripe on the commons by that time."

Cornelia, in any event, soon took a long step into the future. In 1856 Horace officiated at her wedding to Dr. William Bamford, a young physician who later saved the life of Robert Louis Stevenson.* Sarah's offspring, Dan and Horatia (she came to be called Shae, and sometimes Rae), watched the ceremony. Its excitement still lingered in a letter that Shae wrote half a century later to the Bamford's daughter Mary:

Yes, I remember when your pa and ma were married. I have a dim vision of Aunt Nelia, all fixed up, standing by the side of "the doctor" at our house, and my father talking to them, and a lot of other people in the room. I didn't quite take in what she was standing there for with "the doctor," who had black whiskers all around, nor what father was saying to them. Afterwards I went on the trip to their home with my parents in a buggy, while your parents went in another buggy by themselves. They rode just ahead of us. I had on my new red and black plaid dress and my red and black plaid stockings. When we got to the place where they were to live I followed "the doctor" out into the woodshed and saw him unpacking crockery from a barrel filled with straw and dishes. He carried the dishes into the house, and my mother and Aunt Nelia washed and wiped them and they were cooking something to eat off the dishes. All this I remember when I could not have been more than four and a half years old.

*See page 298.

The first thing I remember about you, you were a baby sitting on the floor playing with some wild flowers that Dan had given you. Suddenly Aunt Nelia jumped up quick and took something away from you. It was a green caterpillar that you seemed about to put in your mouth.

I can still see that barrel of dishes in the woodshed and the plates half-hidden in the straw, and the green caterpillar, and the baby on the floor with the flowers, as well as if those things were of last week's happenings. Years are short periods of time after all. Oh, well, I don't feel so very different—I still feel that I am I. I'm glad to have lived, and I'm glad to keep on with living. And perhaps there are nice things afterwards.

Did you see today in the *Chronicle* how the inhabitants of Mars have finished their Canal? An astronomer says so! I'll enclose the article.

Well farewell to Mary, who once liked to eat caterpillars of green hue.

Affectionately,
Aunt Shae

Apart from the inevitable crudenesses of pioneer existence, the Richardsons conducted themselves in California much as they would have done back in Massachusetts—they lived in impoverished gentility on the leavings of Horace's parishioners and gratuities from the parents of his pupils. In a story she wrote for *The Congregationalist and Boston Recorder*, Shae was to recall the humiliation and fury that such impoverished respectability could instill in a small child:

Father says our trials and afflictions are sent to make us better, but I don't see how it can make me any better to have to wear Ophelia Podd's old dresses.

They have donation parties in our church; and every time they have one Phelia's mother gathers up all the old dresses that Phelia has outgrown, for she's bigger than I am, and does them up in a great bundle and sends them along to the donation party. Then mother fixes them over a little and makes me wear them, and the girls at school say: "Why, that dress is just like Phelia wore last term!"

She is a real good girl herself—I'm not talking against her you know—and never tells the girls the dresses were hers; and the girls can't tell sure that they ever were unless mother makes me wear two or three of them in succession. I don't think mother is near proud enough.

Once Phelia had a very noticeable blue dress that was all embroidered in blue silk on the waist and sleeves, and, when it came to me, mother said it was so pretty that she would not alter it a bit, except to make it a bit shorter in the skirt. I didn't want to wear it at all but mother made me. She said I ought to be thankful to have it to wear.

People bring us all sorts of things at these donation parties: sugar and flour and soaps and dresses and hats and meat and tablecloths and wood and coal and bed quilts and ever so much rubbish besides. Some of the things are done up in bundles and after the folks are gone, we children have lots of fun pulling them open.

Once I opened a bundle when no one happened to be looking, and I did not think what was in it was proper, so I made way with it. It was Eliza Smith's old hat. The very one she had worn to church for a long time! I suppose she had a new one, and thought this old one would do for me to wear to school. To wear Phelia Podd's old dresses and Mrs. Steen's old cloak (made smaller to fit me) was bad enough without having to wear Mrs. Smith's Eliza's hat!

I couldn't bear the thought of it, so I "removed" it, but it caused me a good deal of trouble afterwards. This is how I removed it. I dug a hole in the ground between two rows of corn over in Mr. Nichols's field and buried it. The very next morning our dog Tonto walked up to the open kitchen door with that hateful hat in his mouth. He had gone and dug it up!

One day Mrs. Smith came to call, and suddenly she said to mother: "How did Theodosia [Shae varied in her stories between calling members of her family by their right names and modifying them, as here "Theodosia" for "Horatia."] like her hat? I've never seen her wear it."

I felt myself grow just crimson, and mother said: "What hat, Mrs. Smith?"

"I sent a lovely hat to the donation party for Theodosia," explained Mrs. Smith.

Then they both looked at me, and I suppose I appeared guilty, for mother said, sternly: "Theodosia, do you know anything about that hat?"

I had suffered so much in my mind since I removed it that I did not think it was much worse to be found out, so I said, plump and square: "Mother, I buried that hat in the ground!"

Mrs. Smith looked almost petrified with astonishment, and mother was very much mortified. Then they made me tell the whole story, and finally mother sent me out with the fire shovel to dig the hat up. It had been in its grave three weeks then, and was all mildewed, and the crown torn off by Tonto's playing with it. I had to bring it in, right before Mrs. Smith, and she held up her hands in horror.

"Such pride! Such sinfulness! The *minister's own daughter!*" she gasped.

I had begun to be very sorry and ashamed of myself, but her saying that rather unsettled my sorrow.

As soon as she got over being petrified, she told mother that if *she* was my mother, she would make me wear a sunbonnet to church all summer to punish me, and take down my pride.

For a while I was afraid mother would, but when she told father, he just burst into a laugh, and mother always laughs when father does, so I did not have to wear the sunbonnet. But Mrs. Smith is offended with the whole family now, and don't come to our church.

A leitmotif of these narratives is that my great-grandmother Sarah was always proposing condign punishment for some misdeed of the children, and my great-grandfather Horace was always persuading her to let them off. He was much too soft-hearted a man to apply to his own family his lifelong, no-holds-barred wrestling match with the devil.

Dan ran away to see a fire, for instance, and then, afraid to enter the house for his hot supper of poached eggs and toast, went to sleep, crying a little, in Tonto's kennel. When he was found there, Sarah felt her husband should make vigorous use of his belt. According to Shae, the exchange between husband and wife went like this:

Father—"Pshaw! Boys will be boys! I'll tell you what, Sarah—you needn't expect you can keep a boy as big as our Dan from a fire. Let him go to the fire. It don't hurt boys—does 'em good."

Mother, sighing, and giving up the point—"I don't see what they want to go for, though."

Now wasn't he a really splendid father?

Shae described him, when he was teaching the district school in the summer months and poring over his books in the winter, as "a very silent, absorbed-appearing sort of a man"; but, she added, "he could never bear to have us children out of his sight."

The minister's children were perhaps not quite the best-behaved children around. One day when Horace was teaching at San Pablo, a farmer pounded on the school door to complain, "Some of them there scholars of yours have been getting into my haystack again. They've pushed half of it down flat on the ground, a-slidin' off it and on it." Horace ordered the culprits to stand, and to remain standing for half an hour. The only three who rose to their feet were his own offspring—Mat, Dan, and Shae.

When told by her mother to wash milk pans, Shae would hint to Horace that she might be more useful cleaning the church; and he, God's fool that he was, would happily take her along, so that she could walk up and down the aisles singing hymns and occasionally flicking at a pew or the pulpit with her dustrag, while mother Sarah stayed home and rubbed her knuckles raw cleaning the pans.

Once Shae even "kind of" stole from her father; but that, she always asserted, was really Dan's fault. She had saved fifty cents to buy her father a birthday present. Dan wanted to borrow the money for fishhooks, promising to repay her as soon as he had caught and sold enough fish:

I did not like to lend it, but he had lent me money sometimes, so I let him take it. But he never caught a single solitary fish all that week, and when father's birthday came, I didn't have any present. I kept thinking and thinking about it, and all at once that afternoon of the birthday, when I was combing my father's hair, the thought came to me how I could borrow the money for a few days.

Father likes to have me comb his hair and put bay rum on his head, and keep combing and combing until sometimes he falls fast asleep.

Well, this day I had been combing away and thinking about the present, and after a while he dropped asleep.

Then it came to me to just borrow fifty cents out of father's pocket, only for a day or two, until Dan had caught some fish and sold them and paid me my money; then when he paid me I would comb father to sleep again and put it back. I knew father had some fifty cent pieces in his pocket, for I saw him marry a lady and gentleman the day before, and the man gave him the money for marrying them. Any other time I would have asked father to lend me the money; but of course you can't ask a person to lend money to buy that *very* person a present!

So I put my hand in his pocket just as soft, and took the money out just as easy, and he never stirred!

Then I bought him a silk handkerchief of a Chinese pedlar who was going by. It was a real pretty one, with a red border, and when I gave it to father he said I was a dear little girl. But I didn't feel as happy as I thought I would. I felt *horrible.*

Two days later, when Dan did catch some fish and pay me, I ran right in the house and said: "Father, shall I comb your hair?"

He replied, "Yes, dear."

And then I combed and combed and combed half the afternoon, and he kept on reading the paper—but he *wouldn't* go to sleep, and I've combed him every day since; what is worse, he is beginning to wonder why I like to comb his hair so well, for I did not always want to do it. I'll never borrow or steal money that way again. I believe I will wrap the money up in a piece of paper and write on it "Horatia's Conscience Money," and put it between the leaves of father's *Bibliotheca Sacra.* Then when he finds it he will ask me about it and I mean to tell him the whole story and have it off my mind.

Shae's accounts contend that most of her misdeeds were really good intentions gone wrong. This is natural; the stories of her childhood were written for publication, and had to be dressed up a bit. I recently came across one of these stories in print along with a letter by Shae's daughter Imogene describing the same incident. By comparing the two versions you can decide for yourself how many grains of salt to shake over Aunt Shae's memories:

At the age of ten, she drove the family buggy to town alone for the first time. By the account she printed in *The Golden Age,* her selfless purpose was to sell six dozen eggs, so that she could buy her father a Christmas present—either a pair of slippers or a dozen white handkerchiefs.

She had no trouble managing the old mare until she overtook a neighbor, Mr. Wilson, who was riding a horse and driving a cow to market. The cow seemed to suspect that an unpleasant fate was in store for her; at every opportunity, the cow would bolt back toward home. So Mr. Wilson tied her to Shae's buggy:

183

And the cow did not make much difficulty, except occasionally, when she would suddenly remember her troubles, and give a jerk backward, shaking the buggy violently, and making old Dolly very indignant.

When at last Mr. Wilson took his cow away, I drove on a little farther down the street to Mr. Norton's store, where I meant to sell my eggs.

"How much?" asked Mr. Norton, good naturedly.

"Well," I said, "I'd like thirty cents a dozen."

But when Mr. Norton went to draw out the box I had stored so carefully under the seat, ever so many of the eggs were broken!

"Oh dear!" I cried, in consternation; "it was the *cow* that did it!"

My heart was almost broken, along with the eggs.

Everything ended happily in *The Golden Age* story. Mr. Wilson, having sold his cow for a good price, gave Shae enough money to pay for every egg in the box, and she was able to buy her father slippers and the handkerchiefs as well.

Here is Shae's daughter Imogene's letter about the same event:

Shae asked her father once, when she was about ten years old, if she might drive into Oakland all alone. So he said she might, and she rose real early and harnessed the horse herself, and drove down clear to Oakland, to sell eggs to buy herself a hat. She bought a black one. It was shiny, and Shae kept it under the bed in a box and used to take the hat out and look at it by moonlight. She thought the hat was beautiful. Eggs were quite high then. The hat cost $3.00 about, she thinks.

There is a little self-delusion in us all, and fiction should not be confused with fact.

Wild Blackberry

We Have Buried
the Baby in a Corner of the Garden

From 1854 to 1866 Great-grandpa Horace held parishes and taught school at Santa Rosa, Ione, Volcano, Petaluma, San Pablo, Russian River, Healdsburg, and East Oakland (then called Brooklyn)—all communities bordering on San Francisco Bay. Wherever he went, his family piled its possessions on wagons and came along. Each move, says Shae, was preceded by a ritual bustle:

Standing about in different rooms were trunks stuffed full of books, and rows of chairs tied together two to two, and bureaus and washstands and clothes-presses dragged from their places against the wall into the middle of the floor, and baskets full of odds and ends, and bundles of this and bundles of that and bundles of the other. The carpets had all been pulled up, and stretched on the line in the back yard, where father was energetically beating them with a broom, enveloping himself in a cloud of dust at every blow. In the dining-room, mother, with dishes of various sizes and shapes piled around her, was placing them between thick folds of paper, and storing them carefully away in boxes; while Mat and I, towels pinned over our heads, were sweeping into a corner the deep layers of dust that had accumulated under the sitting-room carpet.

One exceptionally long move covered a hundred and twenty miles, and the three-wagon train took four days for the trip. Dan could not persuade the driver of the wagon in which he rode to let Tonto sit beside him; instead the dog had to run behind, attached by a line. On the third day, a passing horseman shouted, "Your dog is dead." Nobody knew how long the wagon had been dragging Tonto's lifeless body by the neck through the clouds of dust.

Some of the houses that Sarah turned into homes were at the edge of redwood forests, the trees so tall that one might have expected their tops to be capped with snow. Others were surrounded by fields of red or white poppies, white or golden oats, or yellow mustard. There might be larkspur, or manzanita bushes with red berries. Horned toads squatted by hot dry roads. Chinese panned for gold in ditches. Digger Indians came begging from their rancherees—collections of huts just outside each white community. Whenever an Indian died, the wailing of the survivors, and the howling of the dogs while the corpse was being burned, carried all the way to town. The Richardson children often heard that distant wailing, and never forgot it.

A deservedly unpublished verse of Mary Bamford's tells how Horace once took up the cudgels for the Diggers when they were attacked by smallpox and the villagers refused to let them approach:

Then out spoke Uncle Horace,
    And said, "Friends, hark to me!
The Indians all are starving
    Out at their rancheree!
Shall we sit selfishly

While Indian children suffer?
Neighbors, this must not be!"

Oh, then the good town-people,
    As Uncle Horace said,
Sent to the starving Indians
    The white man's gift of bread!
Poor little Digger children!
    I hope they all were fed!

Now, Indians come to see folks,
    And beg their food, instead.

Something about those last two lines makes me wonder whether Cousin Mary, however sorry she might have felt for the Diggers, quite understood where the responsibility for the Diggers' plight lay.

Wherever the Richardsons happened to be domiciled, they raised their own livestock and vegetables. The children liked to eat the meat, but hated the idea of having the animals slaughtered. They treated the newborn, especially, as both pets and companions. What is more disarming than a brindle calf that pushes its head between the bars of a fence and rubs against a child's sleeve, looking up with soft, inquiring eyes? Dan fed one calf its milk first from a nursing bottle and then from a bucket every day and when the calf was due to become veal, he managed to secure a remission by promising to go barefoot until his savings in shoe leather equaled the market value of the animal.

Despite the children's affectionate guardianship, the Richardson stock led perilous lives. Dan innocently fed mildewed raisins to a cow of which he was particularly fond, causing it to bloat and die. A sow went mad and ate two of her litter. A wild dog attacked the family's Brahma hen on her first clutch of eggs, so damaging her feathers, flesh, and feelings that she deserted the nest and incontinently expired.

One rainy day Dan, then ten, climbed into his father's boots, which came up to his jacket, and set across the cowyard to collect two new white piglets as playthings. Unfortunately, the boots stuck in the muck, and Dan would have stuck there too if he had not pulled his legs free, fallen flat on his back, and then waded ignominiously back to the house, leaving the boots standing there filling with rain.

On other rainy days, Dan and Shae played dentist in the barn. She would walk ears of corn over to him, these representing "ladies come to have their teeth pulled." Dan would screw a monkey wrench tight on one of the kernels—"that's a tooth"—give a pull, and out it would come. Thereupon, recalled Shae, "I had to holler like everything for the lady, because it hurt her so."

Once they took an unauthorized walk through a neighbor's grain field, the tall stalks parting so docilely before them that Dan exclaimed, "Let's play we're the children of Israel, passing through the Red Sea!" 188

At that instant, however, the owner of the field spied the intruders, their heads barely showing above the stalks, and shouted, "Get out of there, you young ones, or I'll cut your ears off!"

Meanwhile, Horace was continuing to work diligently for the Lord. Besides preaching and teaching, he found time in 1857 to help revive a Baptist periodical called the *Pacific Recorder*. Soon afterward he played a small part in founding the state's first Baptist Seminary, in Berkeley. Sarah drove herself as mercilessly; but her body was less sturdy than her husband's. In her first four years in California, she carried the burden of making homes for her family in half a dozen towns, always under conditions more primitive than she could have imagined from Massachusetts. Her constitution, as people said in those days, was not up to it. I remember my mother remarking on the curious coincidence that both her Richardson and her Taylor grandmothers were transplanted from happy backgrounds to uncongenial places. "Grandmother Richardson," she said "yearned as strongly for the 'rocks and rills' and steeple spires of her New England as did Grandmother Taylor for the plantations and gracious living of the South. And my own mother was equally stricken when torn away from her 'beautiful Mexico.'"

In Santa Rosa, on January 5, 1858, Sarah bore her first California child, Henry Peabody, of whom Grandpa Richardson as a grown man could only recall, "I remember our little brother Henry very faintly. I know that I was left in charge of him once when he was crying, and I stilled him by putting my thumb in his mouth." The following July 3 — a long gap of time, one would think, even in those days of laggard communication — Sarah wrote her sister in San Francisco:

DEAR SISTER CORNELIA:

You have doubtless, ere this, seen in the Santa Rosa paper, the death of our darling baby. He died on Monday eve and the next morning Horace wrote a line to you & the Dr. informing you of the sad event and also of the funeral, which was to be on Wednesday morning. We hoped that you could both be present, but as you were *not*, and we did not *hear* from you, we concluded that the stagedriver neglected to deliver the letter given to his charge for you.

We thought our poor little Henry better that morning, as all his symptoms seemed to indicate, and I think he would have rallied, had not his constitution (which, for reasons easily accounted for, I believe has always been frail), been too weak and exhausted. There was an unusual brightness about him in the afternoon which was the only symptom that gave us alarm of immediate danger. His little life went out gently and without a struggle. Oh, how stricken are our hearts! How *large* a place do such little, dependent beings fill! We miss him everywhere! It was *always* a pleasure to administer to his little wants, he was so *patient, so good*. But we would not call him back. All is *just* and *right*. I feel that we have a new *attraction* in heaven, a new tie to the spirit-land.

He died to sin, he died to care,
　　But for a moment felt the rod,
Then rising on the viewless air,
　　Spread his light-wings, and soared to God.

May I meet him there. We have buried him in a corner of the garden. The children are much grieved at his loss.

My health is, I think, improving. We expect to be *alone* on celebration day. I wish you could be here. Hope your health is not still suffering in consequence of your last visit. Horace says your baby is a very fine, thriving child. I hope the precious treasure will be spared to you long. Kiss it for me and believe me,

> Yours, though in affliction,
> SARAH

Eighteen months later, on February 22, 1860, at Russian River, Sarah bore her last child, Alfred Bennett. In the next two years, the family moved twice more—first to Ione, and then to Petaluma. At Ione, Sarah began to have hemorrhages. "I remember," Dan was to write Shae in 1915, "father's anxiety and the fear which began to creep into our home. . . ."

On April 11, 1862, Sarah left this world to join her lost Henry in the spirit-land. Dan was then eleven, Mat thirteen, Shae nine, and Alfred, or Allie, two.

For the next three years the four children lived at Petaluma with the Bamfords; whether Horace was there as well is not clear. Aunt Cornelia's hand, in any event, was heavier than his. Under her determined tutelage, Shae soon became expert at starting the fire, setting the pot to boiling, and cooking beets and turnips. Her greatest tribulation was washing the greasy black pots that had held the cabbage.

Dan and Shae were even instructed in piano. "Danny played at the growly end," Shae remembered, "and I played at the tinkley end. Our teacher sat and looked at us and kept saying, 'Thumbs under! thumbs under!' when we were playing *up* the scales, and she kept saying, 'Third finger! fourth finger!' when we were playing *down* the scales."

Motherless, they still managed to have their fun. Dan celebrated Shae's tenth birthday by dropping red pepper on her tongue while she slept. She repaid him with a vengeance:

Aunt Nelia sent me into the boys' room for something, and I noticed that the ceiling looked strange. It was made of thick canvas, stretched from one wall to the other. It had rained so hard in the past twenty-four hours that the water had come through the roof, but it did not drip on the floor, because of the thick canvas. It just collected there, and the ceiling right over Dan's bed looked all baggy, weighed down with water. That night when Dan and Allie were sound asleep I brought in a pitchfork from the barn and slipped into the room and stuck the tines into the canvas. But oh, dear! I think there must have been a whole cloud up there, 190 and it came down over me, myself, as well as Dan and poor little Allie. I screamed as loud as I could; and Dan jumped up, and screamed louder than *I* did. Aunt Nelia came rushing in with a lamp, and Dan sat up there in bed, all shivering and wet, and said: "Oh, oh! the world is being drowned out, and we haven't got any ark!" I said: "It ain't; it's only just a cloud that fell out of the ceiling."

On the first of January, 1865, Horace took a new wife — another Sarah, whose last name was Haines. All I know of her is Mary Bamford's comment: "I tell you it is a hard job for a public school teacher to marry a poor minister who has a family of *grown* children!* Aunty Richardson (No. 2) tried to do her best, usually, but it was a hard job. Don't you ever undertake it."

The family next settled in East Oakland, which was to be their home from then on. For a time both Horace and his new wife taught school. In 1866, however, Horace took up the career that was to earn him the sobriquet of Bible Richardson.

In that year he became a canvasser for the California branch of the American Bible Society. The job consisted of selling or giving copies of the Bible or the New Testament to anyone who would take them. The Society listed any person owning neither, whatever his earthly estate, as "destitute."

Horace cannot have earned much more from the new job than the minimum he needed to keep himself alive, including such bed and bread as might be offered by the remote settlers who were his constituents. His new Sarah had to continue teaching school to hold the family together.

But the greatest drawback of his assignment was that it kept him from home for weeks or even months at a time. Horace Richardson was a philoprogenitive man, and he missed his children as much as they missed him.

Still, he labored manfully, unloading the Scriptures on one remote county after another. Reads a typical report to his employers: "Over all this territory that was accessible, sometimes in close proximity to the ocean side, and then again up some of its tributaries, hundreds and thousands of feet above, finding here and there a family, a camp, or an individual, have I scattered the precious leaves of life in English, German, Danish, Swedish, Spanish, Portuguese, Italian, French, and Chinese, speaking and preaching often their blessed truths." The precious leaves of life were printed in many languages, foreigners making up a large part of the mining population, but when Horace spoke and preached blessed truths, he spoke and preached in English, that being the only language he knew.

His efforts at salvation frequently took a numerical turn: "Here," says one Society account, "is what has been accomplished since October

191   *Well, not quite. Great-aunt Helen was eighteen, the others younger.

last, and during a *severe* winter, by Rev. H. Richardson: Number of miles travelled, 1,276; families visited, 2,043; families found destitute, 168; families supplied, 56; persons supplied, 66; Catholics supplied, 38 [the Society apparently drew a clear distinction between *persons* and Catholics]; Bibles and Testaments given, 118, valued at $44.25; Bibles and Testaments sold, 344, valued at $639.95. [By this reckoning, the Bibles and Testaments he sold were valued at nearly two dollars apiece, as compared with less than forty cents apiece for those given away. Either Horace gave away only the cheapest volumes, or the Word of God appreciated mightily in the marketplace.] Whole amount received on contributions, $613.35; number of circulars distributed, 523; letters written, 45; sermons and addresses, 30."

"I was told," says one of Horace's letters to the Society, "that there were two families far up an exceedingly high mountain. I lightened my wagon of a large part of its precious burden, and then, myself on foot, leading my horse, attempted to mount the height. The effort was a hazardous one. At one time, horse, wagon, and all were sliding down in spite of my best endeavors to the contrary. Providentially, however, I succeeded in locking my wagon, until I could unload it of all its large Bibles but two. With these two, I managed to scale the mount, passing meantime the wreck of a wagon, one of the mules killed and the driver injured, reach the families, and furnish each of them with a family Bible, one of them being entirely destitute of one, though having seven children in their family."

After serving the Society in California for eight years, Horace joined the newly organized Nevada Bible Society in 1874 to canvass "the entire state." After a year he retired to his East Oakland home, where he died, penniless and in debt, in 1876.

Though all the family suffered from the long absences of their father, it is fair to assume that the one who suffered most was his last-born, Allie, who from his fourth year until at least his fifteenth saw but little of Bible Richardson. Allie grew up sickly; the one remaining picture of him is reminiscent of *The Sorrows of Young Werther*.

In 1879, not yet nineteen, he joined an expedition to the Arctic. He never returned.

The Genial Flute

In my study, opposite the beehive clock that Grandpa Espy did or did not carry across the plains in 1852, you will see resting on wall brackets— under a head-study in oils of my mother as a three-year-old, done by my Great-great aunt Cleora—the corpse of an ancient flute. It was acquired in college by Daniel Richardson; and except for the not infrequent occasions in his youth when he had to pawn it to keep himself afloat, it remained at his side as companion and comfort for the rest of his life.

Take the flute up and finger it. It has, you will notice, only six stops; its present-day equivalent has eight. Its barrel of brown-stained wood is bound together with hoops of brass. Despite the bindings, the wood is cracking.

Grandpa Richardson was the kind of person who *should* have played a flute: a chiaroscuro sort of man, dappled, an ever-shifting, astonishing succession of sun and shadow. He loved solitudes; he loved people. He was a romantic; he was a rake. He could lie by the hour like a snake in the sun, and then move faster than the eye could follow. He was a Renaissance man, universal in his interests; yet his accomplishments were minor.

His physical growth stopped just under the middle height; his hair and complexion were fair; his eyes, blue and long-lashed, drooped at the outer corners. He was a trifler; he was a hedonist; he was a poet in the style of the day:

'Twas such a night as this, sweet love,
  The moon was in the west,
And timid stars hung then, as now,
  Along Diablo's crest;
Just there you stood—love in your eyes—
  A rosebud at your breast . . .

Like his sister Shae, he went through a period of recording his adventures. The difference was that she brought back her childhood, while he brought back his youth. The more ridiculous a mishap, the surer he was to report it—doubtless for a very small fee—to some periodical. And like Aunt Shae, he kept his clippings. He never bothered to identify, and seldom to date, the periodicals for which he wrote. Some are completely anonymous; I can determine the others only because the name appears on the clipping itself. The outlets for his ramblings included, however, the New York *Illustrated Times;* the San Francisco *Chronicle;* the *Golden Era* (generally under the pseudonym of Cornelius Poe); the *Argonaut;* the *Californian;* the *California Horticulturalist; The Farmer and Dealer;* and *The Wasp.* He may have written for *The Overland Monthly* and *Harper's Monthly*—at least my mother said he did—but I find neither publication named in his scrapbooks.

In 1871, Dan and a traveling companion whom he calls Mathew spent their summer vacation in the Yosemite Valley, where, he reports, "a man from Visalia and a student joined us, and together we dwelt in harmony in two canvas tents beside the river, and in front of the great Yosemite fall:"

All in all, we were very happy. Above and below us on the river were campers from every part of the state, and in every camp except our own there was a pretty girl. A jollier crew never waked the echoes of that wild Paradise. For ten days our felicity was complete. These were the good old times, when but one road led into Yosemite. Men went there to get rid of the smoke and noise of the city. In huge boots and blue shirts, unshaven and unshorn, they stood face to face with nature, and went away better men for the interview. A new wagon road leading into the valley was about to be opened, however, and we were destined to witness the inauguration of a new era.

A grand ball was arranged to celebrate the opening of the new road, and for the occasion the stagecoach brought in load after load of kid-gloved young gentlemen from such metropolises as San Francisco and Stockton. This presented young Dan and his companions with a grave problem: they had no formal clothes for the dance:

Indeed, we were a hard-looking set. With slouched hats, gray shirts, and brogan boots, with faces unshaved, and the dirt and dust of the road still adhering to us, we looked like pirates. A familiar way that Mat, who did the cooking, had of wiping things off on us was beginning to show its effects upon our persons. The student had three distinct impressions of the bottom of the coffee pot in the middle of his back.

"Something occurs to me," said the student. "I believe I know where there is a white shirt. That guide who took us up to Glacier point yesterday told me that John Muir, the geologist, gave him one last spring."

"Can you get it?" we asked.

"I will try."

"I think," said Visalia, knitting his brows and speaking very deliberately, as if trying to recall some isolated fact from oblivion, "I think I know where there is a black coat."

We were all attention.

"I saw one," he continued, "down at Hutchinson's a few days ago, in the cook's room, hanging near a window; I believe I can reach it if it is still there."

"Magnificent!" exclaimed the student; "all we want now is a pair of pants."

Before we went to sleep that night it was decided that, on the following day, each man should start out on a foraging trip, the results of which were to be shared equally between us. To me was assigned the duty of providing a pair of pantaloons, and my instructions were to beg, borrow, or steal, but not to come back to camp without them. I succeeded, without resorting to desperate measures, and was first to get back to camp on the following day with my prize. Mat came next with a vest and a large green necktie, and lastly Visalia and the student put in an appearance, each with a bundle of some description under his arm. We compared notes, and found that we had enough to dress one man.

The pantaloons had evidently been made for a giant. They came clear up to the student's armpits, and there was then, as he remarked, room enough left in them to accommodate a bale of hay. The shirt and vest worked very well; but the coat which Visalia had secured was short and narrow, and absolutely refused to cover up the great folds in the voluminous pantaloons, and its sleeves did not reach much below the elbow on the smallest man among us. Taken as a whole, it was decided that the outfit looked best on Visalia, and it was consequently decided that he should go in and take the first dance, the rest of us awaiting our turns outside.

About nine o'clock we went down the river and crossed over the bridge into the town. Everything was life and motion. The hotels and stores were lighted, bombs were bursting, and everybody in the valley — Indians included — was out in his best war paint and feathers. A temporary dancing floor had been laid near one of the hotels, enclosed by canvas and evergreens, and a band stationed within sent music out into the night to mingle with the murmur of the waterfalls. We could see the shadowy figures of dancers through the canvas, and hear the patter of little feet. What made it all really unbearable was our confirmation of the fact that the town was full of swells, in claw-hammer coats and kid gloves, who were going in and out from the dancing-room, and making themselves merry with young ladies on whom we believed we had a primary claim.

Visalia was, however, equal to the emergency. He took our blessing and left us, disappearing through the door of the tent. For half an hour our suspense was fearful, and then a baggy shadow flitted past on the canvas, and we knew Visalia had found a partner. A few moments afterward he made his appearance, looking savage and desperate.

"What is the matter?" we asked.

"Nothing, nothing," he replied, "it's your turn next, I believe, governor," addressing the student, and he began to divest himself of coat and vest as rapidly as possible.

The figure cut by the student when he had donned the garments which Visalia threw him was something indescribable. I have never been able to understand how he had the moral courage to go into the ball-room, and can only account for it on the supposition that he did not know what a fright he was. Visalia forgot his ill humor, and lay down on the ground to laugh, and Mat and I suffered as we never have suffered since. The student, however, was not to be dismayed. He threw himself into the breach, and we lost sight of him. We imagined that we heard a smothered laugh as he passed through the door, but we forgave the claw-hammers, knowing that nothing human could bear the sight unmoved.

We could hear, however, from our position outside, that the titter which greeted his entrance gradually grew into a laugh, and we were in momentary expectation of seeing an animated pair of pantaloons bounce out through the open door.

Nothing of the kind happened, however, The student had gone in to have a dance, and he proposed to carry out the programme regardless of consequences. Marching straight up to one of the prettiest girls in the room, he asked her hand for the set which was forming, and she promptly rose and took her place beside him on the floor. "The act of that brave girl," as the student afterward expressed it, "should live in history, for it averted a tragedy. If she failed me, I had fully made up my mind to kill every smirking claw-hammer in the room, and I knew I could count on Visalia for a helping hand."

When the music started up, we could see fellows slipping out through the door, holding on to themselves as though stricken with colic, and a pent-up yell would occasionally ring out on the night like a cry of agony. The figure was soon ended, however, and the student returned to us flushed and happy. It was my turn next. I was not possessed of the audacity of either Visalia or the student, and trembled at the ordeal before me; but there was no honorable way out of the dilemma, as we had entered into a solemn compact to stand by one another. I declined, however, to don the unmentionables in which the student and Visalia had figured, contenting myself with the shirt, coat, and green necktie.

My advent in the dancing-room, like that of my predecessors, was greeted with something more than a smile by the loungers around the door; but, to my surprise, the ill-concealed derision drove away my timidity and filled me with a species of desperate confidence. It excited my resentment, and enabled me to understand the incomprehensible audacity of the companions who had gone in before me. On reaching the inner sanctum, my first encounter was with a charming creature named Smith. We had made each other's acquaintance the day before under the Nevada Fall, and were on the most friendly terms. She did not even glance at my brogan boots. but held out her hand, with a bewitching smile: "Why, Mr. Richardson, how late you are!"

"I had a little business," I faltered.

"And where is Mr. Visalia? I thought I saw him here a little while ago. And what has become of the student? I have not seen him for half an hour. And your friend Mat has not put in an appearance at all. I thought you four were inseparable."

"Mat fell into the river on the way down," I stammered, "and he had to go back to change his clothes."

"Mr. Richardson," said Miss Nasturtium, advancing toward me in a coquettish manner, and laying her hand on my arm, "what a pretty green necktie you have on! The student wore one just like it when he was here."

"And what a nice stylish coat you have!" chirped in another girl.   198

"Mr. Visalia wore one of the same cut, and with the same candle-grease stain down his back, when we last had the pleasure of his company."

"And what a nice—" But I saw the jig was up, and did not permit Miss Nasturtium to finish her sentence.

"Listen, ladies," I said, "and I will acknowledge the corn. The boys are outside in the brush. This suit of clothes you see is a combination affair, and we are trying to work it on the installment plan. Think gently—pity our affliction. In the name of the best we could do, be merciful—be—"

A merry peal of laughter cut my words off short, and immediately there was a rustling and scampering, and in less than three minutes a committee of four or five bewitching creatures stood around me in nubias and wrappers, and sternly demanded that I should lead them to the hidden retreat of my companions.

Resistance was useless, and I complied. I will not tell you of the scene that followed, for I cannot. Suffice it to say, that the boys were dragged from their hiding places among the rocks, and marched into the ball-room, in all the glory of their mountain attire. I retained the good clothes, however, and John Muir's shirt, and was happy. But the clawhammers—they were the maddest fellows you ever saw. The girls would hardly notice them. And when "Home Sweet Home" announced that day was breaking about the brow of old El Capitan, we marched off up the river, arm in arm, to our camp, proud and satisfied that for one night at least we had been "cocks of the walk."

Old stories like that one relay hints about my own character and personality that I might be better off not to know.

The Bloody Battle
of the Lower Lake School

The foregoing events took place while Grandpa Richardson was still in college; His school, the University of California, was founded in 1868. Grandpa's class of '72 was the first to go through all four undergraduate years. It was natural that, as an undergraduate, he should think as a child and act as a child. The following year, however, he was graduated, and, being now a man, put away childish things. In evidence, he located a school in the settlement of Lower Lake, a rural community in the Napa Valley, and settled down to teach. The determination with which he approached this challenge can be best appreciated from his own published account:

I had never taught before, and did not know exactly how to commence. The district, moreover, had just been organized, and I was the first teacher. Everything was crude and primeval. There was not even a schoolhouse yet. Down by a little lake in the heart of a wood, an abandoned log cabin had been designated for this purpose, and here I was told to organize my flock. Furniture there was none. We rolled in logs for the children to sit on, and my desk consisted of an empty syrup-keg. Empty, I say, although the thing had a way of rising at times — especially on hot days — which induced doubts upon this point. The woodpeckers had bored so many holes in the shake roof that it became necessary to pile brush on top to keep out the sunlight, and my big girls stuffed wild grasses and fern leaves into the glassless and solitary window-sash at one end of the structure. Immediately in front of the door, which was massive and never shut, lay the wreck of an immense steel trap which the former occupant of the place had used for catching grizzlies, and just beyond it, nailed high up against the trunk of an oak, were the spreading antlers of a buck.

I soon found out, in fact, that my lot was cast among a race of hunters. The larger boys had a way of sauntering down to school in the morning with shot-guns and rifles on their shoulders, and the grand "stack arms" in the cow-shed would have done credit, on occasions, to an Oakland military company. This kind of business made me a little nervous at first, although I soon became accustomed to it, and even carried a gun myself before the term was finished.

Fortunately for me, there were no arms in sight on the first morning, else I should have taken to the brush like a quail. There were three or four boys in my class — wiry, muscular mountaineers, who could have whipped me easily in the event of war. One of them had already killed his man — an Indian, in a sheep-herder's quarrel — and was looked up to as a hero by his admiring companions. There were likewise two or three buxom lasses in my flock who took no back seat — as I afterwards found out — when it came to a question of muscle and grit. Two of them were very pretty, and I was secretly in love with them both during the entire term, but never dared say so for fear some of the young bucks in the neighborhood would murder me. Besides, I could not decide in my own mind which one I preferred.

There were, all told, about thirty youngsters in my school, varying in age from six to twenty years. Most of them came down on horseback, and it would have done you good to hear them whooping in the cañons and screaming through the woods as they came and went. For a long time their movements were a mystery to me. They seemed to spring up in the morning like wild things from the bushes, and disappear at night in the same marvelous manner.

All this mystery, however, was destined to be made clear, for my contract provided that I should "board around." How much this means can only be understood by the man of vast and varied experiences. To me it meant that I should learn all the sheep trails and hidden paths through the hills; that I should make the acquaintance of busy house-wives, diversified babies, and suspicious dogs; that I should know every-body's business, and eat all kinds of food; that I should sleep in strange places and in strange company; and that I should learn to go to bed in the dark, and dress like lightning in the nick of time on the following morn-ing. The acquirement of this latter accomplishment gave more trouble than all the others. The homes of my patrons were simple and rustic. Few of them contained over two rooms, most of them but one. When bed-time came, the men folks would withdraw to the corral or go out a little way into the brush, upon which the women would retire and put out the lights. It then behooved the masculine biped to sneak in and undress himself in the dark. It was a delicate and trying ordeal for a timid man—one requiring blind faith in providence and an intimate knowl-edge of the topography of the room Subdued giggles would occasionally reach his ears as he struggled with a boot or stumbled over a chair; and on one occasion there was a wild outburst of fiendish female laughter when the schoolmaster's bed went down with a crash.

If going to bed was surrounded with such difficulties and dangers, the act of rising was not less perilous. Woe be to the young man who slept with his face turned from the wall! The women rise first in this mountain land, and early in the dim dawn they cast an eagle eye about to see that the coast is clear. Turn over, young man, and go to sleep, or some one will dextrously toss a horse-blanket or a sheepskin over your face; and then, when the old woman has gone down to the spring and the young girls are out milking the cows, you rustle around and get into your clothes, for you may not have another chance. These rosy lasses have a streak of humor in their composition, and sleepy fellows have been known to stay in bed until noon before they could "clear"—all because they failed to embrace the early opportunity given.

After getting fairly under way with my school, all went well for sev-eral weeks. There appeared to be no insubordination or disposition to give me trouble, and everywhere I was greeted with cordiality by the bluff mountaineers when I met them in their homes or on the roads. One morning, however, on going down to the schoolhouse a little earlier than usual, I was surprised to find the great oaken door closed and barred.

Tethered here and there in the bushes were the horses of most of the pupils, but not a child was in sight, and perfect stillness reigned in the little clearing. This was such an unusual state of affairs that my suspicions were at once aroused. Going closer, I attempted to open the door. A wild shout of laughter immediately went up from the assembled youngsters on the inside.

"Open the door!" I commanded.

"Hi yi! Whoop la! Open it yourself!" came back the response.

Peering in through a crack, I could see the larger boys and girls on guard at the window and door, both of which were strongly barricaded, while the younger children were huddled together in the corners. For some little time I was undecided how to act. Should I attempt to enter by force with these odds against me, or go for assistance?

Should I consider this matter as a serious breach of discipline, or give the boys a tussle and let the thing go as a joke?

Of one thing I was certain: if I did not conquer now I should lose prestige, and probably all control of the school. Upon the outcome of this affair depended not only my future influence, but my ability to remain in the district. To go for help would cause them to despise me. Better make a square fight and get whipped.

First, however, I would try parley. But parley would not work. They flatly refused to come out or open the door unless I should declare the day a holiday and send a boy down to Lower Lake to purchase a supply of nuts and candies as a peace-offering.

This I would not do. The latter part of the condition I could not do if I would, because of financial stress. So war was determined upon.

Going back into the woods a little way I procured a stick—the heaviest I could carry—and charged the butt end of it with all my force against the window barricades. The splinters flew and there was a whoop of defiance from within. Again and again I charged it, and then there was a crash, and I could see that the old wagon-bed which they had braced up against the window on the inside had gone down. Springing instantly into the opening, I succeeded in getting my body half-way through, when I was met by a dozen arms, and a lively skirmish took place on the sash, nearly breaking me in two. As a result, I was violently expelled, my coat was split up the back to the collar, and my hat remained in the hands of the enemy.

In the second round I directed my battering-ram against the door. For a while it resisted my best endeavors, and the boys on the inside were laughing in derision, when a luminous idea struck me. Extending out over the schoolhouse was a limb of the oak tree to which reference has already been made in this article. To throw a rope over this branch and suspend my battery was a simple matter, and I soon had a ram at work which made the old log house tremble. Bang, bang, bang it went; the door began to groan and grumble; the younger children screamed with terror, and the older ones yelled in unison; and then came a grand splintering and before the dust cleared away, I was standing in the middle of the schoolroom in triumph. Immediately three or four of the large boys seized me, and a desperate struggle took place. There was no disposition to strike blows on either side, but the boys were bent on putting me out of the building, and I was equally determined to stay in. Although overpowered from the start, it was still possible for me to make a very respectable resistance, and the enemy did not succeed in evicting me until my clothing was pretty much all torn off, and a number of scratches, bruises, and bloody noses testified to the intensity of the struggle.

My breath was now exhausted, and I sat down to take a rest. The boys in the meantime had replaced the fallen door and cut down my battering-ram. During the fracas most of the smaller children had escaped to the woods, and I could see their scared little faces peeping into the clearing from the surrounding circle of trees and bushes. While thinking the matter over, and wondering if it would not be a good idea to hitch a horse to one corner of the building and pull it down, a little girl approached very timidly from the direction of the schoolhouse, and handed me a scrap of paper.

"Nancy Clark put this through a crack," she said, "and told me to give it to you."

I opened and read as follows:

Git in at the winder; we will help you.
                    Nancy.

"This would seem to indicate," I thought, "that I have friends in the garrison," The "we" was somewhat indefinite, it is true, but it certainly meant more than one. "If I can effect another lodgment in that shanty," I argued, "and there are two persons on the inside who will stand by me — male or female — we can hold the fort."

Approaching cautiously from a blinded corner, I peered through a crevice at the rebel crew inside. All told, they were nine — five boys and four girls. The boys, I noticed, were guarding the door, while the window was left to their female companions. This latter had not been barricaded since I demolished the wagon-bed, my early repulse at that point having led them to the conclusion that it was not necessary. Nancy stood nearest to the opening, her face flushed with excitement, and her lithe, graceful figure as alert as a cat. Around her were grouped the other girls — no doll-faces, by the way, but healthy, rosy lasses, with plenty of firm, shapely muscle; girls who could handle a rifle or an ax, ride a mustang or lasso a steer.

"If these radiant creatures," I thought, "have concluded to desert the rebel cause and join my standard, I will win this battle yet."

I was ungallant enough to have some doubts as to their fidelity; but reflecting that I had nothing to lose and everything to gain by so powerful an alliance, I resolved to throw myself into their hands. Procuring an immense club, I renewed my assault on the door with all the vigor at my command. To demolish it without the aid of the swinging battery I knew was impossible, but another purpose was shaping itself in my mind. When satisfied that the attention of the garrison was fully fixed upon the door, I suddenly dropped the club, and slipping quietly around the building, sprung into the open window and down into the arms of my Amazonian friends before a masculine hand could be raised to stop me.

The scene which now ensued was the liveliest, I ween, that the old log schoolhouse ever witnessed. The boys made a dash for me, but the girls rallied to the defense like Spartan heroes, and gallantly stood off the assault. Securely entrenched in a corner with four gritty girls to defend me, I was prepared to defy the county. For half an hour the struggle lasted, and then everyone was out of breath. Taking advantage of the lull in the storm, I mounted the syrup-keg to make a speech.

"Boys," I said, "you have done nobly, but your sisters are better men than you are. I think that we have had fun enough. Let's call this thing quits, and get back to work."

"You ain't mad, then?" queried one of the rebels, an active youth of about sixteen, who had taken a leading part in the revolt. There was something in the gravity with which the question was put that excited my risibility; but before I could frame a reply the head of the syrup-keg caved in and I came to the floor amid a general laugh.

"Hooray for the teacher!" shouted a barelegged youth; and a chorus of whoops and approving yells greeted the proposition.

The tide had now turned completely in my favor, and all resistance was at an end. At my suggestion the boys put the room in order, the little ones were called in from the brush, and studies were resumed. When the noon-hour came, I noticed Nancy and several of the other girls holding a whispered conversation under the trees; and then one of the boys was mounted on a swift pony and hastily dispatched over the mountain trail. Three-quarters of an hour later he returned with a bundle on his saddle, and I was waited upon by a select committee of young ladies, and requested to accept the loan of a suit of Pete Blethen's Sunday clothes until they could repair my own badly dilapidated garments. They asked, furthermore, that I would repair at once to the woods and make the exchange, as they were provided with needles and thread, and proposed to put my wardrobe in order without further delay.

It took the girls most of the afternoon to sew me up, and in the meantime but little pretense was made of keeping school. So the youngsters had their holiday, after all; but I don't know who had more fun out of it — they or I.

Only three or four years after the episode here described, another young teacher, seventeen-year-old Julia Jefferson, taught her one year of school five hundred miles to the north, at Oysterville. Dan's daughter was eventually to marry Julia's son. If those two parents-in-law ever sat down to compare pedagogical notes, I'd like to have been there.

20

There Is Always
Fruit on the Banana Trees

Grandpa Richardson taught school for five years in the backwaters of California—not only Lake County but Los Angeles and Fresno were then backwaters—before he determined, in consultation with his flute, to try his luck in Mexico. I have no idea what put the notion into his head. Though he never hesitated to recount personal experiences, however embarrassing, for the entertainment of his readers, he was almost as reticent as my paternal grandfather about what really went on inside him. Whatever his motivation, he persuaded a clutch of newspapers and periodicals in California and on the East Coast to denominate him their special Mexican correspondent, which meant they would buy what they liked from him. Dan could scarcely count on such hit-or-miss income to keep him alive in a country where he lacked both friends and influence—even his Spanish was halting—but in that forenoon of his life, he was nothing if not an optimist.

With a friend whom he disguises in his chronicles under the name of Marion, he took ship for Acapulco in late August of 1874. They reached that port, on the Pacific Ocean some three hundred miles south of Mexico City, in early September. The plan was to push on to the capital at once. Dan, however, was in no hurry; by his own account, Acapulco suited him fine:

We were just from the bustle and roar of San Francisco, but here all was quiet—no noisy carts and drays, no pushing, impatient crowds, no stock boards, no politics. A wide straw hat and a cotton shirt, bare feet, and a palm-thatched roof—what else could mortal wish? The citizen works here when he feels like it, and if he never feels like it, he has the assurance of Mother Nature that he shall be neither starved nor frozen out. There is always fruit on the banana trees, and the sun is always warm. At night these lazy fellows sit at their front doors and thrum stringed instruments, or go sky-larking around, making love to each other. What do they care for wealth or power, or the greedy struggles of the outside barbarian?

Apparently grandpa's puritan upbringing was under heavy pressure; like the man in the fable, who buttoned up his overcoat when the north wind blew, he was tempted to slough his clothing under the beneficent rays of the Mexican sun. Marion, however, was made of sterner stuff. Within two days of their arrival at Acapulco, he had assembled a caravan for the overland trip to the capital. Included in the party were a German adventurer, a Philadelphian, several native merchants, and "a Mexican poet" (wherever grandpa traveled, one of his companions turned out to be some species of poet). Communications with the interior being by pack animal alone, the party also included several muleteers, or *arrieros*. At first sight, Dan mistook Alejandro, the *conductor* of the expedition, for a pirate:

He was dressed in leather jacket and pantaloons, and wore spurs and an immense sombrero. At his side hung a long, heavy knife, or *machete,* and a horse-pistol looked out from beneath his red sash. From head to knee he was bespangled with glittering silver buttons, and his boots were yellow.

The caravan covered five leagues the first day, arriving that evening at the village of La Venta:

The huts were made of poles heavily thatched to turn the rain, but open all around. They reminded me of chicken houses. A light burned inside of every house, and as we rode through the town, we could see right into the bosoms of families. No domestic operation was hidden from human view, and for a while I felt like an eavesdropper. We soon learned, however, that they were not at all sensitive on that point. We stopped in front of one of the larger huts, and a dusky damsel came out to bid us welcome. She was bare armed and bare breasted, and her clothing was scanty and poor, but as she stood there holding a blazing pine knot above her head, its light reflected from her white teeth and flashing eyes, her braided hair falling low down her back, and her voice as soft and sweet as that of Laughing Water, we fell in love with her to a man, and our envy of Alejandro, to whom she was talking, would have frightened that individual if he had known it.

About midnight a fearful racket awakened us, and, starting hurriedly up, we could see by the light of the moon a group of ten or twelve half naked Indians, charging, as we thought, right down upon the porch where we were sleeping. They were bare headed, and carried their long wicked-looking knives in their hands, ready to strike. My first impression was that these wild citizens were coming for our midnight scalps, and I made a hasty dive for my revolver, but fortunately my trepidation was unnecessary. The Indians swept past us with loud cries, and disappeared in the direction of the river. Somebody had been killed, and the friends of the murdered man were seeking the slayer to avenge the act. Fortunately for the murderer, he had the start, and escaped into the brush . . . [It turned out next morning that the murdered man was one of grandpa's own muleteers, Ponciano by name. He had been treating a girl of the village to a glass of *orchata*, which was not a nice thing to do. Ponciano's head was nearly severed from its trunk by a *machete* stroke.]

When we entered Dos Arroyos next evening, an air of desolation seemed to hang over the village. As soon as we could find anyone on the street we asked the occasion for it, which was as follows: Two days before, a company of Federal soldiers had marched into the village and demanded of the Alcalde (mayor) a quantity of supplies. The Alcalde refused to comply, upon which he was knocked down and dragged by the hair out of his own courtroom. The principal men of the town interfered and remonstrated with the soldiers for their barbarity. The soldiers then deliberately fired into the unarmed crowd, instantly killing ten men and mortally wounding a woman and child on the street. The Alcalde himself was cruelly butchered by the hand of the superior officer . . .

The third day brought the travelers to a forlorn station called *Agua de Perro,* or Dog Water:

It consisted of a single open shanty, far up in the heart of the mountains. There were twelve in our party, but the naked host greeted us cordially, and, in the spirit of genuine hospitality, invited us inside with the pigs and the chickens. A donkey was domiciled in one corner, and as we stepped in he brayed; but whether it was done in a spirit of hospitality or defiance we could never determine. Our advent made it necessary to kill a hog, which the host at once proceeded to do in our midst, and in the course of a couple of hours the hostess came in from a little back shed, and placed our supper upon a mat in the middle of the floor. There were no chairs, knives, forks, or spoons, and all the eatables—pork steaks, beans, tortillas, and coffee—were in one earthen dish. We were required to sit down upon the ground, and help ourselves with our fingers from the common plate. Having already learned the necessity of laying aside all scruples in journeying through the Indian country, and being exceedingly hungry, we complied, and a more enjoyable meal was never eaten. During the progress of the meal two of the larger dogs got into a fight over a bone and waltzed across our table, but it did not disturb our equanimity further than to occasion a regret on the part of the poet that his coffee had been upset . . .

It was a night of fleas and horrors. I had tried in vain to suspend myself from the rafters in a very narrow hammock, and, having fallen out two or three times, finally concluded to lie still upon the ground and give the fleas a chance. I was just beginning to doze a little when a stentorian grunt awakened me, and I felt myself violently turned over. Scrambling to my feet, I peered through the darkness and discovered that my enemy was a hog. He had not intended to be uncivil, but had accidentally rooted me over in his search for a comfortable place in which to lie down. This, at least, was the charitable construction which I put upon it, for I felt humble. For the first time in my life I admitted that "man and beast are brothers"; nor could I persuade myself under the circumstances that I had any rights which the hog ought to respect.

There followed days of pitiless rain; of near-drownings in flooded rivers; of stupefying storms of thunder and lightning. All this I skip. I skip even grandpa's chilling experience of being mistaken and almost shot for a robber, save for the relief of its conclusion:

The warlike guardians of the pathway finally agreed to let us pass on one condition: if we would come forward one at a time and place ourselves in their hands, they would escort us through the village and let us depart. It is not a pleasant experience to ride through a Mexican town like this at midnight under any circumstances; but when you chance to bestride a Guerrero mule with a tendency to go tail first, and a blanketed rascal runs along on either side with a revolver at your ear, and the rain and the lightning blind you, and you feel helpless and at the mercy of all things diabolical, the experience becomes grim and loses all sentiment.

The travelers arrived after ten horrendous days at their destination, the capital city of the Republic of Mexico. So it was decreed; for otherwise my grandfather would not have met my grandmother; nor would my mother have been born, and transported by devious ways to the village of Oysterville.

Oysterville

A Short Man, a Blond Man, a Damyankee

Though Grandpa Richardson has long been mouldering, his flute remains, waiting patiently against my study wall for someone to pluck it off and try his lip on it. So it waited more than a hundred years ago, sitting as surety among the bottles and jars of a dingy Mexico City *fonda* when grandpa's credit ran dry.

For it turned out that silver dollars did not grow upon the Mexican trees; nor were any golden *onzas* to be found lying about the streets. Yet grandpa and Marion found it no less imperative than it had been back home to eat, which was impossible without food, and to sleep, which was at least uncomfortable without a bed:

Trades we had none, and as common laborers, even if employment offered, we could not earn enough to buy one square meal a day. Strangers in a strange land, without influence, friends, or money, we began to be in want, and hunger stared us in the face.

Yet when we recalled our vainglorious boasts on leaving home, and the light estimate which had been placed upon the advice and warning of loving friends, we were resolved to see the adventure out, and ask no odds of friend or stranger. The day after Marion informed me that we were finally and absolutely "broke," we remained supperless in our room, and spent the long evening writing cheerful messages home. "Forgive this short letter," Marion wrote to his aged mother, after devoting a number of pages to our flattering prospects; "we dined this evening with the Australian Consul, and are a little tired and sleepy." I added a postscript endorsing the lie, and after laughing ourselves hoarse, we went to bed.

Marion mortgaged his watch to a pawnbroker next day, and from the proceeds we were enabled to pay another week's room rent in advance, and there remained upon our hands a surplus of two dollars. This lasted but a few days. There was a little *fonda,* or eating house, on an alleyway leading from the Cinco de Mayo to the Plaza de Armas, kept by a stalwart* Indian maiden whose two brothers acted as waiters, and here chocolate or coffee with steaming tamales was sold for a *medio.*

"Would it not be possible," I suggested, "to ogle this dainty damsel into giving us a little credit?"

She had smiled upon us a number of times as we passed in our small coins for coffee, and, emboldened by the recollection, Marion assumed the responsibility of stating our case in a few brief words. She listened kindly, and was pleased when he called her *encantadora;* but alas for our hopes and the aching voids within us!

She did a cash business.

If, however, we had some such collateral as a watch, an overcoat, or a guitar to leave with her as a pledge of good faith, she would not object to allowing us a reasonable amount of time. Saddened at this new evi-

---

*Considering the amorous adjectives usually applied by grandpa to any female of the species, the proprietress must have been built like Tugboat Annie.

dence of the sordid practical in dreamy Mexico, we went back to our room and took an account of stock. It was not extensive. A few necessary articles of clothing, a little jewelry, and my flute. The latter article seemed most available. It lay on the open music-book where Marion had last been playing *andante*. It was our one solace. How many lonely hours it had helped beguile, and how often its plaintive tone had voiced the homesick yearnings which came with the night and the stillness! Marion took it up gently and played a few notes from the old college song "O, think of the days over there."

But it was not a time for sentiment. Twenty-four hours had elapsed since the cravings of the inner man had been appeased, and so the flute was borne away and stood up among the bottles and jars behind the Indian woman's counter. "Sold for a mess of pottage," it seemed to say, as it looked reproachfully down upon us from its ignoble eminence; but redemption there was none. For a week we ate in peace and then the brown damsel levied another assessment. The flute was lonesome, she said, and something of further value must be placed beside it. This was regarded as a notice to quit, and we returned no more.

But we were not yet done with the businesslike proprietress. Her brothers, the waiters, were trained and carefully instructed to lie in wait for us on all occasions, and demand the cash redemption of the flute. They dunned us on street corners, in churches and hotels and public squares, until we took to dodging up back alleys and making wide detours to avoid them. Marion declared his belief that it was the spirit of the dishonored and indignant flute which prompted our persecution. And to be sure, its voice was a little plaintive grown when, months later, we redeemed it from captivity.

It was no longer possible to pay the room rent, and we were told to "skip." One by one our remaining personal effects were turned over to the pawnbroker, and for several weeks we lived in the most uncertain and migratory manner. An occasional opportunity would present itself to earn a few dollars by translating newspaper paragraphs for the native journals, and once our hearts were gladdened by the receipt of a small remittance from a San Francisco daily; but these rays of sunlight were few and far between.

For days at a time we did not know where the next meal was coming from, nor where we would rest our heads at night. As good fortune would have it, however, actual want never overtook us. Something always turned up at the last moment to relieve the immediate distress. It was vacation time, and a number of students attending the law and military colleges were nearly always in our company. These light-hearted fellows, proverbially impecunious, were proof against all low spirits, and many a merry lark we had on short allowance and empty pockets. Twenty-five cents was frequently made to furnish a meal for a crowd, and at night five or six of us often accommodated ourselves to one small bed. Someone would first go up alone to the hotel and hire a room. It was generally one of the cheapest and at the top of the house. The rest would then drop in one by one and dispose of themselves as best they could. The bed clothes were divided, one mattress was dragged out upon the floor, lots were cast for the softest places, and all was soon quiet.

There is no knowing what might have been the outcome of this anomalous state of affairs had not an old-time schoolmate and friend arrived from the coffee groves of Colima as the representative of his state in the National Mexican Congress. But a few years before, we had studied irregular conjugations from the same book, under the spreading trees of the old school back home. Immediately interesting himself in our behalf, a happy change was soon effected in our circumstances.

At this time the Castle of Chapultepec was undergoing repairs, and its historic halls were unoccupied save by a few guards and their families. This structure crowns a rocky hill situated about three miles west of the city. Its surroundings, and the view to be had from its summit, are unsurpassed for beauty, and the tradition and legends of a poetry-loving people have been woven about it for centuries. Years ago, when the waters of Lake Texcoco washed its base, it was the resort of the battle-scarred Aztec warriors from the campaigns. Later it became a fortress, and then the site of a school under the republican regime. The presidents and rulers of Mexico have often made of it a suburban retreat, and the unhappy prince, Maximilian, spent much of his time here, beautifying and laying out the grounds. Americans remember it as the scene of the last desperate struggle of the campaign of '47.

In our numerous rambles in and around Chapultepec, Marion and I had frequently discussed the possibility of obtaining lodging within its walls, but the permission of those high in authority being necessary to secure this end, the project had been abandoned as hopeless. For our newfound friend, however, it was an easy matter to procure for us the necessary permits, and Marion came rushing up one evening with a mysterious blue document in his hands which proved to be an order upon the warden of the castle for a room sans lucre, and liberty of the grounds.

To be transferred thus suddenly from the Arab life of the noisy streets to the halls of Montezuma seemed incredible! No more dodging angry landlords; no more skipping about under the mellow moon without where to lay our heads; no more doleful naps on cold stone floors with our overcoats for winding sheets; but, in the place of all this, the shades of heroes, and the galleries where emperors had held high revel! Unlike our predecessors, baggageless and without ceremony, we assumed possession of our royal quarters. The dishonored flute still stood among the plates and bottles of the coffeehouse, and the clutch of the pawnshop owner was upon our chattels. But what of that? Kings before had been in debt, and ours was not the temper to be depressed at trifles. Consistency was no jewel in our code of ethics; and, if it had been, we would have pawned it long ago. In this respect at least we did not differ from the other crowned heads of the world.

For six long happy weeks our reign was undisturbed. Marion went daily to the city where our generous friend had found him work, but I remained at home. My royal province was to cook, make the beds, and clean the house; but with these cares upon me there was still time to read and dream and study. Day after day I stretched myself along the sunny slopes, or wandered beneath the forest arches which extend away from the castle base to Molino del Rey.* At night, after Marion's return, it was our custom to pace the long corridors overlooking the valley. What glorious sunsets we saw from those old gray walls, and how the veil of enchantment hovered over the world beneath as the hazy shadows shifted over lake and forest, and finally climbed the snow peaks far beyond! No pen can describe this wondrous valley. Like Irving, dreaming away his time in the deserted Alhambra, our days and nights were filled with romantic novelty. Every rock and tree and cave had its historic interest, and its tale of wonder. There were many relics of the unhappy empress, Carlota. In the chamber, next to the one we occupied, stood her grand piano, its lid closed down and locked, and the dust lying heavy upon its damask cover. The baths which Maximilian had built for her remained as she had left them at the base of the southern cliff. There were paintings and statuary, and coats of arms. But we took little pleasure in them. An air of desolation was about them, suggestive of empty pageantry, and the folly of human ambition.

In later dispatches, Dan told of scaling Mount Orizaba, 21,000 feet high, and sliding back on a mat, covering in fifteen minutes a stretch that had taken five hours to climb. He told, too, of penetrating the gloomy, smoking crater of Popocatepetl, where one of his party was overcome by sulfur fumes, and had to be hoisted, dangling like a corpse, up the two thousand-foot crater wall.

Why had they left so agreeable a location as Chapultepec Castle? By reason of good, not ill, fortune. As has been noted, Dan was able within a few months of pledging his flute to redeem it, "its voice a little plaintive grown." The reason was that he had struck up an acquaintance and then a friendship with John W. Foster, minister of the American Legation. In the spring of 1875 Dan was promised a post as secretary of the legation. So fortified, he was able to dash back home to Oakland for a hero's welcome, bask in the envy of his friends, and return to Mexico City to report for work on July 28, 1875. He remained until March of 1879, serving in turn as secretary, consul general, and chargé d'affaires.

On May 1, 1876, he married a nineteen-year-old American expatriate named Annie Medora Taylor. He used to say that he saw her one day washing her hair, and vowed that he would eventually make her his. The odds against such a consummation were enormous; certainly, prior

---

*A group of thick stone buildings about two miles southwest of Mexico City. On September 8, 1847, it was the scene of the bloodiest battle of the Mexican War. The United States troops lost over 700 killed and wounded; the Mexicans, over 3,000.

to his appointment by the legation, he could not have afforded to support a wife, nor would he have had the social contacts necessary to meet an eligible prospect. Annie Medora had lived in Mexico since she was eleven, and combined in one fiery body the anti-gringoism of her Mexican acquaintances and the hatred of all things Yankee instilled by her Confederate parents. Her mother had died in 1872, and her father, apparently the representative of an export firm, was often absent on business, leaving Medora and her three younger brothers in the charge of a French couple who tried to convert her to Catholicism. In this effort they were unsuccessful; she refused on one occasion to kneel and kiss the bishop's ring; on another she agreed to go to confession, but when asked what had happened there reported only that she had slapped the priest's face.

Add that Annie Medora Taylor swore daily that she would never marry "a short man, a blond man, or a damyankee," each epithet an exact description of Dan Richardson, and you will see that grandpa was working under handicaps. His storming of Annie Medora must have been scarcely less risky than the Yankee attack on Chapultepec Castle a generation earlier. However irresistible he may have been to women, I still find it surprising that he made the conquest in less than a year.

Both my grandmothers died before I was born, and both are mysteries to me; but my Grandmother Richardson is the greater mystery of the two. There is a contradiction in my feeling about her. On the one hand there is the quiet, forbearing wife and mother whom mama remembered as quiet, loyal, and of unquenchable good cheer under seemingly unbearable family circumstances. On the other hand there is the fiery southern girl who refused to kiss the bishop's ring or take confession — the girl who had been brought up to sleep with a loaded revolver under her pillow, because of the wild land in which she lived, and continued to do so, under very different circumstances, to the day she died. The time must have come when that loaded revolver worried grandpa. Not that there was any likelihood of her shooting someone by accident — she was a superb shot, and would never have hit the wrong person. There were occasions, however, when grandpa may have had good reason to fear she might hit the right one.

22

Oh! Is It to Be Thus If So I Had Rather Die

JAMES TAYLOR married
FRANCES,
and begat again
JAMES

James married
MARTHA,
daughter of COLONEL WILLIAM THOMPSON,
granddaughter of SIR ROGER THOMPSON,
and begat
GEORGE;

George married
RACHEL,
daughter of JONATHAN and MARGARET (CATLETT) GIBSON,
and begat
RICHARD and EDMUND;

Richard married
CATHERINE,
daughter of JAMES A. and FRANCES (BERRY) DAVIS,
and begat again
RICHARD;

Edmund married
SARAH,
daughter of FRANCIS and SARAH (HAYNES) STUBBS,
and begat
MARY;

Richard married
MARY,
and begat
WILLIAM HENRY HARRISON;

William Henry Harrison married
CATHERINE SMITH ROBINSON,
and begat
RICHARD;

Richard married
RACHEL MEDORA PRYOR,
daughter of JOHN CANNON and ANN (BULLARD) PRYOR,
granddaughter of DAVIS and SUSAN (BALLOW) PRYOR,
and begat
ANNIE MEDORA;

Annie Medora married
DANIEL SIDNEY RICHARDSON,
who begat
HELEN MEDORA;

Helen Medora married
HARRY ALBERT ESPY,
who begat . . .

On the tenth day of July, 1855, in Frankfort, Kentucky, a twenty-one-year-old bank teller of romantically mournful countenance (according to my reading of his photograph), Richard Taylor by name, a native of Clinton, Hickman County, wrote and doubtless rewrote a momentous letter to the Honorable John Cannon Pryor, a former judge in that county, but by 1855 living in Florida or Mississippi. Richard's letter, with several others exchanged in the Taylor-Pryor family during the fifties and sixties, was destined to be carried from Kentucky to Texas, from Texas to Mexico, from Mexico to California, and finally from California to Oysterville, Washington, where after more than a hundred and twenty years it still survives, tied in a bundle with its companions, in the left-hand corner of the topmost drawer of a bedroom bureau. The style of the communication may be orotund, but its purpose is clear:

HON.
    JOHN PRYOR
        DEAR SIR
Considerable time has elapsed since an engagement of marriage, (indeed when we were but children), was made between your daughter Medora & myself.

This engagement has proven more than a passing dream of childhood, each year that has gone by since the first exchange of our childish affections has served but to strengthen & refine them into a deep & earnest attachment. It occurs to your daughter & myself that the time has come when I may bring the subject directly to your notice, & ask your consent to the consummation of our engagement. I am not unmindful of the great responsibility the request involves & am fully conscious of the extent of the favor I solicit of you, & if the promptings of my heart are an index to my judgment, you shall never have occasion to regret your acquiescence to our arrangements if your inclinations should be favourable to our wishes. I enclose a letter from Mr. J. B. Temple, & will take pleasure in furnishing you with such other references as will assure you that should you consent to our marriage her happiness would be as secure as if she were under your own protection.

        I am very respectfully
           DICK TAYLOR

The seconding motion from Mr. Temple is not extant, but I do find one from James I. Fall:

HON. JOHN C. PRYOR: —
    DEAR SIR—
At the request of Mr Richard Taylor I write to you on a subject, in which we all feel greatly interested. As you are aware, an engagement exists between Mr Taylor & Medora. That engagement was made more than a year ago, not without the knowledge of several of Medora's friends—myself among the number. So soon as I ascertained its exist-

ence I told Medora that it was not my intention to throw any obstacles in the way of the fulfilment of her wishes; but that she must immediately write to you, and inform you of the affair—otherwise I could not allow them to correspond. This course seemed best, because young persons— young ladies especially—should be taught to confide, freely, such matters to their parents.

I did not interfere with their arrangements; because Mr. Taylor's family is of indisputable and eminent respectability; and because he himself is a gentleman, and a young man of superior business habits— indeed it is seldom that you find one, who is, in all that constitutes the gentleman, of more unexceptionable worth and standing. Although young—about 21 years of age—he has lately been elected Teller of the Br. Bank of Ky. in this place; and that after his fitness for the place had been thoroughly & practically tested by the officers of that Bank.

It would, perhaps, be improper for me to say more, concerning Medora's interest in this matter, than that I am sure her happiness, through life, is involved in her attachment to Mr. Taylor and in the fulfilment of her engagement with him.

Very truly yours,
JAMES I. FALL

What was a sixteen-year-old girl doing alone in Frankfort, at a time when her father had removed to the Deep South? The answer is sadly simple: Medora's mother was dead. Medora, the only girl in the family, was the youngest of six children—sixteen years younger than her eldest brother John. Having no idea of what else to do with her, her father shipped her off to finishing school.

Medora, called always by her second name, was the granddaughter of David Pryor, a Virginia veteran of the Revolutionary War. Her father was a peripatetic type; he lived at one time or another in Kentucky, Mississippi, Florida, and Louisiana, and died in Texas of a plague. Medora's eldest brother, John, returning from a gold-hunting expedition to California, was crossing the Mississippi on February 27, 1849, when his boat overturned; he drowned rather than shuck the gold-heavy belt he carried around his waist. It would not surprise me if Pryors are still diving for his body. Another brother, Isaac Thomas, sired Colonel Ike T. Pryor, whose Texas ranch was at one time among the largest in the world.

Our family owes to the Pryors the lovely given name Medora, now passed down uninterruptedly for six generations.* The first known Medora in this family sequence was the subject of the letter just quoted. I suspect she was named for the heroine of Byron's 1814 poetic tragedy, *The Corsair,* in which a Medora, the beloved of a captured pirate

*Rachael Medora (Pryor) Taylor had Annie Medora (Taylor) Richardson, who had Helen Medora (Richardson) Espy. Helen Medora had Medora Espy, who died without issue. To keep the series of Medoras unbroken, I called one of my daughters Freddy Medora, who called her first child Medora Ames. In the same spirit, my sister Dale named her only daughter Sydney Medora.

(supposedly modeled after the French-American buccaneer Lafitte), expired on hearing a false rumor that her lover had been slain.

Such gooey romance must have been irresistible to gravid antebellum matrons deciding on a name for a daughter. They would not have heard that during the gestation period of *The Corsair* Byron appears to have impregnated his own half sister, who called her child Medora. I don't know whether Byron's baby — if his she was — was named after the fictional heroine or the heroine after the baby.

So we know that Richard Taylor and Rachael Medora Pryor grew up together in or about Clinton, Kentucky; that there was an early attraction between them; that chance took him to Frankfort to work, and her there to finish her schooling; and that in Frankfort their relationship ripened into love. One suspects that the parents of Dick and Medora were acquainted, and expected some such consummation. Dick's letter to John Pryor must have won favor, to judge by Medora's communication with her father less than two months later:

Sunday, Frankfort, Sep. 2nd 1855

MY DARLING FATHER

I wrote to you a few days since but did not write a long letter so thinking you are always glad to receive my letters I will write again and intend writing every sunday. Oh! father if I am not with you I think of you daily and nightly and am always wishing to do something to add to your happiness.

My last letter was mostly about my marrying so in this I will say but *little* about it, but *now* my darling aged Parent think upon it. Had you not rather see me married and settled down with a kind husband if you were called to die than a *wanderer* in the world "no place is like home" and in a short time Dick will bring me to see you and may be it will not be long before we move south for you to live with us. We are willing to do anything to add to your happiness yes dear Father we are your kind children at heart you will see that. Dick is as kind as your owns sons his disposition is so kind and affectionate. Father I am buying my wedding clothes my clothes and my account this summer will come to about $350 Father I have *never* had any linen underclothes and all grown ladies and almost all girls have them during the last three years my store accounts have been about $125 not one cent more and your $41 ⅔ is a small sum for a girl one year and now I really think I ought to have a nice outfit and I know you will make Mr Stewart send me some money Oh! Father I feel very badly here without *one* cent and Daddy my own and almost only brother wrote me word that I *should not* have any money but that I *should* come home Oh! did a Brother ever treat a sister thus?

Father please write me send what things you wanted me to get you last winter we will get them and bring them down with us you wanted some socks and *we* [changed from "I," and underlined] will get them.

Father Mr Sanders was in Frankfort some three weeks since you remember having sent me some shells by him he said he would send me the shells as soon as he returned home but they have *not* come yet. He taked [*sic*] of you very affectionately and said he would write to you very soon he is quite an agreeable man he sent much love to you.

I will soon close it is almost church time do write soon to Dick and myself. I am going to write again next sunday. *All* send their love. I am still your devoted daughter

MEDORA.

Well Dear Father since I closed this letter I received a letter from you which delighted me greatly yes dear Pa *we* are a thousand times obliged to you for consenting to our marrying *here* We will leave here the 3*d* of October and will not let Paddy know anything about it Oh! how strange how strange it is that a brother should treat an only Sister thus Oh! if I could see him he would I know change I am going to write him a long letter in your next Father I know how he feels about my marrying but I know it is for the best enough of this.

Well Father concerning M*r* Stewart's sending me $1000 this year he tells an untruth he sent Cousin Jimmy $641.63 to pay for my schooling and at the *utmost* he has sent me about $60 so Father $701.63 in all he told you that he would send me $201 but he has *not* sent me but $20 in the last 4 months do dear Father make him send me some immediately remember it is *now* only 25 days and I am going to give my supper my self and do you not know that if I pay my debts after I am married *every* persons [*sic*] will say that M*r* Taylor had to pay them oh! is it to be thus if so I had rather die to think that I am to be treated thus I wish to send this in the morning so I will close do *do* write soon to your own devoted child.

MEDORA

[On back of last sheet] *Remember how Cousin William Pryor treated me?*

Many of the questions raised in Medora's letter remain unanswered. Did her father send her—perhaps through Mr. Stewart, whom one assumes to have been some sort of estate manager—the money for her "nice outfit?" Did Dick and Medora buy father his socks? (I notice that it was now September; he had asked for them the preceding winter.) Did Mr. Sanders send the shells? Did "every persons" indeed say that Mr. Taylor had to pay the wedding costs? How *did* Cousin William Pryor treat Medora? There is only one of her questions—a rhetorical one, to be sure—which I can answer with assurance. The answer to "Oh! did a Brother ever treat a sister thus?" is "Yes."

alder
Oysterville,
Washington

The Ship Is Foundering,
but the Cargo Is Saved

Back in 1935, when I was comparatively erect myself, it depressed me to have a distant, aged Taylor cousin confide, "Of course I am crippled, but the Taylor women have been very erect in their carriage. We attribute it to our military ancestors."

Considering the way I stoop now, the Taylor blood in me must be running pretty thin. If Martha Taylor's effective use of hot mush as a weapon against Indians in the seventeenth century is any criterion, the women in the family used to enjoy a good fight as much as their menfolk did. And the menfolk enjoyed nothing more.

The progenitor of my ancestral Taylors, says tradition (I enter that caveat because I have never seen proof of descent), was the Norman Baron Taillefer, who was slain at the side of William the Conqueror on Saturday, October 14, 1066, during the battle of Hastings. Bulwer, in *Harold: Or, The Last of the Saxon Kings*, describes Taillefer's death as follows:

In the midst of Duke William's cohort was the sacred gonfanon, and in front of it, and of the whole line, rode a bold warrior of gigantic height, and he rode

> Chanting aloud the lusty strain
> Of Rolland and of Charlemagne,
> And the dead who deathless are
> Who fell at famous Roncesvalles.

He seemed beside himself with the joy of battle. As he rode, and as he chanted, he threw up his sword in the air like a gleeman, catching it nimbly as it fell, and flourishing it wildly, till, as if unable to restrain his fierce exhilaration, he put spurs to his horse and dashing to the front of the detachment of Saxon riders, he shouted, "A Taillefer! A Taillefer!" and by voice and gesture challenged forth someone to single combat. A fiery young thane started forth and crossing swords with him, Taillefer, again throwing up and catching his sword with incredible rapidity, shore the unhappy Saxon from the helm to the chine, and riding over his corpse, shouting and laughing, he again renewed his challenge. A second rode forward and shared the same fate. The rest of the English horsemen stared at each other aghast. Leofivine, the Saxon King's brother, came in front of the detachment, not drawing his sword, but with his spear raised over his head, and his body covered by his shield. Taillefer rushed forward, his sword shivered on the Saxon shield, and in the same moment he fell a corpse under the hoofs of his steed, transfixed by the Saxon's spear. A cry of woe, in which even William joined his deep voice, wailed through the Norman ranks.

Well, all that is as may be. The first Taylor ancestor I can claim with certainty, James, came to Virginia with his wife Frances in 1667, and there bore a dozen children, of whom my six-times-great-grandfather, also James, became a colonel of a regiment of colonial militia, fought happily in the Indian wars, represented King and Queen County in the House of Burgesses, served as surveyor general, and died unaware that two of his great-grandchildren, James Madison and Zachary Taylor, were to become Presidents of the United States. His son George set a martial genital record: ten of George's sons served in the Revolution, nine as commissioned officers. Two of these, Edmund and Richard, are my four-times-great-grandfathers. Mary, Edmund's daughter, married Richard, Richard's son.

Edmund was a captain in the Virginia state line, and that is all I know about him. His brother Richard was commissioned a captain in the Virginia navy in 1776, and served actively for more than six years. At one time he commanded a squadron at Hampton Roads; as captain of the schooner *Liberty* he was able to surprise and secure four enemy merchantmen in the Rappahannock; again, commanding the *Patriot*, he engaged the British privateer *Lord Howe* off the Virginia coast. It is said Taylor might have had the worst of it had not the U.S. brig *Northampton* come to his assistance. The *Howe,* finding the odds against her doubled, very sensibly retired.

In November 1781, Richard received a grapeshot through the knee that was to disable him for life. The hit came during an engagement with a British cruiser off the capes of Virginia. The day being still, and both vessels wallowing, Captain Taylor determined to attack the Englishman in open boats. As these approached the enemy, they were the target for volley after volley from the British guns, but the aim was poor, and it looked as if the Americans would have no trouble getting into close quarters and boarding the English ship. Unfortunately, however, according to one account:

One of Captain Taylor's young and enthusiastic sailors cried out in foolish bravado to the English gunners, "Why don't you elevate your metal?" (that is, elevate the breeches of their guns), whereupon the British, taking the hint, poured a well-aimed volley of grapeshot into Captain Taylor's boat, killing a number of his men and wounding him severely. He was compelled to beat a retreat and abandon all further attempts to capture the enemy.[*]

That was the end of Richard's active service, but the Commonwealth of Virginia made him a commodore, and honorary commander in chief of the Virginia navy, which consisted of his two old ships, the *Patriot* and the *Tartar*. In 1794, he resigned and removed to Kentucky, where he settled on 5,333 acres granted to him by the United States for his services during the Revolution. Here he was visited by the Marquis de Lafayette in 1824, and here he died in 1825, declaring triumphantly with his last breath, "The ship is foundering, but the cargo is saved!"

Two sons of Commodore Richard Taylor bore his Christian name.

---

[*]William Kyle Anderson, *The Robertson-Taylor Genealogy.*

The first, born out of wedlock but reared as one of her own by Richard's wife Catharine, was known as "Hopping Dick," because of lameness resulting from a wound received in battle with the Indians. General William Henry Harrison said of him, "If I wanted a man to storm the gates of hell, I would send Dick Taylor."

The second Richard, called "Black Dick" to distinguish him from his illegitimate brother, left no record of achievement, except that he did become a colonel, which must mean something. Through his son, William Henry Harrison Taylor, he also became my thrice-great-grandfather; but I doubt whether that future event is noted on his tombstone.

All right. Richard Taylor had William Henry Harrison Taylor. William Henry Harrison Taylor returned the favor by having another Richard Taylor, my great-grandfather. The marriage of Dick Taylor to Rachael Medora Pryor is a prime example of one of those complex family inter-knottings — not just square knots and bowlines, but granny knots, cousin knots, and uncle-niece-nephew knots — that still provide an agreeably arcane area of study for aging spinsters among my Southern relatives. Here are a few of its intricacies (which, if you are not an aging spinster, you have my permission to skip):

✛ Joshua Davis, one of Dick's forebears, was a connection of Jefferson Davis, and a great-grandfather of President James Monroe. Joshua's wife Catherine was a kissin' cousin of Captain Alexander Doniphan, an ancestor of Harry Truman.

✛ George Taylor, Dick's twice-great-grandfather and progenitor of the ten Revolutionary combatants previously mentioned, was the husband of Rachel Gibson. Her father Jonathan was President Madison's godfather, while her maternal grandfather, John Catlett, was, along with George Taylor's father, President Madison's great-grandfather.

✛ Dick — and I am back now to my Great-grandfather Taylor — had an uncle, Edmund Taylor. Edmund's second cousin once removed was Zachary Taylor, President of the United States. Zachary's son Richard became a general in the Confederate army, while my own Richard Taylor could never make it past captain. Zachary Taylor's daughter Sarah married Jefferson Davis. Uncle Edmund meanwhile married first a daughter of Henry Clay's brother Porter, and, second, a Miss Hart, a niece of Henry Clay's wife Lucretia. By this second wife he had Thomas Hart Taylor, likewise to eat out my great-grandfather's heart by becoming a Confederate general. Lucretia Clay was a cousin of Missouri's crusty old Senator Thomas Hart Benton, commonly known as "Old Bullion." Benton's daughter Jessie married J. C. Frémont, who played a prominent part in the capture of California during the Mexican War and in 1856 was the first Republican candidate for the Presidency, running on an antislavery ticket. (Having an abolitionist in the family must have been a shock to Old Bullion.) Thomas Hart Benton the senator was great-uncle to Thomas Hart Benton the painter.

✢ Uncle Edmund's third wife was Martha Southgate Taylor, a relative. His fourth was Elizabeth Fall, daughter of the Reverend Philip Fall who, rounding out the circle, in 1855 united Edmund's nephew Dick with Rachael Medora Pryor as man and wife. Uncle Edmund's new niece, my Great-grandmother Medora, was also the blood niece of Mitchie Pryor, the second wife of Randolph Jefferson, Thomas Jefferson's slightly better than half-witted brother. Mitchie, an extravagant and determined woman, ran through whatever property Randolph's own poor management had left him. She was referred to by a contemporary* as "a Jade of genuine bottom."

✢ Uncle Edmund's fourth marriage made Medora not only his niece through marriage but his sister-in-law as well. It added likewise to his stock of brothers-in-law, of whom one, William Fall, married Edmonia, sister of Dick—my Great-grandfather Dick, that is. The first child of William and Edmonia (Taylor) Fall was Albert, destined to become senator from New Mexico, secretary of the Department of the Interior under President Harding, and recipient of a $500,000 bribe in the notorious Teapot Dome scandals of the 1920s.

Back now to my own Great-grandfather Dick. All my life I have known that he was a Confederate captain, and that when the war was over he exiled himself and his family in Mexico. One Pryor cousin insisted to me that Richard had been a prisoner of the Union forces; that he had killed his guard with a shovel; and that he had then fled across the border.

Yet when the time came to report Dick Taylor's war record, I discovered that I knew nothing about it at all. Since he was born in Kentucky, since he was married in Kentucky, since my grandmother was born in Kentucky, I had taken for granted that he must have enlisted in a Kentucky regiment. Yet inquiries there revealed no trace of him. As last, as I brooded over the Taylor Bible, the obvious answer leaped out at me: though Richard's first and second children were indeed born in Kentucky, his third and fourth were born, in 1860 and 1862, in San Antonio, Texas. Clearly, it was from Texas, not Kentucky, that Richard had joined the army. An inquiry to the Texas state library brought by return mail the following information:

Name and Rank: Richard Taylor, PVT
Comm. Off.:   Duff, James, Capt.
Organ.:   Co. of Alamo Rifles, 30th Brig. TST
Enlist: Sept 1861

---

*Joseph C. Cabell.

Remarks: R and F 87; Comm. Jan 11-62; HQ San
                      Antonio Jan. 1-62; 1 mu. roll for
                      month of Dec. 1861.

I was now convinced that to trace this dashing Confederate through his scintillant military career would require only a few letters of inquiry to official sources. So I wrote the letters, and did learn a few facts. I learned, for instance, that TST stands for Texas State Troops. I still don't know what R and F 87 means.

What I could not learn was just what sort of *fighting* Dick did. San Antonio was far from being a center of war; quite to the contrary, it was, say some, a gold-rush town, a city of gilded sin—though I am sure sin shunned the areas frequented by Rachael Medora's family. With the rest of the South under blockade, San Antonio was a port of entry for guns, for ammunition, for the necessities of life, and for all the rich man's luxuries that somehow manage to pullulate in the midst of even the most brutal war. Whatever Europe could produce in the way of wasteful consumption was on display in San Antonio. The rest of the South might live on grits; but King Cotton held high carnival in the city on the San Antonio River.

Still, Richard Taylor must have seen action. By May 7, 1862, he had become a second lieutenant in Duff's company, which served primarily as a border guard against Indians, Mexican marauders, and Confederate deserters. He was mustered in with a horse valued at $150, gear worth $50, and a six-shooter and saber priced at $100. In November he became a captain. That, however, is as far as he got. As I study the scant records available, I begin to suspect, indeed, that with every day spent in the field Captain Dick became more certain that at heart he was a home-loving, uxorious type, not meant for war's alarms. In the spring of 1864 he received a thirty-day leave of absence for the purpose of removing his family from San Antonio to Ellis County, and after that the military seems to have found him as hard to catch and hold onto as a greased pig. On the ninth of June he wrote his commanding officer from Austin, "I have been on the road eleven days & am now water bound here. Have no idea how long I may be detained as the Colorado is not to be ferried & Still rising. You can therefore see that it will be impossible for me to get back to Brenham within the time granted me. If you will be kind enough to give me an extension of time for 30 days more I will be enabled to arrange for the comfort of my family during the war, otherwise I will be forced to return at once & without them."

By August 20 he was still not back at his Brenham headquarters, and Brigadier General H. E. McCulloch complained indignantly:

There is one case to which I wish to call special attention in which it seems to me great injustice has been done the service to accommodate *one* officer. On the 27th May last I granted Capt. Rich*d* Taylor a leave of absence for 30 days, he made application to Dist. hqrs and got an extension of 30 days more, and has since rec'd an extension for 15 days more from the same source, making 75 days, and is now detailed on court martial at San Antonio, while his company is here under the command of his Lieutenant, and he in the mean time has been a candidate for County Clk in Bexar County, thus showing a disposition to avoid the Service entirely. Under all these circumstances I respectfully ask that he be ordered to return to his co. at once that justice may be done the service and other officers of his co. and Regt.

A scribbled note in a different hand appears below the foregoing. It reads, "Order Capt. Taylor to his Co." Whether he actually returned I cannot swear, but I do note that "Richard Taylor, Capt. Co. A., etc., resigned Oct. 25, 1864."

All this is fragmentary, and it may be that between leaves of absence Captain Dick Taylor was killing Yankees like San Antonio mosquitoes. The only reassurance I have on that score comes from Colonel Harold B. Simpson, USAF retired, director of the Confederate Research Center and Gun Museum at Hillsboro, Texas. The colonel says, "Your great-grandfather's service record is not as bad as you believe. I would take the charges made by H. E. McCulloch with a grain of salt. He was a mediocre officer at best."

Look, I never *did* put any credence in those charges of McCulloch's. I could see just by looking at his handwriting that the man was a born liar.

Still, it is puzzling that Dick Taylor, one of the few hundred Confederates who exiled themselves and their families to Mexico after the war, was one of the very few dozen who never came back.

Family bible

My Dear Dear Darling

However dubious the military record of Captain Richard Taylor, he at least took up arms, which is more than most of his descendants can say. Still, we can claim he was also the last of us to be thrown into jail. Or perhaps it was a stockade; the record here too is vague.

All I know about that period is contained in that packet of letters in an Oysterville bureau drawer.

Fragments from old letters are like a lightning flash on a stormy night, so brief that there is time for only a glimpse of the landscape before everything is blacker than before. There are references to unknown persons and events; to contexts that can only be guessed at. Just what did Richard do, for instance, that ran him afoul of the law? Was it his unregeneracy as a rebel? Or was it a crime? Colonel Simpson, mentioned a page or so back, speculates that his difficulties "may have originated from his service with an irregular Civil War unit involved in something the Federal government or the post-war carpet-bag state government considered atrocities. Shooting a negro state policeman, for instance, would have made him highly popular with the citizens, but very unpopular with the State authorities."

I find nothing in the record to confirm cousin John Pryor's contention that Dick killed a guard with a shovel; but there is nothing to disprove the assertion either. We know only that he fled to Mexico some time between October 1864, when he resigned from the army, and September 5, 1865, when his wife wrote him as follows:

San Antonio, Sep. 5*th* 1865

MY DEAR
DARLING HUSBAND

Your last letter was written 28th Jully & it now being September I am quite anxious & really uneasy. I look daily *yes* hourly for a letter bidding me come the days all seem longer to me & I am lonely indeed. I feel I have nothing to live for or care for here all on earth to me so far away maybe you think me cruel with four so *lovely* children as ours but you little know my feelings In your letter of Jully 28th you said I would be with you in early fall of course that ment September or October & of course your next letter will tell me when & how to come oh! I pray it may. Mr Colowell is here but the Powder Co. money amounts to but little it being but $160. I am really uneasy I do not believe I will have enough money to take me to you even if I sell my things at a good price which is doubtful I will trust to providence & will not despond — am trying to come by the 1st of Oct —

Next Monday is your birth-day & sad I feel as the time approaches as you have always been with me on your birth-day & we have been so happy will the time ever come again, last year you were at home & our dear country in a prosperous condition the men have all changed & it is hard to tell which is the *real yank* — I am proud to say the southern ladies are unchanged. Gen Sheridan has [word illegible — possibly "come"]

235

here — There are about 10,000 troops here they are quite ordaly, but you know what we think of them & how we *love* them —

The children are all well Annie goes to the Convent & Tom to the colledge Dick Pryor stay with me. I send the children to the Catholic schools for in our future home there will be nothing else. Do write me often I must be there soon. do let me come & please get Mr Gonzolez send me a check on his home here if you are doing business for him. I must close I am going to send this letter to you by Mrs Capt King to Matmoras & there she will mail it to you. Goodbye my dear dear darling husband & I pray the time may not be long before you send for me. All the children send love & kisses to papa God bless & watch over you is the prayer of your devoted wife

MEDORA

The letter at least makes clear that Medora was still worrying about money in 1865, just as she had worried about the financial burdens of her impending wedding ten years before.

Dick probably entered Mexico early in July 1865, as part of the expedition headed by General Joe Shelby. Magruder had asked Governor Murrah of Texas to empty the state prisons to swell the expedition, which may be as good an explanation as any of how Taylor happened to go along. Vagabonds included, Shelby's command could not have exceeded five hundred, though he was to boast later to Emperor Maximilian that he could place a thousand fighting men at the beleaguered Austro-Frenchman's service.

The expedition could scarcely have been an impressive sight as it entered the Republic of Mexico. Some of the men wore jeans and boots; others were clad in threadbare Confederate gray. Some walked under packs; others led horses and mules laden with saddlebags and camping gear. Officers' ranks were determined by ballot; an unpopular major was demoted to corporal, while several lieutenants were breveted captain and major. Shelby seems to have been of several minds about the purpose of the expedition: he talked with the insurgents about helping them against the French-imposed Emperor Maximilian; he talked with Maximilian about helping him against the insurgents; he considered establishing a base from which to resume the war against the Union, and apparently toyed also with the idea of taking over all of Mexico for the United States. As a practical matter he had his hands full simply keeping his troops in order on their way to Mexico City, where they arrived in the middle of August; in a little more than a month of marching and skirmishing more than fifty men had been killed and at least twice that number wounded.

The idea of permitting an organized armed force of foreigners within their borders had little appeal for the Mexicans, whether Maximilianistas or rebels. Even if the Confederates' own purposes had not been suspect, they might at any moment provide an excuse for a new intervention by the mighty power to the north. Within a few months, therefore,

Shelby's force was disbanded, and his men had to make their living as best they could as immigrants.

The English-languge *Mexican Times* lists Richard Taylor as arriving in Mexico City August 25, 1865. On December 6, 1865, Medora wrote her husband again from San Antonio:

MY DEAR
DEAR DARLING —

I received your letter on the sunday it was dated 12*th* Oct. the letter by Col Barns I have not received you cannot imagine how happy your letter has made me I had almost given up all hope for months had passed since I heard at all, & the prospect of your doing so well makes me feel so different. I was afraid you would have to return to the U S — & you could not live here my darling & no where else in the U.S. — there is an arrest for you you never did any thing to [be] arrested for but you could not have justice so my darling dont come. Col Sucket Judge Divine Gen Haws & Maj Macklin were induced to return but are *now* in *irons* in ft Jackson How I long to be with you I cant be happy until I see you. oh! I have so much to tell you. I am not pregnant as we suposed (sic) so I can come as soon as you write for me.

The children want to see you so badly how much they talk about dear Papa Oh! when will we come do let it be soon —

I am writing two letters to be mailed at different places for our letters are intercepted I wrote one yesterday also — so I pray God some of them may reach you for it would kill me to see you arrested — know you would not have *justice*. Oh! my darling how much I pray for you. pray for yourself and now my darling may God our heavenly Father bless you & watch over you & lead you in the right way is the prayer of your own devoted and lonely wife

MEDORA

Direct your letter to sister Fannie

According to the previous letter, Medora had not heard from her husband since well before July 28. How could it take her until December 6 to discover that she was not pregnant? Had he slipped back north for some midnight assignation on the banks of the Rio Grande?

But no matter. Some time in 1866, Medora and the children joined Dick Taylor in Mexico City. On September 23 of that year Dick's sister, Edmonia Taylor Fall, wrote:

DEAR SISTER MEDORA AND CHILDREN —

I was so glad to have an opportunity of seeing the children before they left Texas for their far, far home. My darling Brother, though you are now an exile in a foreign land, I trust to God we may some day be reunited. I won't allow myself to think of the distance that separates us; it is almost like thinking of you as dead. You have *warm* friends in Texas. My heart is often made to throb with pride and pleasure at the eulogies passed on you. And the character you are making for yourself in your foreign home is one that gratifies us extremely. But as I often said to Captain Gayley, one of your comrades in the army, "People could not help admiring and loving such a man as you are; so brave, so generous, and so true."

I do not know yet what business Mr. Fall will go into, but will get at something very soon. We have but one child [Albert Fall], and a very darling little son he is to us.

Most of the Americans south of the border tried to make a living as farmers or traders. Uncultivated land was available on generous terms, and some was fertile. Carlota, a farming community of Confederate exiles, named after the empress, was said to produce "greenpeas, tomatoes, cabbage, turnips, egg dishes, fresh beef, pork, bananas, oranges, lemons, and one hundred other varieties of fruits and vegetables, fresh and in abundance." There were drawbacks, though—"yellow fever during the rainy season—dysentery—malaria—typhoid—pellagra—and outside privies deep in rain-drenched clumps of cane brakes." Not surprisingly, many of Shelby's men, along with other Confederates who had sought to make a new living south of the border, grew discouraged and began drifting back home. They had not come here, remarked one bitterly, to scratch the soil for living and raise half-Mexican brats. Mexican bandits were not content with robbing a man once—they returned to him again and again, like fleas hoping for just one drop more of blood. On a trip between San Luis Potosi and Mexico City—a distance of two hundred miles in a direct line—Colonel Beverly Tucker of Virginia fell prey to bandits five times, losing first his watch, then his shirt and trousers. The third time around, since he no longer had money or even a wallet to carry it in, he was struck on the head with a sabre, losing most of the sight of one eye. The fourth time, his stage coach was stopped and all the passengers were compelled to lie flat while their belongings were rifled. Tucker had only his boots to lose; he was nude when the stage was stopped once more, outside of Vera Cruz.

Dick Taylor was no farmer, and he had no intention of becoming one. He settled in Mexico City, where he scrambled for a living, apparently (though this is only an assumption based on his prewar career) in the export-import business. My guess is that the family lived in lodgings, not a home of their own. Yet he never seems to have even considered returning to the States. Perhaps he did hit that guard over the head with a shovel after all.

On June 14, 1867, Medora Taylor bore in Mexico City her second daughter, Medora Law. Said the *Mexican Times:*

PROTESTANT RITUAL. The first Protestant Ritual celebrated in this city, so far as we can learn, took place at the residence of Capt. Dick Taylor, on last Sunday. It was the christening of MEDORA LAW TAYLOR. The ceremony was performed by Rev. Wm. S. Southgate; and the sponsors were Mrs. Mary O'Bannon; Mrs. Mary Smith; Mr. Santiago Smith, and Mr. Geo. W. Clarke. Miss Medora made her entree upon this world's stage on the 19th June* two days before the gallant Diaz and his heroic army entered the capital; after her mother had been driven from her residence by the 12 and 18 pound shots of the besiegers to a hotel in the centre of the city; and at a time when an order was out, issued by the tyrant Marquez, for the imprisonment of her father and every American in the city. The fortitude of the mother upon that trying occasion was an example worthy of the days of ancient Rome and Greece.

We wish all the parties may be present at Miss Medora's next important ritual — her wedding.

As it turned out, Medora Law lasted only into her third year. Her elder sister, my grandmother, previously called Annie Maria, thenceforward became Annie Medora, and like her mother and sister was called by her second name.

By the end of 1870, most of the Confederates who had sworn never to return to their homeland, including the doughty General Shelby himself, had slipped quietly back across the border. "There is not at this moment," wrote Thomas H. Nelson, then United States minister, "a single notability remaining out of the many confederate refugees."

Well, Dick Taylor may have been no notability, but remain he certainly did. One of the few ambitions life has left me is to learn how he earned his family's keep. Certainly their life was not all *pulque* and *fruta;* as the following letter indicates, Captain Dick had to hustle:

Acapulco
26th April 1872

MY DEAR DEAR MEDORA:

We arrived here on day before yesterday, very nearly played out.

After leaving Yquala, the last place from where I wrote you, we got along very well until the evening before our arrival at Chilpancingo. The day was exceedingly hot and I was perspiring very freely going up the mountain. Just as we arrived at the top we met a severe Norther, and before I could get my greatcoat untied I felt my breast was getting tight (as you know I left with a cough) and in ½ hour, no one ever had such an ague as your poor old hus. By the time we arrived, a distance of 4 miles, I was in a raging fever out of my head by 10 oclk. At 11 I fell into a broken sleep, out of which I was awakened by an officer striking me in the side by a walking cane, saying, get up *cabron.*I asked him who he was & what in the devil did he want there; however by that time he had commanded all of his companions to come into my room. He ordered

---

*The newspaper was wrong. As attested by the family Bible, Medora was born the 14th of June, so she was a full week old before Diaz arrived. General Porfirio Diaz, the most prominent figure in the successful struggle against Maximilian, soon fell out of favor with the new government of Benito Juarez, and was sought for several years as a criminal. He led a successful revolution in 1876, and in seven terms as president brought a measure of stability to the republic.

myself & a Mexican gentleman, one of our companisons, to be tied & taken to prison. I protested, telling him I was sick; he said I lied, that he knew who I was. I then said, Sir, I will go but not tied. However, after two hours of such *bola* as you never saw, he found out that he was mistaken. It appears that I had the honor of being taken for Genl. Diaz in disguise, & my friend the Mexican for Col. Mena.

I never have been so brutally insulted in my life but what could I do but submit to 40 armed Indians commanded by a Drunken officer. The Governor made every apology the next day, but which was of little satisfaction to a sick gentleman who in the dead hours of the night was made to play attendance for two hours going in and out in the night air to a half drunken officer. The effect of this was to have almost killed me. At 9 next day I took two pills but they would not stay. I then asked one of my friends to open the little bottle of chlorodyne & give me 10 drops. They were so frightened about me that they gave me 30 drops, which is 10 drops more than the directions say shall ever be given. The consequence was that, it having a large portion of chloroform in it, in 10 minutes I was asleep & in about 1 hour I waked up vomiting like a dog, throwing up very thin green bile, and the straining almost setting me frantic with my lungs. Fitzharris made a plaster & put all over my chest clean round under my shoulder blades. I went to sleep & woke at 12 without fever, but oh so weak & parched that I thought that If I get to Acapulco it will be by the providence of God, that I could only get on to the horse by assistance & rode 8 leagues that afternoon, the heat being about 130 & not a tree. I took that night two quinine pills & next day two more, and arrived here without having eaten but two bowls of chicken soup & a wing & leg in four days & nights, my poor mouth broken out both inside & out with fever blisters as large as a *medio*. All I could do was to ride along the road & suck orange juice to keep me from choaking.

On our arrival here the night of the 24, I went to a German drug store & got two pills of blue mass (as our baggage did not get in with us) took it, & the next morning two doses of Seidlitz powders which worked me for 12 hours about 8 times.

By advice of the Old Gentleman I took a sea bath last night & dose of cough medicine & this morning feel like a different man having only coughed once & having a good appetite. He told me to eat plenty of fish & vegetables and keep in the house & take a bath every night, all of which I will follow.

I tell you dear old self that I liked to have gone up. I now feel no fear, am very weak & have lost about 11 pounds. I shall never, never forget the kindness shewn to me by every one except Avana, who is nothing more or less than a dirty selfish scrub.

The Mexican is the best nurse I ever saw & never failed to get up two or three times a night to look out to see that I was comfortable. His name is Vicente S. G. de Ysiguerre, and without exception one of the finest gentlemen I ever knew.

Rachael Medora died six months to the day after her husband wrote the foregoing letter. Four years later, immediately following Annie Medora's marriage to Daniel Richardson, Dick Taylor and his two sons, Pryor and Richard, removed to Port Limón, Costa Rica, where one by one they succumbed to tropical fever—Pryor in 1879; father Dick in 1880; and son Richard in 1886.

Wm. Little clock

25

Where Did You Get That Hat?

The wedding between Annie Medora Taylor and Daniel Sidney Richardson in May of 1876 can scarcely have been a gala affair, both bride and groom being poor as a *raton de la iglesia,* but the American Minister gave the bride away, and presented the young couple with a silver nut dish, which must still be around someplace, though nobody in the family remembers seeing it recently. If the Minister thought the nut dish relieved him of his responsibilities toward the Richardsons he was wrong, though, for just two years later Annie Medora gave birth to Helen Medora in the American compound, and he could do no less than give his goddaughter a pair of pearl and turquoise earrings, which are still around—dear me, they are now almost a hundred years old.

If I don't tell about Dan's and Medora's honeymoon, it's because I don't know. They lived in the compound, as I say, and like all young couples in the foreign service they had to entertain with no money to entertain on. I am sure they were very much in love. Though I suspect grandma never did give a general amnesty to short men, blond men, and damyankees, she probably convinced herself that Dan was really tall, and dark, with a Texas accent. Besides, they had the best-tempered, best-looking, brightest infant daughter ever born to seal the reunion of the States, and it could be only a matter of a few months until Dan was made ambassador to some romantic country—not England or France, maybe, because you had to be rich to be ambassador to England or France, but some modest little place like Spanish-speaking Madrid or Buenos Aires, or maybe even Peru. The Richardsons weren't proud.

But then things never work out quite the way they are supposed to, at least in my family. The baby—called Helen instead of Medora to distinguish her from her mother—was barely eight months old when Daniel's father Horace died. You will recall that Horace, though a mighty hunter before the Lord, shared to the full the general family ineptness at collecting worldly goods. He went to his reward leaving behind him a few rentable houses, an abundance of tears (shed by his two unmarried daughters and a teen-aged younger son) and a still greater abundance of debts, which became the responsibility of Daniel as the new head of the family. The post of consul general in Mexico City in the 1870s had many pleasant features, but a high salary was not among them, and Daniel had to say farewell to the afternoon teas that he could not afford to give anyway. He had to forget the post that was to have been his some day in Madrid or Buenos Aires. In short, he had to quit the diplomatic service, go home to Oakland and make some money.

At least he left in style. He had come up from Acapulco, four years before, huddling with his friends against irruptions of *ladrones.* He returned to the same port with a bride, an infant, a nurse, four peons to carry the baby's litter, and fifty cavalrymen to ward off bandits.

Annie Medora, who had passed her formative years in Mexico City, found the Bay area of San Francisco barbarous by comparison. Her first shock came as she was picking her way carefully down the gangplank to the pier, wearing, as was her custom, a sombrero. A barefoot urchin called out, "Where did you get that hat?" — the refrain of a then popular song. Medora was so taken aback that she tripped; her husband had to catch her arm to save her from falling. That same evening, at dinner, she was appalled to see men, their jackets off, eating potatoes, their jackets on.

A few days later, settling in the Oakland home that had been Horace's she inquired for a laundress, and was given the name of a "colored lady around the corner." That night, says family tradition, "a puzzled and homesick girl wanted to know if even washerwomen were ladies in this country."

Medora Richardson's early portraits reveal a slender, dark-haired girl of vivid coloring, with a straight, short nose, high-fashion cheek hollows, and brown eyes alive with merriment. The lips had not yet begun to droop, the eyes to sadden, the hair to lose its luster.

But she had no interest in displaying this loveliness outside her home. The social affairs around which the life of the Bay area revolved bored her; she would have preferred bullfights.

She did leave home occasionally to dine in the Latin quarter of San Francisco. Her favorite restaurant was Perini's — to be destroyed in the fire of 1906 — where the little French maitre d' danced attendance on her because her eyes crinkled at him as she spoke his tongue.

But Mexico remained her heart's home. When General Diaz fell ill at the time President Garfield was shot, grandma's whole concern was for the sick Mexican; her Richardson in-laws explained to her, using charts, that our own President was her husband's sixth cousin once removed, but she could not have cared less whether Garfield lived or died.

Because she would have done almost anything to please her husband, she attempted to read *Uncle Tom's Cabin;* but as she turned each page her color heightened and her eyes blazed hotter. At last she flung the book across the room, crying, "Lies! All lies! We loved our darkies! An intelligent owner would not treat a good horse like that!"

Though Daniel was as fervent a Yankee as Medora was a rebel, there is no indication that their conflicting views ever caused a strain between them. She remained forever too much in love to quarrel with him about anything — except other women.

It is a measure of his sway over her that she actually let him take their children to the dramatized version of *Uncle Tom's Cabin.* The only impression my mother, then seven or eight, came away with was that Eva went to Heaven in an elevator.

Grandpa Richardson was as gregarious as his wife was solitary. He was also as full of energy as a windmill in a hurricane. He arrived home from Mexico responsible for the following household:

✛ His own wife and child;

✤ His eldest sister Helen, who never married and was to live with him for the remainder of her life;

✤ His second sister Mat, who had borne a son and daughter to her husband, Carlos White, and then had watched White degenerate into a ne'er-do-well, a drunkard, and finally a madman;[*]

✤ His younger sister, Horatia, still unmarried;

✤ His brother Alfred, just turned nineteen.

The last two named were quickly taken off his hands. Aunt Shae married James Carlin the following Fourth of July, and later in the year, as mentioned earlier, Allie left for the Arctic and disappeared.

Through the intervention of John W. Foster, still minister to Mexico, and later secretary of state, Dan quickly became general superintendent of the San Francisco Post Office, a job he kept for thirty years. It was his responsibility to administer the post office, the titular postmaster being replaced whenever one political party succeeded another in power. In 1885, still paying the last of his family debts, he took on a second job as adviser to the Japanese diplomatic corps in the United States, a post which he was to hold until his death thirty-seven years later, interpreting the inscrutable Western mind to the simple Japanese. (My brother Ed, who inherited the samurai sword that Grandpa Richardson was given by the emperor of Japan, has recently turned it over to me to hang above the Richardson flute.)

It would have taken a high-speed camera to catch Grandpa Richardson, to judge by this undated copy of a clipping, from *Facts on File:*

Dan had an almost boyish impulsiveness in taking hold of enterprises. One of these was in marshalling his personal friends from the counting room, the post office, the schoolroom, and similar places, and having them, with their own hands, unused and unaccustomed to labor as they were, build a house for a poor young Englishman whom he wished to befriend. At the end of the day the house was built, the family moved in and the bruised and lame self-appointed workmen hobbled home.

He seemed always to be hammering two things together, tearing a third apart, repairing or remodeling a fourth.

His interests and friendships were innumerable. He was for sixteen years treasury of the Astronomical Society of the Pacific; I wish I could locate the telescope that once pointed heavenward on his roof, though I don't see how I could hang it on my wall beside the flute and the samurai sword.

As a writer, he was friendly with such as John Muir, Charles Warren Stoddard, and Bret Harte. My mother mentioned Ambrose Bierce as an occasional visitor, but I hope he was very occasional; I cannot imagine that Bierce and grandpa would have liked each other.

---

[*]Their daughter Mabel, by all accounts a dazzler, refused to marry for fear of passing her father's faulty genes on to her children.

Joaquin Miller, the poet, was a close friend. "He always called daddy 'the gentle boy,'" mom recalled. "He would come dashing up to the front gate on his horse—a queer-looking man he was, too, with his big, soft hat, long boots, and flying hair—shouting at the top of his lungs for the 'gentle boy.' Usually he only wanted to make sure that daddy saw the sunset before it faded."

My mother was still in her early teens when Joaquin Miller lost his sight, and it became one of her tasks to read aloud to him. I have always suspected that his passion for Victorian poets colored her own, and perhaps narrowed her later choices.

Dan joined writers of the area for long, chatty evenings. A teetotaler, he matched every glass of his companions' wine with a glass of milk. Philosophical and literary quodlibets were the staff of life to him. When in the midst of a discussion, he had no idea what he was eating; it was an occasional diversion of his friends to send his main course away before he had touched it, knowing that he would leave feeling fully fed.

Grandpa's own literary growth, it has always seemed so to me, stopped when he was about nineteen. In the early 1900s he published a book of verse, *Trail Dust*. I think he would not complain at my selection of one particular verse, "Home to California," as showing both the nature and the limitations of his talent:

O, the wildness of the Way!
O, the call of bird and stream!
O, the lights and shades that play
Where the winding rivers gleam!
Throw her open; Donner Lake
Slumbers in the cup below;
All the pine trees are awake
Shouting to us as we go:
Whoop! She shivers on the rail;
How the canyons laugh and roar
When she hits the curving trail
Tipping downward to the shore!
Far below the valley sleeps,
Warm and tender; I can see
Where the Sacramento creeps
Willow-bordered to the sea.

In some ways his sensitivity ran deep. When his infant son Tom lay dying, grandpa, a free thinker (how that would have appalled his father!) had him baptized to ease Medora's lacerated Episcopalian heart. Yet he felt shamed; "*My* God," he told a friend, "does not damn the souls of innocent babes."

If love of practical jokes connotes immaturity, Grandpa Richardson was immature. Once, sitting in an oyster bar overhanging San Francisco Bay, he ordered oysters on the half shell, dropped them through a knot-hole into the water below when the waiter's back was turned, and continued reordering until he had done away with a half gallon of oysters. Since he had to pay for the oysters, it would seem to me that the joke was on him.

Another time, he wrote in woman's guise to a matrimonial bureau, describing his female charms so convincingly that lonely men by the dozens sent requests for rendezvous. In each case, grandpa wrote back, setting an appointment at Woodward's Gardens, a local zoo, and asking the correspondent to identify himself by wearing a carnation in his buttonhole. Grandpa would then seat himself happily on a bench, and watch while the victim paced up and down in increasing frustration, waiting for a prospective bride who would never arrive. That joke never seemed funny to me.

Among Grandpa Richardson's merits, the art of making more money than he spent was conspicuously lacking. His point of view about money was the same as about watermelons. At a riverside picnic he would bid his guests eat only the rosy center. "Why bother about the rest?" he would say, setting an example by throwing the fruity rinds into the stream.

How admirable a figure Grandpa Richardson was I leave to the moralists. But oh, Dan, what a lot of fun you had!

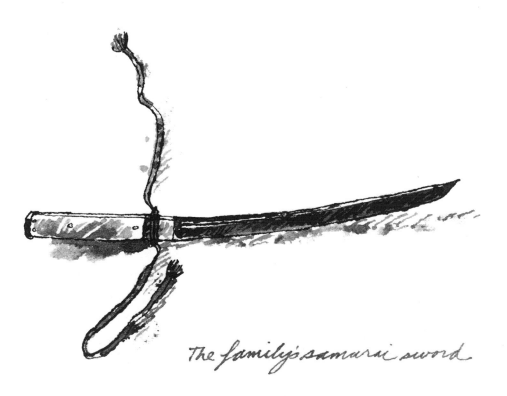

The family's samurai sword

"Mother Hubbard"
Caused the Most Merriment

Families of the Richardson stripe may have been run-of-the-mill in the nineteenth century, but I have never come across anything to compare with them in the twentieth. Great-uncles, great-aunts, uncles, aunts, and cousins coruscated about Grandpa Richardson's home so incandescently that my mother, a girl still uncertain of her worth, must sometimes have had an impulse to clap her hands over her eyes.

There was one exception. Aunt Helen, Dan's eldest sister, a spinster, lived ghostlike among them; humankind dismayed her. Her shadow was visible more often than she was. If cornered, she reacted with quiet courtesy; but a visitor who looked away from her to glance out the window would find on turning back that Helen had vanished. At the sound of a strange footstep, she would hide in her room; if outdoors, she would disappear behind a hedge or fence.

But "what wonderful books," my mother recalled, "she would give us to read! And if I found her alone with her cat, she would talk in her soft voice by the hour—stories of her girlhood in Massachusetts—of the blueberries, and the old well with a bucket—and then of the trip around the Horn."

The rest of the family mama saw with sunlight glittering from their armor. For example, her great-uncle Sidney, Horace's brother: "Slender," mama called him, "graceful, an eighty-year-old king of men; I can see him now with his great broadcloth cape and soft black hat, and long curling hair to his shoulders. He would quote Horace, Livy, and Plato to me, and shake his old head at my father: 'Dan—Dan—how you are neglecting this child's education!' When I was sixteen, much to my bewilderment, he began greeting me with 'Ne'er did Grecian chisel trace/A Nymph, a Naiad, or a Grace/of finer form, or lovelier face.'"

Sidney, a Harvard graduate, was teaching classics in a Mobile military academy when the Civil War broke out. The student body marched off as a single company to the fighting. "His heart was with the South," mama said, "which created a split between him and his brother Horace. His handsome mien and cavalier shine always struck me as an anomaly, when his hours were spent so fully with the Latins and the Greeks."

Aunt Cleora, wife of the eighty-year-old "king of men," was a compulsive, and competent, painter. Her still lifes and landscapes were not Turners or even Winslow Homers, but West Coast galleries sold them and they were frequently exhibited. Some twenty of them today hang in the old Oysterville home; my favorite, I think, is a pastel of an abandoned two-wheel cart, its body tilted so that the outer ends of the shafts rest on the ground. Her softly sensuous re-creations of cherries, strawberries, peaches, and plums warm the dark wood of the dining room.

Mama in her childhood was dazzled by her father, her great-uncle Sid, grandpa, and Nathan Stein (of whom more presently). But it was the women who set the cultural and intellectual tone of the Richardson household. By today's standards, women in the 1880s and 1890s were chattels. If so, somebody forgot to tell grandpa's sisters and his cousin Mary Bamford, who wound up with the curious title of Poet Laureate of Oakland.

The eldest scribbler was Mat. After a disastrous first marriage, she had to write frantically for newspapers and magazines to keep herself and her children fed, clothed, and roofed. Yet she managed to make her way to Boston to learn the art of elocution, and thereafter traveled up and down the West Coast giving "Prose and Poetry Recitals for the Benefit of Churches, Temperance Organizations, or Dramatic Societies, at a compensation consisting of one half of the net proceeds." Even had her husband been a community pillar, Mat would have elocuted. She performed well:

It would be difficult to decide which piece she declaimed the best, though "Mother Hubbard" caused the most merriment. Mrs. White is a very fine elocutionist. — *San Mateo County Journal.*

Her voice, distinct and sweet, was modulated at will, at one moment inclining the hearer irresistibly to tears and the next compelling smiles, laughter, and applause. — *Seattle Daily Post-Intelligencer.*

"How We Hunted a Mouse" was an excellent exposé of man's boasted superiority over the opposite sex, and "The Old Actor's Story" was full of touching pathos. — *Olympia Critic.*

Meanwhile the husband who later went mad was doubtless wavering on a saloon stool a thousand miles away.

Life could not have been easy for Mat, but the last thing she wanted was to leave it. As she wrote for a Colorado newspaper in 1889:

For myself, I cannot bear to think of lying under the ground in some quiet graveyard, returned to dust, forgotten and unmourned, while all the marvelous possibilities of human thought, invention, and discovery are going on around me. It would not be so hard to die if one could somehow know all these interesting things, even though he might not participate in them. Laugh, reader, if you will, but I should want to see what improvement had been made in the illustrations of the *Harper's* and the *Century* after a hundred years had passed; I should like to know how much more swiftly the trains would carry people from Boston to San Francisco; I should be eager to find out who had taken Howells' place in the affections of novel readers; what great political parties existed, who had become the people's idol, what another century had accomplished for the "solid South," and whether the negro had become a power in the land, now that slavery had so long been a thing of the past. Ah, there is no end to the things one would want to know. The Socialists, in their desperate efforts to level wealth and power—where will they be when the twenty-first century dawns? And the "mind cure" and "faith cure" doctrines—will they be placed upon a solid basis, which none can gainsay? Will the doctors have discovered an infallible cure for cancer and consumption? . . .

And the dentists—will another hundred years of experience teach them how to pull out a whole set of teeth without administering chloroform, yet so painlessly that one would sooner have them out than not? Will the false sets of teeth made in the distant future retain the vermilion hue which now characterizes the gums, "giving one away" the moment he smiles? Or, will the new teeth of the new era be such an improvement on Nature's supply that men and women will rush to the dentist at the first jumping tooth, have out the whole miserable lot, and "store teeth" put in their place? Ah, how rich the coming dentist will be, if the latter guess proves correct!

Then there are the churches; will they have learned at last that in union there is strength, or will they still divide into a dozen denominations for every little town?

Again, there is that marvelous "sixth sense," that strange but undeniable power which enables some persons to read the thoughts of others by a touch of the hand. What may not future scientists discover here? How interesting the explanation of a sense which, though dormant now in most persons, may some day be recognized as belonging to all, and greater than any of the other five! . . .

As for that life of mystery which comes after this, we can only hope that within its scope will be the possibility to look down sometimes and watch with interest the busy world of which we once formed an infinitesimal part, and which we loved so well.

Mat died at forty, just six months after these speculations appeared. She will never know the answers to the questions she asked, and to most of them you and I will never know the answers either. But I think she did guess wrong about teeth.

The most inveterate scribbler of all on the distaff side was Aunt Shae, source of most of my anecdotes about how a minister's children grew up in pioneer California. Her outlets included *Golden Days, The Portland Transcript, The San Francisco Examiner, The Interior, The Congregationalist and Boston Recorder,* and *The Youth's Companion,* then known as *The Companion.*

Aunt Shae was the family favorite, and I wish there were space to give her a chapter to herself. Convulsions, suffered during the birth of her daughter Allie Imogene, left her with a severe hearing handicap—condign punishment, said the neighbors, for hanging out clothes to dry on a Sunday. Yet there was no self-pity in her. She not only laughed at herself, but led others to laugh at themselves as well. She was as deaf as a post, yet her sallies kept roomfuls of relatives and friends in good cheer for hours. After the death of her first husband, she was also as poor as a Baptist church mouse. During this period she made shawls for a living. It was then, too, that she wrote most of her articles and stories. They added little to her income; a handwritten list at the back of her scrapbook shows that her lowest fee for a story was $1 and her highest $6. But her own story had a happy ending. On February 6, 1887, the day of the heaviest snowstorm ever recorded in San Francisco, a businessman named Nathan Stein called on her to look over the shawls she was making and selling for a living. Within months they were married, and Aunt Shae lived prosperously and contentedly for the rest of her life.

I had hoped to discover that Nathan Stein was connected with the family of the writer Gertrude Stein, who grew up in the East Oakland area. He was not. He was, however, an early executive of the Wells Fargo express company, and later of the bank of the same name. He was said to have "witnessed the great gun battle when Wild Bill Hickok killed six men without batting an eye." In 1900 he succeeded his twin brother Aaron as secretary of Wells Fargo and assistant to the president.

But from the Richardson viewpoint, the key fact about Nat Stein was that, like all his in-laws, he considered himself, however efficient he might be as a businessman and charming as a gentleman, to be intrinsically a poet. No one could restrain him from offering up a hundred or so rhyming lines when Kansas became a state, or Wells Fargo had an anniversary, or Mills College a graduation, or overland stage drivers a reunion. He was an inevitable acquisition for the Richardson menagerie.

Salal
Cemetery Border
Oysterville

Road's End

27

Love in a Boarding House

Several years passed before Dan and Medora found a permanent home. Mama's earliest memory was watching from the window of their first house, on Montgomery Street in San Francisco, as the lamplighter stopped his horse each evening at one lamppost after another, igniting the lamps with his taper. There were other memories:

An old, blind soldier stood on the corner of Market and Kearny, and I remember his telling my mother that he always knew my father's quick, ringing footsteps amongst the crowds. I believe he did, for his face always lighted as we approached. I wonder how many felt the cool of silver from daddy's too-open hand. . . . Often daddy would stop by the violet vendor on the corner, and there would be the pungent steam of chili pepper and the sweetness of violets—a strange, alluring blend in the foggy air. . . . How I loved to hear the tamale man sing as he wheeled his cart down Market Street, "Tamale, tamale, 'tis good da cheek-in tamale." . . . There was Sing, the Chinaman, with his long queue and laughing face, and the baskets of vegetables hanging one at each end of a pole that he balanced over his shoulder as he dogtrotted from house to house. . . . Chinese jute mill workers passed at noon by the hundreds. One had a red pigtail, and my day was incomplete if he failed to appear. But I hated it when my nurse took me through the steep hills of Chinatown. Such smells—such noises—and once there were two little boys asleep in a box suspended by a hook from the ceiling. I saw a Chinese boy fall and cut himself on a coal oil can. The fact that he bled puzzled me; I had thought all Chinese were made of wood. . . .

Two experiences that brought her no joy were church and school. Her mother was Episcopalian. Daniel's parents had been the most puritanical of Baptists. Daniel himself was not much of anything, except that he appeared to believe some vague Beneficence kept an eye on Its creatures. Yet the Richardson children regularly attended Sunday school—whichever school was handiest. Before she reached her teens, mama had been exposed to Methodist, Episcopal, Presbyterian, Baptist, and Congregational Sunday schools. The Methodist school, which she attended in her fourth year, impressed her most: "There was a young lady there," she recalled, "who had a most beautiful way of using her handkerchief, creating an absorbing ambition in me—to blow my nose as she did."

To her dying day, Grandma Richardson never felt at home in Yankee surroundings. She found democracy, at least in its social manifestations, repugnant to the point of seeming bestial. She centered her life on her family and a few intimate friends; outside lurked not simply savages, but monsters.

Mama attended San Francisco's first kindergarten school, but only because a friend of the family ran it. Her father dropped her there each morning and came for her at noon. "I thought there must be something wrong with children," she wrote years later, "for I never was allowed out at recess time. It was understood that I should not mingle . . . the beginning of a lifetime of feeling behind closed doors."

Grammar school was even worse: "There was the old 'Sweat School' on Thirteenth Avenue, and the Franklin on Tenth Avenue—both houses of inquisition to me, where the pupils drew numerals and did problems, and used common towels and drank from one cup—and where the teachers thought a child 'queer' who had by memory verses from Tennyson or Shakespeare or Milton. A nightmare place, from which I was rescued at fourteen and put into a private academy."

Rooms on a city street not being "good for children," the Richardsons spent the weekends across the Golden Gate at Sausalito—wading, finding tiny crabs that pinched, floating among the rocks in a rowboat, lunching among the trees.

At about the time mama entered the academy, the Richardsons removed to the Oakland side of the Bay, living as Horace had before them, in one of their four houses, and renting out the other three. They moved into whatever house happened not to be rented, and had their carpets cut to fit any of the four.

Soon thereafter, they found a permanent home in the hills behind Oakland. Here for a time they found peace. When there were no visitors, the family often sat on the front porch in the evening, watching the dusk creep over the gold of the poppy fields while a faint, special aroma emanated from inside the house—a fragrance holding hints of tar weed and cigar smoke. Grandpa, my mother remembered, would sit on the porch idly playing his flute, or grandma in her wing-armed wicker chair would sing drowsy Spanish airs, her hair black against the blooms of the white rose tree, until the increasing coolness drove them indoors.

Grandpa Richardson commuted to San Francisco each day. He could have traveled to and from the ferry by horsecar, but that form of transportation was too slow for him; he preferred to walk. When a double-decker electric car replaced the horsecar, my mother, who, unlike her father, was no friend of progress, felt as if she had lost a friend. She missed that beautiful yellow contraption, with glass windows on each side, two fat, plodding horses in front, a jovial, accommodating conductor, and a mysterious box at the rear where people dropped their money.

Dan, reacting against his own childhood restrictions, took every opportunity to escort Helen and her brother Sid, three years younger, to the circus, but their reaction disappointed him. They were more frightened than delighted. Nor was he much more successful with his Fourth of July fireworks displays; these drew children from blocks around, but only made his own daughter and son uneasy. The pleasure he gave the neighbors' boys and girls may have made up partly for what his own could not accept; one day he announced proudly, "Well, the sinful man of the neighborhood can still be trusted with children. Tonight I'll have the sons of two ministers and the daughter of a deacon with us at the circus, since it might hurt the good names of their parents to take them."

On special occasions Helen and Sid accompanied their father on the San Francisco ferry. Mama was particularly taken with the molasses man. "In those days," she recalled, "we boarded the lower deck by a gang plank and walked up stairs, and there stood this swarthy Mexican with a peg leg, a white apron, and a tray of chewy molasses candy, wrapped in oblong packages of pulled sticks, fast together. Every Thursday and Saturday night daddy brought a package home."

The ferries were two-storied affairs, with the men's smoking apartment below and the women's cabin above. The engine was at the center, with the pistons and wheels visible inside a glass enclosure. Mama could never understand what made Sid stand spellbound, nose pressed to the glass, watching the wheels go round. Men threw out lines with bait for the sea gulls, and then drew the surprised birds to the deck. "Daddy objected to this careless cruelty," mama recalled, "and tried to prevent his children from seeing it; eventually he was instrumental in having the practice outlawed."

Grandpa was a loving, outgoing, and imaginative father. Mama always regretted that he never put his bedtime stories about the Hamfat man into print. (Yet she never repeated any of those stories to her own children.) She sometimes wondered whether, as the eldest child, retiring and shy, she might have been a less satisfacotry companion to him than her sister Ruth. "When Ruth was tiny," mama recalled, "daddy would carry her around on her shoulders while she chanted doggerel like

'A girl can laugh, and a girl can flirt,
And a girl can make crochet;
But she can't light a match on the seat of her pants,
'Cause she ain't built that way.'

"Daddy made up such nonsensical rhymes by the yard just to hear Ruth spout them."

With two jobs and an income from rentals, Dan should have done fairly well. Yet even at their home in the hills they had to take in boarders for extra cash. These were generally either Japanese of the ruling families, recommended to grandpa by the consulate, or students at a nearby Baptist institution called California College. The boarders' quarters were in a frame house connected by a verandah to the Richardson home, and they ate with the family.

Ed Espy matriculated at California College in 1893, and his brother Harry two years later. The parental Espys insisted that their sons make their home with a family of impeccable Baptist antecedents. The Richardsons appeared to be an ideal choice, Daniel's father Horace having preached the Baptist Word for more than thirty years. Dan, needing the extra income, did not mention to them that his views and his father's had little in common.

Uncle Ed came to the Richardson home, looked around, liked what he saw, and happily settled in. He lost no time starting to flirt with Helen, then seventeen. For several months he waited on her; but there is no sign that his intentions were serious, and his social manner, tending toward the domineering, did not cause any rosebuds to bloom in her breast. When papa matriculated, she saw him the first day of school sitting under a eucalyptus tree, reading. "What a handsome boy!" exclaimed mama to her friend Eve. That night he presented himself at the Richardsons' as a boarder, and he and Helen fell in love forever.

On papa's side, at least, no wonder. Helen may have had human frailties — in the local swimming pool, for instance, she would slide out of her monstrous bathing garb and swim happily in the nude, while bystanders determinedly turned their eyes away; I have always wondered how she got back into those wet garments, or whether some maid stood at the edge of the pool, eyes screwed shut, holding at arm's length a great turkish towel. But it was hard to believe her flesh and blood were of common clay. She was shy, which made her seem spiritual; she was dreamy; she was romantic. Above all, she was pretty. Her medium-brown hair curled naturally in the style of the day; her large blue eyes drooped provocatively at the outer corners, like her father's. She stood five feet two inches, weighed a hundred and five pounds, measured nineteen inches at the waist, and took immense pride in the fact that she wore a number three shoe. Perhaps small feet were linked in her mind with aristocracy; the San Francisco Chinese, she knew, bound the feet of upper-class girls to keep their feet stunted and the girls useless for daily chores.

I am not sure she would have met her own father's criterion for the choice of a wife. "Never commit yourself," he said, "until you have taken the girl camping and seen her in bathing dress." I understand the reason for the first injunction, but, considering how little the bathing dress of the day revealed, I am confused by the second.

Papa shied at love like a colt at its first saddle. He mewed, he moped, and he left for Oysterville in the summer of 1897 without having declared himself. As was the ladylike fashion of the day, Helen went into a decline. Her friends whispered of consumption, a disease that was making its way among the Richardsons and their friends. Ed, by now a practicing lawyer, became concerned about her, and as a man of action took steps. He sent papa a wire: PROPOSE TO HELEN IMMEDIATELY OR I WILL TAKE CARE OF IT.

That ambiguous message brought papa back on the next train, and while the maid was still hanging up his hat and coat he was in the living room offering Helen his hand. Harry, devout and idealistic, regarded all well-brought-up young women, and certainly his own fiancée, as holy chalices. Still, he had been reared on a farm, and was well aware that the differences between man and woman were designed with a purpose in mind. He was aghast to discover that his dear Helen had literally no idea where babies came from; nor could he muster the courage to enlighten her. At length, in desperation, he confided his dilemma to her mother. 258

Mrs. Richardson, shoring up her courage, explained sex to her daughter—and with considerable enthusiasm, judging from the glowing passion Helen expressed in correspondence surviving from the days and nights of my parents' early marriage. The marriage was consummated on Thanksgiving Day, 1897. My father and mother renewed their wedding vows with love and gratitude each Thanksgiving day for the next fifty-seven years.

As a helpmeet, Helen had drawbacks. To be sure, her mother had taught her the art of cooking. She knew how to set a table and to arrange flowers in a bowl. But until her marriage she had never swept a floor, beaten a rug, or washed a dish. "Never learn to wash dishes," her mother had advised her, "and you'll never have to."

Which shows that even mothers can be wrong.

Mama's marriage—she was nineteen, papa was twenty-one—came at an opportune moment. Helen worshiped her father, but a rust spot on his shining armor was becoming increasingly hard to ignore. To put it bluntly, grandpa found it impossible to turn his back on desirable and available members of the opposite sex. Perhaps because Grandma Richardson's hair was so dark, he was especially vulnerable to females of the flaxen-haired variety. Mama was still in her middle teens when her mother received an anonymous note accusing Dan of a long-standing, intimate relationship with one such beauty. The charge turned out to be true—and the woman in question to be grandma's best friend. Mama, in her room two doors down the hall, could not help hearing raised voices at night in the parental bedroom; her father had good reason for his frequently voiced concern about the loaded revolver under his wife's pillow.

Yet Helen remained devoted to her father. I remember her criticizing him only once, in an oblique passage that went something like this:

"Daddy turned up the highlights of our home, but the essential footlights were mother's loyalty and unquenchable good cheer. The highlights often flickered or were missing altogether, but the footlights never wavered. Dear little mother—patient, loyal, faithful! She was lost in daddy's brilliance, but for sweetness and fidelity his character could not match hers."

More than general disapproval of her father's roving eye lay behind those obscure remarks. They stemmed from a deeper disillusionment, one that mama was incapable of voicing to others, or even admitting to herself.

The trouble was that Sam Gaches, papa's schoolmate at both Centralia Academy and California College, had a sister Eva, also a California College student, who became my mother's intimate friend. Soon after my parents' marriage, Eva and Sam moved into the Richardson home.

Now Eva was a young lady whom men could not pass without a wild surmise, and Uncle Ed became her instant slave. Sid, Helen's younger brother, pursued Eva like a madman, proposed to her the day after she entered the house, and threatened suicide when she laughed at him.

But Grandpa Richardson calmly brushed such callow competition aside. He appears to have soon been spending more time in Eva's room than in his own. As soon as Ed discovered the affair, he ended his visits to the Richardsons. When Sid discovered it, he left home and never returned, even to attend his father's funeral a quarter of a century later. As for Dan's wife, drained of rage after a long series of episodes leading up to this climax, she quietly decided the time had come to die.

Mama, fortunately, heard nothing of the scandal until later, when she was living hundreds of miles away, with her emotional focus locked on a family of her own—a beloved husband, daughter, and son. She was thus partially cushioned from the shock that sundered the rest of the family. She did not abate in her love for her father, or even—and this was a phenomenon that few of her friends could understand, and some never forgave her for—for Eva. But in neither case could the love be a white seamless garment again.

Dan insisted that Eva remain in the Richardson house. Why she agreed, and why grandma allowed her to, are mysteries I may be able to resolve if I ever find time to read the thousands—yes, thousands—of family letters scattered in boxes, trunks, suitcases, and folders about the Oysterville house. In any event, Eva was still there when Grandma Richardson died in 1902. Grandma's last words to my mother were:

"Make sure that I am buried wearing my wedding ring. That girl downstairs may have Dan, but she can't have *that*."

Grandpa and Eva were married within a year after my grandmother's death, so exacerbating the scandal that many of their friends refused to attend the wedding reception. The family was shattered. Beulah Hunter, the girl Sid later married, hated grandpa with such bitterness that she would not have permitted a reconciliation even if Sidney had wanted one. It was Beulah who kept him home from Dan's funeral. Mom's younger sister Ruth, only nine at the time of her father's second marriage, was sent away to boarding school and never lived at home again before her marriage to Herman Hagedorn in 1912.

Daniel Sidney Ford Richardson died in Berkeley on September 11, 1922, aged seventy-one years. He had been suffering from heart trouble for some time, and on his seventieth birthday had written a cheerful *vale* that began

> Three score and ten! Not far to go,
>   O feet that long for rest;
> The sun that led along the way
>   Is sinking in the west . . .
>
> And yet the path, O tired feet,
>   Was not all toil and pain,
> There were such flowers along the way . . .
>   Such lark-songs in the rain!

What dawns we knew! What sunsets burned
  Against the bars of day!
What ecstasies of life and love
  Were with us on the way!

The immediate cause of his death was probably the Washington Disarmament Conference of early 1922. The Japanese had wanted him there as adviser; against his physician's advice, he agreed to make the trip to Washington, provided that he did not have to leave his private car to attend the official conferences. He stayed in the car in the railroad yards throughout the sessions and died soon after returning home.

Judging from the newspaper obituaries, he must have been several men in one. One account said he was born in a mountain cabin on the Russian River; another, that he crossed the plains in 1849; a third, that he was a native of England.

Papa helped his father-in-law intermittently in the San Francisco post office, but spent most of the time supervising the operations of Grandpa Espy's remaining gold mine, in the Siskiyou Mountains along the northern border of California. The mine lay in an area of grand and isolated mountains, inhabited by tall cedars, fast streams, and abundant game. Hilt, the nearest town, was ten miles away, and the only access to the mine was by pack mule. Even in my time, a quarter of a century later, the road to the mine was so narrow and crooked that often we could round turns in our Ford only by stopping and backing up for a fresh try. On the steepest grades, the gasoline, which was normally carried from a tank beneath the front seat to the carburetor by gravitation, flowed the other way, the carburetor being higher than the tank; we would then back down to a place wide enough to make a turn, and proceed up the hill backwards. The road reached a dead end a mile from our cabin, and we had to pack our supplies the rest of the way.

Water pressure flushed out the gold. The water flowed down a ditch to a dam, where gravity drove it through a pipe ending in a flexible tube like a fire hose. The water emerged from the hose in a furious gush, tumbling dirt, pebbles, and even sizable boulders before it into a wooden box with a bottom like a giant washboard. The heavy gold came to rest between the ridges of the washboard; the lighter material washed on downstream.

In summer, the ditch was often dry. Workers crawled down it, tossing out sticks, old leaves, rocks, and other trash, occasionally sending a startled fawn dashing ahead, or pausing to put a revolver bullet through the head of a coiled rattlesnake.

During his first summer at the mine, papa:

✢ shot his only deer; imagining reproach in the eyes of the dying creature, he swore never to kill again except out of need.

✢ took his first and last swallow of spirits. "I had been told," he explained later, "that whiskey took getting used to; but my first swallow tasted so close to ambrosia that all my good angels joined in jerking the bottle from my hand. From then on, whenever I saw a whiskey bottle I moved to the other side of the room."

✝ grew the Vandyke beard that was to be his trademark for the rest of his life. Years later, he came home from the mine one summer with his beard almost clipped off; I remember how amazed I was at the squareness of his chin.

In the summer of 1900, mama accompanied papa to the mines, bringing the two children that had arrived so far—Medora, three years, and Harry Albert, Jr., one year. The wilderness did not bother her—frequent expeditions to Yosemite with her father had made her an expert camper—but she told the cook she wished he would stop burning the biscuits. "Harry," he explained, "likes them that way." Papa had been too polite to complain.

At camp, mama wore her hair in a single thick braid down her back. This braid, when hanging free, was irresistible to the cabin cat, a brindle who would leap, catch the rope of hair in its foreclaws, and swing happily until thrown off. For the rest of her life, mama tolerated cats, but I cannot say she loved them.

On their way back to Oakland, the family traveled by mule to Hilt, where they spent the night at a hotel. The gold-hunting had been good, and papa was carrying a sizable amount of the metal—the romantics in our family say $50,000 worth, the realists say $5,000—in a money belt, which he wore against his skin. Before the family retired he pushed bureaus and beds as barricades against every door and window, then donned his nightgown over the money belt. In the small hours, mama slipped out of bed to give Albert his bottle. Papa, waking just enough to sense movement, leaped up, and seized the supposed intruder in a death grip—or at least a grip that knocked the wind out of mama. This may have been fortunate, since it gave them both a moment to reflect before she recovered her breath enough to tell him what she thought of him.

Papa cleared the Hilt ditch every summer for the next thirty years, because the law required him to do so in order to retain title to the property. But after 1900 he never again mined there for gold. There was trouble in Oysterville, and he had to return home.

28

Is This What You City Folks Use
for Champagne?

Grandma Espy died of a stroke in April 1901. Grandpa then converted his property into an estate company held half by himself and half by his children. These took fright when almost at once he married for a second time. Grandpa, they concluded, needed watching.

There was no question about who was the logical person to go back home and watch. It was papa. Obviously, Uncle Ed could not go; he was in the first flush of a promising law career.* Uncle Will could not; he was still a freshman at Oregon State College. Uncle Cecil could not; he was only a fifteen-year-old boy. The two older sisters, Dora and Susan, were married, while Verona was even younger than Cecil.

That left papa. At the end of 1902 he pulled up his California roots and returned with his wife and their two children to Oysterville. The stay, he was assured, would be brief; grandpa was almost seventy-six years old, and could not be expected to last long. "In a year or two," papa's brothers and sisters assured him, "you'll be back in Oakland." But fifty-seven years passed, and he never returned there.

His heart must have known that he was destined to live out his life in Oysterville. The Espy Estate Company immediately sold him the family ranch and the erstwhile parsonage of the Reverend Josiah Crouch, all for a $10,000 note.

The H. A. Espys took a steamer north in late November. From Astoria they crossed the Columbia River to Ilwaco, a passage which required three hours because of alternating tides. At Ilwaco they boarded the narrow-gauge railroad that grandpa had helped to finance. The scheduled time to Nahcotta was forty-five minutes; but when the conductor learned that Harry and Helen had not seen the *Petrimpus* (a German bark that had recently been wrecked in the breakers), he insisted on stopping the train and sending them across the dunes for a close look. While mama and papa floundered through a quarter of a mile of snow-white sand to view the remains of the vessel, the conductor dandled young Medora and Albert on his knees, or chased them up and down the aisles.

"We delayed the train for half an hour," mama used to marvel, "and I was almost afraid to come back. But the other passengers didn't seem to mind a bit!"

Grandpa's hired man was waiting with a carriage at Nahcotta. The hired man returned to Oysterville by the daily stage, and the Espys appropriated the carriage. They traveled this last lap over a road of soft sand. A strong northwest wind wiped out their carriage tracks fifty feet back. "The trip was only four miles," said mama, "but I would have called it twenty. At one point the horse shied and ran into a young alder tree. The tree bent, passed under the carriage, and popped out the back with a sound like a cannon shot. Pa was a wonderful horseman and the sand held back the team, or we would have had a real runaway."

---

*In 1906, Uncle Ed, by then a California state assemblyman, died of tuberculosis a few days after having himself carried on a litter into the Assembly to vote for his bill banning horse racing. The measure failed, but passed the following year, and horse racing was outlawed in California for the next quarter of a century.

They arrived on a day that papa probably considered completely satisfactory; there was no rain, just a heavy mist. But an unfriendly storm pushed a high tide into the bay that night, and next morning mama woke to find the house surrounded by water. Looking out one window, she saw a girl in a sou'wester and slickers rowing a flat-bottomed boat down the street; looking out another, she saw waves lapping through the picket fence into the yard.* In the background, the ocean was roaring. Mama would have liked to shut her eyes and never open them again, but Albert was crying, and she had to get up.

In those first days, she was to recall, "People made excuses to come to the house. Curtains were pulled back if I walked down the street; children ran indoors, and I knew they were telling their parents that the curiosity was coming. I got the impression that everyone was very sorry for papa. They thought he had picked up some sort of toy he'd grow tired of soon.

"Papa was awfully sweet, but in trying to protect me he sometimes ended by making me seem queerer than ever. He would usher people into the living room, whispering, 'You know, my wife wasn't raised like you and me.' So the neighbors were ready to inspect me from top to toe to see what was the matter.

"When I wanted to run from people," she said, "the memory of poor Aunt Helen, continuously in hiding, would rise before me; her example was so extreme and pitiful that I would force myself into the open."

On balance, mama was doing an injustice to herself and the citizens of Oysterville as well. Their interest was generally friendly and respectful—at times they were even spellbound. It never entered my mother's head that people who had spent their lives in an isolated village might consider her a woman of glamour and even mystery. Mrs. Wirt, who was to become mama's good friend, once commented to my sister Dale, "Your mother had four good-looking daughters, but not one of them could hold a candle to her. When she first came here she was the most beautiful girl I had ever seen—nor have I ever seen one since that could come up to her."

Some of the stricter neighbors may have suspected the solidity of her religious convictions. Mama refused flatly to attend the wild revivals or the baptisms in the bay that, the saloons being gone, provided the village's chief entertainment.** "The same sinners were saved again and

*High tides were not confined to Oysterville. In 1908, a Raymond newspaper reported: "Rev. Wolfe of the Raymond Methodist Church has solved the problem of raising chickens on the tidelands. He has just completed a floating house for his chickens which insures a safe, dry place for them when the tide is high, while at low water they can feed outside. Rev. Wolfe did not say whether or not he had supplied his flock with tide tables."

**In her later years, mama found solace in religion. My brother Edwin tells me there was a period when, lacking other leadership, mama conducted Sunday services, reading from the pulpit the sermons of such preachers as Harry Emerson Fosdick.

again, hallelujah, amen," she said. "Papa didn't mind; he had been raised in that tradition. But I put my foot down. I said, 'If you want to make a *real* heathen of me, just insist that I go to one of those revivals.'"

The Baptist minister then occupying the Oysterville pulpit was Robert Yeatman, an Englishman who retained his Cockney accent and preached in a long-tailed coat divided down the center in back. At the first service my mother attended, an eighteen-month-old girl crept behind him in the middle of his sermon, and began crisscrossing his coattails. When that amusement palled, she swung from them. Mr. Yeatman ignored her, and mama was apparently the only member of the congregation who considered the incident out of the ordinary.

In the rear pews, children sat eating peanuts. Grandpa Espy's attention was caught when a yearling banged his nursing bottle against the pew. Ordered grandpa, raising his voice above the sermon: "Syd, next Sunday when you bring that child to church, put a sock on the bottle!"

Mama asked the Reverend Yeatman to dinner, which for her was a 6 P.M. meal. He showed up at noon. Mama was in the process of blacking the old wood range, applying a coat of impermanent dye. So she had nothing to cook on, and the unfortunate man had to go home and return six hours later.

It took mama a while to accept the fact that high style in Oysterville consisted of using a dried bull's pizzle for a walking stick; that the village children played with blown-up cow bladders instead of toy balloons; and that one family, regularly buying its false teeth from Montgomery Ward, checked each new denture through mouth after mouth to find the one it fitted best. She was indignant, too, the first time she glanced out the window and saw a hulking Dunkard marching down the road, reading with exultant fervor from the Psalms, while his ninety-pound wife, well into the last stage of pregnancy, trudged after him with a fifty-pound sack of flour across her shoulders.

In general, the social life of the village operated by laws she could not understand, much less master:

"Everyone," she recalled, "came in by way of the kitchen. It was their way of being friendly; but it flustered me. One day, when the babies were small and I was tired and the breakfast dishes weren't done, a woman I barely knew dropped by for a visit. It was a cold day, and I thought I should at least put a piece of wood in the stove. In the confusion I deposited the hot stove lid on my chair and sat down on it. I nearly hit the ceiling. This same woman came in one day and saw my after-dinner coffee cups sitting on the shelf. 'What are those things,' she asked, 'what you city folks use for champagne?'"

(My sister Dale is indignant with me for reporting that mom sat on a hot stove lid. But anyone can be forgiven for sitting on a hot stove lid once. Twice would be a different matter.)

From early childhood on, books had been my mother's favorite diversion and escape. In Oysterville, they became an essential solace and source of support. When my friends laugh at me for reading while I wash, or as I walk down the street, I blame the habit on my mother. Though I never saw her do so, no doubt she read while washing dishes. Oysterville had few other diversions to offer. I would guess, however, that the village also blocked from her mind anything written after 1902. If she had remained in Oakland, she would undoubtedly have been reading Yeats and Eliot, while at Oysterville she was still quoting Arnold and Tennyson.

Reading may have been a support, but it could not have been the source of the iron hidden behind mom's fragile facade. "Mama," says Dale, "had the greatest inner strength I have ever known. Delicate as she was, she performed more manual labor in this house than any of her children have done anywhere. She papered the bedrooms, painted the floors, and laid the carpets. She used to say she performed such chores herself instead of asking papa because she liked to see things accomplished fast. Papa always did a beautiful job, but he was so meticulous he took forever. She was quick in her movements and got things done in a hurry, but there were always more things to do. Aunt Susie said, 'There should have been three women to do the work mama did—run a huge house and a large family, and be attentive at all times to a man who kept erratic hours.' "

Mom despised the drudgery of making beds, sweeping floors, and carrying out night-pots (which we called pōs). She was not orderly by nature. ("Orderly!" sniffed Aunt Beu, "Why, Helen never did reach an accommodation with housekeeping. When she dusted, she would not use a regular cloth; instead she took one the size of a lady's handkerchief, and wrapped it around her index finger.")

Mama didn't complain about what she had to do. My brother Ed recalls that "most homes I visited seemed in utter confusion compared with ours." Uncle Cecil's wife, Ruthie D., unlike Aunt Beu, "was very critical of mama for keeping things too neat, especially toys, clothing, funny-papers, and so on; Ruthie D. felt we should have been treated more like *children.*"

Whether mama made the beds perfectly or not, she made the home

itself "a joyful memory," as Dale puts it. The house always contained greenery, even if she had to resort to plucking thistles or huckleberry stems. She loved to cook, incidentally, almost as much as she loved to read. Her meals reflected her mother's Mexican upbringing. Whether the main dish was spaghetti, pot roast, ground beef, crab, or frijoles, it would likely be flavored with sliced onions sautéed in bacon drippings, combined with puréed tomatoes and finely chopped peppers. The food often was pink from the tomatoes; we frequently had Spanish cream for dessert; and occasionally I bit something that turned my mouth into a bonfire. Of all the niceties of civilization, she at first most missed figs and French bread. Papa always tried to find these for her if business took him to a sizeable town.

Mama set the dinner table meticulously: if not with linen, at least with white cloth; if not with crystal, at least with goblets; if not with sterling, at least with silver plate.

One day, having arranged the setting to her satisfaction, she left for a moment to replenish the wood in the kitchen stove. On her return, she heard the table grunting, and saw it pitching like a dinghy in a storm; with each tilt, dishes slid to port or starboard, and glasses splintered on the floor. A hog was happily rubbing its back against the table's underside. Mama beat the rear of the beast with a broomstick, but it went on contentedly scratching. Fortunately, Medora, then aged ten, knew better than her mother how to handle a hog; she ran for a bucket of swill and waved it before the creature's nose. Eagerly grunting, it followed her back to the sty from which it had escaped.

Asked once what were the happiest days she could remember, mama replied, "When the children were little." She meant the first children, though her love for us later ones as well was so all-encompassing that it would have seemed fierce in a less gentle woman. The firstborns, though, died too young—Albert at four, and Medora, two years his senior, at seventeen. Albert's few years were before my time; I am told that he was as blond as a silverside salmon, and could not pronounce his r's. While Medora would roll them out—"Mr. Foster went to Gloster, all in a shower of rain"—the best Albert could do was, "Mistah Fostah went to

Espy home

Glostah, all in a showah of wain." He caught this speech defect from his mother; she had inherited a slice of Grandma Richardson's Kentucky accent, as distorted by Texas and Mexico. She also said "cigareet" instead of "cigarette"; perhaps her mother, or her nurse, had confused the word with "cigarillo." Ed—and I, to a lesser extent—still have difficulty with our medial r's. When he says "arrive," it sounds to me like "awive."

At three, Albert once dashed out the door—he was always dashing—explaining over his shoulder that he was off "to call on Mrs. Wirt and God." The second call followed the first by only a few months; he died in a Portland hospital of an undiagnosed stomach ailment. The family returned to Oysterville in the midst of a snowstorm, one of the rogue sort that strike the peninsula no more than once in five years, but then bring normal human activity to a near halt. Suzita, a year and a half old, had never before spoken Albert's name; but when she reached home she ran to each door and window, crying "Alber', Alber'," and continued to seek him for weeks afterward.* Thereafter mama had a morbid dislike of snow; she considered it a shroud. And indeed it began to snow the day mama died. For the next three days Oysterville experienced its heaviest snowfall in ten years.

Medora was not only the firstborn, but mama's strong right arm. Just as it was she who conned the pig from the dining room, so it was she who, seeing one-and-a-half-year-old Ed teetering on the edge of a second floor window sill, slipped up behind him and caught him around the waist before he could become alarmed and fall.

Shortly before her seventeenth birthday, Medora, a student at Portland Academy, fell while skating, and received a concussion from which she appeared to recover within a few hours. Later she began to develop headaches, and after six months she died in her sleep. Mother took to bed following the funeral, and lay there for weeks, the shades drawn; she would let only papa see her. Though the day came when she laughed again, she was touched for the rest of her life with melancholy. One day I heard her murmur, unaware of my presence, "There is comfort in a grave."

She bore seven children in all, the last at thirty-three, when her doctor, a bumbling ass, warned her solemnly that another pregnancy would be a death sentence. There were no intrauterine coils, no Pill, no oral sex in mama's world. For her as for papa, a lusty thirty-five, that was that.

For the remainder of mama's life she was subject to mysterious indispositions, migraines being the most common. Yet the relationship between my mother and father, by whatever standard I can adduce, re-

___

*Suzita died of pneumonia in Portland, Oregon, on December 27, 1932, just before sulfanilamide made the disease curable. I took my first transcontinental flight to attend her funeral. A Ford trimotor plane bore me as far as Salt Lake City, and a single-engined Rube Goldberg machine the rest of the way. Mona, the fourth child, was born in Portland December 10, 1904, and died in Oysterville, July 4, 1970. The three youngest children, all still living, are Edwin, born in Portland December 30, 1908; Willard, born in Olympia, Washington, December 11, 1910; and Dale, born also in Olympia, November 13, 1911.

tained its radiance. To each of them, the other made up for all that was wrong with the world.

Nor did her love for the rest of us lessen; if anything she became even more protective, even more fiercely ambitious for our futures. Her heart was as inexhaustible as the pitcher of Philemon and Baucis. Perhaps because her father had proved less than her romantic ideal, she may have been particularly grateful for her own husband's unshakeable fidelity. ("For one thing above all I thank God," papa in his old age told Edwin. "I have always been faithful to your mother.")

Mama never ceased to insist that Providence had inexcusably cheated the two men who in turn dominated her life. Her father should have been secretary of state, and she was indignant that fate had denied her husband the governorship of Washington. Such men, she declared, were race horses, not meant for the harness and plow. At every opportunity she reminded us—in a somewhat obscure analogy, since we had never seen anything but one variety or another of draft horse—that we were race horses, too, and that she and papa expected us to run. This particular form of romanticism was a source of merriment to papa, and I must say that she took his teasing in good part.

It is pleasant to remember that when they had a chance to sit by the library fireplace and chat, with us children either listening or going about our own affairs, the subjects were not always serious. It might even be surmised that serious subjects, in our presence, were avoided.

They used to chaff each other, for instance—though papa was usually the chaffer, and mama the somewhat defensive chaffee—on the dissimilarities of their ancestral, religious, and even moral backgrounds. (Until her middle years, mama leaned more toward the Episcopalianism of her mother than the Baptist faith of her grandparents and husband.) "No Baptist has ever become President," she would challenge. "Agreed," papa would reply, "and there have been a lot of Episcopalians in the White House. But you count the populations of the jails, and you will find a lot more Episcopalians than Baptists there too."

Two events put an end to these arguments. First, in 1921, Senator Warren Gamaliel Harding, a Baptist, *did* become President, which destroyed mama's argument. Next, as before mentioned, Secretary of the Interior Fall, also a Baptist, went to jail for taking a bribe. His denomination set papa's sails back flapping. But since Fall was mama's first cousin once removed, she was unable to gloat. The aged Taylor female cousin previously referred to (page 227) wrote me in 1935, "You know . . . in any family as large as ours there had to be a black sheep. I forget them and always attribute their badness to the other side of the house."

Once the connection between politics, church denominations, and morality had become moot, the subject was no longer mentioned in my parents' idle conversations around the library fireplace or the nursery stove. But their investigations of family history, and their speculations about it, went on . . . and on . . . and on.

29

Young Man,
God Put That Moon up There

Lateness was not an occasional aberration for papa; it was a way of life. He saw no objection to milking the cows at 3 A.M.; and, given his druthers, he'd have dozed in his rocking chair through the night (waking occasionally to reread a newspaper editorial, or perhaps to write a letter in his cramped longhand, crowding the lines together and then turning the page on its side to fill in the margins), and would then have slept most of the following day. He customarily planted corn so late that the ears were ready just in time for Christmas dinner.

He found a seat near any stove where coffee was burbling; the number of cups of coffee he drank in a day was never totaled; one eyewitness stopped counting after papa drank twelve cupfuls on a morning visit to his father.

It would be tempting to attribute papa's irregular life-style to his heritage of tides and oysters. The tides lost fifty minutes a day, and the working life of the village had once followed the schedule of the tides. Theoretically, the differential between flood and ebb increased or decreased according to the waxing and waning of the moon; but one outsize wind might shift the balance by a foot or more. Moreover, the gathering of oysters ceased completely in the summer, that being spatting time, when the gravid oysters were soggy, unaesthetic, and, said local superstition, lethal.

But there has to be another reason for papa's odd hours, since he never was a working oysterman. As a small boy he must have accompanied his father onto the beds, and certainly he was familiar with oyster farming. But though in the teens and twenties he assembled the agglomeration of oyster beds then known as Espy's folly, he did not work them; there were no commercial quantities of oysters there to work. Oh, he regularly walked the beds in hip boots and raincoat; if he found a surviving native oyster he would open the shell with his oyster knife, and swallow the contents with a gourmet's delight. If he came across a cluster of native oysters, he would bring them home in a gunnysack he carried for the purpose; he could always locate enough for a family meal, or even for a dinner party. These solitary expeditions, usually involving several miles of trudging over rippled sand and slogging through shallow sloughs, provided a relief from the drudgery of farming; he could act out a fantasy, seeing again in his mind's eye the great reefs of oysters that his father had viewed in 1854. He could dream of the day when somehow those oysters would return.

He had a perverse compulsion to check the oyster beds at night during howling storms. As he aged, mama came to worry about these nocturnal explorations. She would go upstairs and peer out the bay window, checking the flicker of his lantern until she was sure he was headed for shore.

Papa's approach to any job was to think it through in advance; delay it as long as possible; do it perfectly, but with the maximum number of interruptions for conversation or coffee; and, if possible, use it as an ex-

273

cuse for delaying going to bed. But his children were not permitted to follow his example. "To bed, to bed, said Sleepyhead," he would quote: "let's tarry awhile, said Slow; put on the pan, said Greedy Man, let's sup before we go." And he would sweep up Dale and me, one under each arm, and carry us upstairs to bed.

For milking he wore a soft, ancient felt hat, full of holes, which he pressed firmly against the flank of the cow being milked. Sometimes he was not home from the barn before midnight. He would then wash carefully, change into clean clothes,* and sit down to supper. On these occasions he would not let mama wait up for him; instead, he ate his warmed-over meal before the nursery stove, where wet underwear, shirts, and gum boots generally hung steaming overhead. "Not anyone or anything," complained Aunt Beulah (she was the wife of mama's younger brother Sid; they tried to make a living by raising cranberries in Oysterville, but finally gave up) "could change this atrocious habit."

He found a moonlit night the ideal time to perform chores he had not got around to during the day, such as tightening the weak spots in a barbed wire fence. "The funniest sight I ever saw," remarked one neighbor, "was Harry weeding beets by moonlight at 2 A.M." During the First World War, when a curfew and blackout oppressed the peninsula, a cavalry patrol once spotted papa on our roof at that very hour, pounding nails into loose shingles. When the patrol leader ordered papa down, he refused to descend: "Young man," he said, "I did not put that moon up there; God did." There was no rebuttal to that, and the patrol trotted on.

When indoor plumbing reached our home, papa adjusted to it easily, save that he always donned his hat before going to the bathroom. Asked why, he replied it still seemed to him he was headed for the privy. "Do you know," he said, "I can still feel that wind whistling around my head." His first meetings with automobiles affected him in much the same way; he had no difficulty managing the machines, but for years said "Giddy ap" when he wished to go faster and "Whoa" when he was putting on the brakes.

Papa was a last-minute churchgoer. ("You lose more time by being too early," he would say, "than by being too late.") Mama would hurry the older children through their toilets and send them scurrying over just as the Sunday school bell rang, causing a brief commotion among the mud swallows that darted constantly into and out of their nests under the eaves of the church. We smaller fry, requiring special attention behind the ears or in other secluded areas, arrived a little later. Papa, however, moved with an unalterable rhythm through washing, changing his clothes, and clipping his Vandyke. The minister, waiting, added hymn to hymn, and did not finally begin his sermon until papa was safely seated. Papa sang in a thunderous bass, which embarrassed my mother

*Psychologists might have their suspicions about the number of times papa changed his clothes each day. He had milking outfits, gardening outfits, and business suits, which he might rotate as many as half a dozen times between rising and retiring.

since he could not carry a tune. In California College, she said, he had been the loudest singer in the men's choir, and was ridiculed behind his back. I can't carry a tune either.

Papa was a last-minute train-catcher too. He continued to converse with standers-by on the platform until the cars actually started to move; only then did he swing aboard.

The only connection between Oysterville and South Bend, where he had frequent business, was from Nahcotta by means of two small steamers, the *Shamrock* and the *Reliable,* which made the round trip on alternate days. When headed for South Bend, papa would saddle his sorrel mare Empress; hitch her to the gatepost; bathe in the nursery in a washtub (filled with hot water carried in buckets from the kitchen); don a clean set of long woolen underwear; pull up his socks and affix them to garters (the socks came up over the lower legs of the underwear, creating a bulge, which no one could see once his trousers were on); dress in his second-best banker's-gray suit ("I don't mind appearing in a shiny suit," he would say, "as long as I know there's a good one hanging at home in the closet"); polish his black, ankle-high, twenty-year-old shoes; and meticulously clip his Vandyke beard before a small mirror placed on the south window ledge of the nursery. Meanwhile, Ed, Dale, or I would be sitting on the roof, following the progress of the steamer up the bay from South Bend. When it breasted the red buoy directly in front of our house, the watcher would call a warning. Papa, impeccable in stiff collar and string tie, would emerge from the south door, unhitch Empress, and swing astride, while mama hurried after to hand up a cup of the watery brew he called coffee. Off he would lope for Nahcotta, sipping as he rode. At the dock he would dismount, invert the empty cup over the pommel, slap Empress on the haunch to start her back to Oysterville, and vault, just as the steamer began pulling away, across the slowly widening space between the dock and the deck. His timing was exquisite; he never missed.

Once, though—on August 3, 1910—he had to skip the *Shamrock,* or the *Reliable,* whichever it was, altogether. He was committed to uniting Uncle Cecil in marriage on that day to Ruth Davis; but his candidacy for the state senate made his schedule unreliable, and he was unexpectedly summoned to an urgent August 3 meeting in Olympia. Ruth refused to change the wedding date to suit his convenience, such a change being an invitation to bad luck; if papa couldn't perform the ceremony, she said, she would find someone else.

Papa's solution was to schedule the ceremony for one minute after midnight, and then to row the twenty miles from Oysterville to South Bend and catch the Olympia train. Events were so ordered. Even grandpa and his new wife Aunt Kate, whose nine o'clock retirement hour was as unalterable as the laws of the Medes and the Persians, stayed up for the event, and the children were wakened to come out in their nightgowns to watch it.

275

At precisely one minute past twelve Ruth Richardson struck up the wedding march on the piano. At precisely one minute and five seconds past twelve, mama shouted, "Stop—stop—Harry is still trimming his beard!" At precisely five minutes past twelve the wedding began, the bride and groom standing in the alcove formed by the bay windows of the living room, which in my later day was to be the nursery. Following the wedding supper, papa rowed off for South Bend; Grandpa, Aunt Kate, and Uncle Cecil returned home; and Ruth, the bride, spent her wedding night at our house. It was a curious bridal night by present-day standards.

As justice of the peace, papa performed all his marriages in his home rather than in the church across the street. He may have felt that, since he was not an ordained minister, it would have been inappropriate for him to officiate at a church ceremony.

When asked to arbitrate a legal dispute, on the other hand, papa always met the contesting parties at the schoolhouse, so that their sometimes unbridled exchanges would not offend mama's ears.

Papa's sentences were as elaborate as a championship chess game, full of subordinate clauses and unspoken parentheses. He could talk indefinitely on any subject, detouring away from it for miles but always returning to his point of departure. I considered this an extraordinary accomplishment, and would follow his phrases breathlessly, waiting to see how he would reach a grammatically correct ending to each complicated sentence. A cow passing the door could set papa off on a disquisi-

tion that would last, if no one interrupted him, for upwards of an hour. He would trace the generations of that cow as the king of Spain might trace his ancestry.

Papa was only five feet eight inches tall, but held himself so erect, and so dominated his surroundings, that he seemed to his children to tower over his six-foot brothers. His skin, where weather had not turned it to the consistency of leather, was astonishing white. His nose, broken twice by the kicks of cows, had set into a Roman line. In combination with the Vandyke over his square chin, that nose imparted an air of authority to his countenance that may not have been completely justified.

In some ways, he was an urbane man, and in others an innocent. Certain late-blooming peculiarities of his father's, whispered back and forth among all the Espy women for years, remained unknown to papa to the day he died. During Prohibition, almost every able-bodied man in Oysterville was engaged in rum-running, and fishing launches often came in past the ocean bar with a catch more precious than salmon; but no one told papa, either because they did not wish to disillusion him or because they feared his conscience and his responsibilities as justice of the peace might force him to turn the lawbreakers in.

Papa's broken nose symbolized a certain ambivalence in his attitude toward cows. I am not sure he really liked them. To cause physical pain hurt him; yet once when Holstein, a rangy black-and-white bovine of the breed so named—commodious of udder but low in butter fat—knocked Ed down with a swing of her horns, papa gave Holstein an instant and impressive beating. He cannot have been deliberately punishing her, since he knew she would not understand the reason; he must simply have been outraged that one of his own cows should fail to distinguish between an Espy and the rest of the animal world.

Papa once spent over a thousand dollars—a staggering sum, in view of our chronic financial distress—to purchase a champion Shorthorn bull named Lambert, whose mission was to raise the quality of the Espy herd. Lambert soon developed rheumatism, and refused to mount a knoll, much less a cow. My father hammered together an upward-sloping ramp, so that bull could mate without having to rear so far; but Lambert could not be persuaded to march up the ramp. Papa next arranged a wide belt as a support for the bull's chest. Attached to the belt was a rope that ran through a pulley, screwed into an overhead beam. Two men hauling on the free end of the rope could lift Lambert's forequarters into the classic mating position. The indignity, however, undid his libido. For thousands of years Middle Eastern peasants have dug pits for the patient cows of rheumatic bulls to stand in. Papa was a bright man. He should have thought of that.

If you plan to have a large family, I recommend my father's system of naming calves. He had, for instance, a cow named Rose. He named her first heifer Rosette; her second, Rosita; her third, Roselle; and her fourth, Roserta. Rosette's first heifer was Rosettette, and so on. No such attention was paid to the naming of the bull calves, since they would be slaughtered in any event before arriving at maturity.

Our "ranch" consisted of perhaps a thousand acres, mostly marshland. Some three hundred acres were suitable for cattle-grazing, truck-farming, and the growing of hay. Our entire herd of cattle could never have exceeded a hundred and fifty head, nor did the milch herd amount to more than two dozen.

Cows have a reputation for placidity, but when they refuse to let down their milk, when they swat the milker's eyes with their tail, or kick his stool out from under him and upset his bucket, they can be irritating. Papa was generally as calm as the cows, but I have known them to exhaust even his monumental patience. His jaw would tremble then, so that the part of his goatee immediately under his lower lip stood out like the pronged heel of a fighting cock. Yet he never struck a cow in anger; I saw him beat one only once, in the aforementioned case of Holstein. Even at his angriest, he never swore, at cattle or anything else. But he was the most powerful nonswearer I ever heard. His more common expletives were "Son of a sea cook!," "Consarn it!," "Dad durn it!," "Dad gum it!," "Dad cuss it!," "Ding bust it!," and "Sou'-wegian!" The ultimate in frustration emerged as "Devil!," or, more commonly, "Devilation!" These harmless-appearing epithets burst from his mouth like thunderbolts.

He hated off-color jokes. Once he stumbled across the fact that a bumbling bachelor of the neighborhood had told a group of Oysterville boys, including at least one of the Espy children, a joke involving the ingenious means developed by God to splice the female of the species with the male. Papa did not shout at the man; he barely whispered; but his Vandyke thrust like a dagger, and we could never persuade that poor bachelor to tell us a blue story again.

Papa was unwilling to throw away a paper with anything written on it. Today, nearly twenty years after his death, his children continue to sort through cardboard boxes, throwing away mouldering bills and magazines and third-class mail, setting aside personal letters for more careful reading.

Though papa clung tenaciously to his land, he never expected to make money from it. He was confident, rather, that it would provide security for his children. We were to have everything he had missed.

Occasionally the Espy Estate Company would dispose of a few hundred acres of timberland or a few thousand square feet of city real-estate, always at fire-sale prices. For a day or two there would be the sweet smell of cash around our house. Papa would come home from South Bend with gifts for the children (generally books) and with a most particular present, painstakingly chosen, for mama. Then he would pay another pittance on his debts, buy more oyster beds, and we would be poor again.

Papa's indebtedness resulted from neither extravagance nor the inability to make money; the ranch provided a satisfactory income from the sale of veal, pork, eggs, milk, and cream. But while he was serving in the state senate in 1910 and 1911, a Nahcotta store in which he had an interest failed. The debts had not been incurred by papa but the creditors had relied on his word, and he spent the next twenty years paying them off. However, when the oyster industry revived in the 1930s, papa was able to lease, for a respectable sum, the beds he had clung to so stub-

Espy Home

bornly for a quarter of a century. He and mama spent their final years without financial worries.

Papa was one of a political breed not yet protected under the Endangered Species Act—that is, he was a Republican. He was a regular delegate to Republican national conventions, and would come home proudly with such mementoes as an autographed book of Calvin Coolidge's speeches. His sole deviation from orthodoxy took place in 1912, when he was one of the rumpsters who nominated Theodore Roosevelt for a third term as President. After papa's death I found in a drawer a campaign button bearing the likeness of a moose head—the Teddy Roosevelt symbol—and a legend: "Founder, Bull Moose Party." I still wear that button in every presidential campaign, and if anyone asks me for whom I am going to vote, I say, "Teddy Roosevelt."

Had it not been for papa's perhaps unrealistic sense of honor, he no doubt would have continued in politics. He was a forceful speaker; he was coherent as well as eloquent, and could make himself heard by a vast audience without shouting. The carrying power of his voice was useful, too, when telephoning, our phone being one of forty on a single hookup. When any subscriber's number rang (our ring was a short and a long and a short), the other thirty-nine subscribers generally listened in, draining away power so that most voices were faint, fighting against background noises of a primitive telephone system. Papa, though, could always make himself understood; mama said he could have carried on a conversation with Long Beach, fifteen miles away, without using the telephone at all. He loved communicating with people, whether friends or strangers; indeed, he found it next to impossible to tear himself away from them. His inability to say good-bye used to drive my poor mother wild. She would sit in the carriage, desperate to be off for the blessed privacy of home, while he continued to chat at the door or gate. I can remember only three other situations in which papa willfully disregarded his wife's wishes—when he explained to visitors, as if apologizing, that "Helen was not brought up like you and me," and when he refused, as he did every night, to go to bed until most Oystervilleans were about to get up. Finally, a quarter of a century later, when mama was a victim of glaucoma and cataracts, he insisted on explaining in a stage whisper, "Helen's blind, you know."

Throughout my childhood papa was frequently sought out by congressmen, United States senators and other dignitaries or would-be dignitaries who wanted his political support. If they found him mowing or raking or nailing up fence wires, he did not hesitate to ask them to shuck their jackets and lend a hand. I have no doubt he derived secret pleasure from seeing politicians develop blisters.

He spent much time—some say too much time—on others' problems.

It might be Tina Wachsmuth rushing to knock on his bedroom window in the early hours of the morning, and then rushing back home; papa would emerge seconds later, adjusting his suspenders as he ran to minister to Tina's old father, who had just suffered another of his recurrent sinking spells.

Or it might be a young half-breed writing for a small loan. "I don't suppose you'll send it," remarked a friend when one request came; "you'll never get it back." Papa replied, "He has borrowed from me a good many times, and has never failed me yet." He got the money back ten years later.

So far as is recorded, he complained only once about the demands put on him, at least in his own mind, by his relationship to Oysterville. On that occasion Medora found him pacing the floor, and asked what the trouble was.

"I don't mind preaching for all the churches and marrying all the young people in the county," replied papa, "but when somebody I don't even know commits suicide and they expect me to dig the grave, I think that's too much."

The conflict between his lingering political ambitions and what he conceived to be his honor reached a climax in 1924. Under intense pressure to run for lieutenant governor, he came down with influenza, relapsed, and wound up with asthma so severe that he could not lie flat on his back for the next eight years. Surely this was a psychosomatic illness, an escape from a dilemma that he could not resolve.

His marathon conversations and his stalling tactics on chores could also be interpreted as forms of compensation. In my grandfather's final years, for instance, papa walked up the street each morning to catheterize him for the release of urine. The process required only a few minutes, yet papa always lingered, often eating lunch there, on the excuse that "it is too hard for Helen to have to prepare a full meal at noon."

Financial and ego frustrations might be sufficient to explain such oddities. But why did he dread to go to bed, making every excuse imaginable, whether it was beets that needed weeding, or roofs that needed shingling, or oyster beds that needed examination by lantern light? The explanation, I think, is as simple as it is appalling:

My father's love for my mother, as hers for him, did not diminish, but if anything grew more intense with the passage of the years.

"When I was little," says Dale, "it was hard for me to understand why mama always got the principal attention when papa went away or returned. Once the horses ran away during a drive on the beach. Papa didn't even think of the rest of us until he was sure his Helen had suffered no damage. The first time we drove our Ford after dark, the lights went out, so you boys walked alongside the car to guide us. You didn't do so well; we ran off the road. The accident didn't amount to anything, but even so, pop's first words were, 'Are you hurt, Helen?' "

Papa's problem was not just that he had wanted to conquer the world for his Helen, and had failed. It was not just that he had suffered the loss of his firstborn children at her side, and then had piled the weight of her mourning on his own. It was more: he loved her with a passionate love; and the time came, in the full flush of his manhood, when she was denied him.

Physical renunciation of the sort that papa accepted without question is so foreign to today's standards that to many it will seem absurd. Nobility is not currently in fashion.

If I were a man of tremendous physical energy; if I had to lie without stirring every night at the side of the woman I loved and desired more than life; if I were unable even to extend a hand and touch that near, dear form—then I think I too would make excuses not to go to bed. I think I would milk the cows or weed the beets at two in the morning. I think I would tramp miles of empty oyster beds by lantern light.

But these speculations are too deep and alarming for me to pursue. It is less disturbing to recall that papa was gallant to pretty girls, and even to not-so-pretty-ones; that he ate with extreme slowness; that he enjoyed oatmeal mush and liked his bacon limp; that he studied the comic strips as carefully as the world news, and frequently read the novels of Joseph C. Lincoln aloud at the breakfast table, pausing to laugh at any particularly amusing exchange.

Papa's self-respect remained as inherent at eighty-three as it had been when he wrote his diary at seventeen. Knowing his own worth, he was equally indifferent to others' flattery or disparagement. When he was caught off guard, a submerged, nonegalitarian part of him might show for an instant, like the flash of a fish breaking the surface of the bay. Once, a tourist knocked on our south door and asked him, "Do you belong to that church across the street?"

"No," replied papa. "That church across the street belongs to me."

30

Grandpa Passes

I doubt whether Grandpa Espy really had one foot in the grave in 1902, as the family contended. If he had, he hastily removed it when papa returned to Oysterville.

That his arrogance and self-centeredness increased with age, however, is indisputable. In his own way, for instance, he certainly had been fond of grandma. So it hit his children like a toppling Douglas fir when, in the late 1890s, he virtually dropped her from his will. Urged to reinstate her, he demanded, "Why must this be done? She never earned anything—it's my money." That she had made a home and a refuge for him; that she had borne him eight children, risking her life eight times; that she had reared them all, save only the stillborn eldest, and had imbued in them an ethic so deep that it shaped their entire beings—all this no longer impressed grandpa. To put it bluntly, he was becoming a trifle dotty.

He of course told it otherwise. "My hearing's gone," he would admit; "I need a cane—maybe two canes—for walking; I don't see very well; I've even had to give up my horse. But my *judgment* is as good as it ever was."

Well, not when it came to women. Less than a year after my grandmother's death, grandpa remarried. The date was January 8, 1902, and the bride was one Rosa McLellan, whose background is unknown to me. She divorced him before the year was out, receiving, it is said, $20,000 from the Espy Estate Company in settlement of all claims. There is no way of telling whether such a payment was her objective from the start, or whether grandpa was just too much for her.

Thenceforward his interest in the younger members of the opposite sex became so overt as to embarrass his family. They sighed with relief, therefore, when, in 1907, he took as his third and final wife, Kate Wichser Miller, the woman who had stayed at his home in 1878 while waiting for her fiancé. By then, Aunt Kate, as Oystervilleans called her with affection, had gone through two husbands, both ministers; so she should have known something about the male of the species, particularly the male of religious bent. Whether she foresaw what would be involved in her marriage with grandpa is another question.

Shortly after her death in 1924, someone remarked that Aunt Kate "must have been the only woman of our time who married three times and died a virgin." Uncle Cecil commented, "You would not have said that if you had known father."

This remark, like others by Uncle Cecil, contained more information than was immediately apparent. Aunt Kate treated grandpa with deference, never presuming even to address him by his first name; but soon after their marriage she confided to Aunt Dora, "I was startled to find Mr. Espy so demanding. I had thought by the age of seventy-nine [she herself was seventy] he would be over all that."

By my calculations, he had to be eighty-one. Anyhow, as a pioneer woman she should not have been surprised. When I was a small boy, an

Oystervillean aged ninety-two married a teen-age girl, who in due course bore him a daughter. Joshed by the young bucks of the village, he quavered proudly, "Just give me the mold, and I can make the bullets."

Grandpa's sexual quirks grew quirkier. Recalls a cousin: "We girls were never left alone in a room with grandfather. The young wives found that he liked to fondle. I don't think he ever actually molested anyone, but he was a definite problem to his womenfolk. We can say God bless Aunt Kate for standing between him and the world in his later years."

My parents removed to Oysterville at about the time grandpa's second marriage was ending. He was a widower for the next five years and he regularly ate his morning and evening meals at their home. He arrived each morning at exactly seven o'clock, and it was mandatory that his food be ready and hot. This was a trial not only for my mother, who was nervous in grandpa's presence (though he appears to have treated her with both respect and affection), but for my father, who would have preferred to continue sleeping until a later hour. Grandpa returned each evening at six. As if the house were his own, grandpa said grace, carved the meat, and served the dishes. He had a special fondness for vanilla-flavored cornstarch pudding. (There is a rumor that in later years, during the First World War, he consumed more than his allotted two pounds of sugar a week.)

After his marriage to Aunt Kate, grandpa ate at home except on such special occasions as Easter, Thanksgiving, and Christmas. This arrangement cannot have been altogether agreeable for him. My mother, like my Grandmother Espy, was a good cook. Aunt Kate, though she possessed other virtues in abundance, could not have cooked a palatable meal for Jesus himself. She always kept a jar of caraway cookies for us children, and we had to smile as we ate them, though they were undoubtedly the worst-tasting cookies ever devised by woman's hand. She baked, said grandpa, "the long way of the grain."

Even my sister Dale, who doted on Aunt Kate, held those cookies against her. Dale complained, too, about having to change from coveralls into a dress before Aunt Kate would let her enter the house. Aunt Kate refused to countenance "females in pants or females chewing gum." Dale never chewed gum, but she spent most of her young life in coveralls, and exchanging them for skirts was a severe trial. (I still share Aunt Kate's repugnance against a female, or a male for that matter, chewing gum; but I have reconciled myself happily to pants on females, as long as the contours enrich the garb.)

Aunt Kate was adamant, too, against automobiles. She swore that her first trip in one would be to her own funeral, and she broke her oath only once, in 1921, when a winter tide had covered the road and she could not return from our house to hers without accepting — most ungraciously for such a generally amiable old lady — a ride in Mr. Lehman's truck, which took water a foot or so deep in its stride.

At all times of the year, Aunt Kate kept her house stifling hot, and wore a dark dress which reached to the floor. Perpetually tied about her waist was a spotless white apron, scored with deep net lace. Outdoors, her face was always shadowed by a sunbonnet.

She was a tiny woman with only one tooth, but that in front. She was proud of that tooth, because she could use it to scratch the meat from an apple.

All in all, Aunt Kate cared well for grandpa in his last years. My sister Mona, who was thirteen when he died, retained a lifelong reverence for him, perhaps because she was a year or so too young ever to have been warned against staying in a room with him alone. She appreciated the fact that he kept horehound candy in a jar and was generous with it. She admired, too, the dark three-piece suit that was his regular attire. "Really," she used to say, "he was quite a courtly old gentleman, and fine looking. He kept all his hair, and it never even turned gray."

I recall him less amiably, partly because he once scolded me for carrying too large an armload of logs from the woodshed to the living room fireplace. "Only lazy boys carry big loads," he told me, "so they won't have to make so many trips." I also heard him say more than once, "One boy is worth a whole boy, two boys are worth half a boy, and three boys are worth no boy at all."

Dale, who is eleven months my junior, remembers him in connection with the picket gate that opened from the lane to his outhouses and yard. To enter, one had first to open the gate; and to open the gate, one had to lift the latch. At five, Dale could reach the latch only by standing on the lower brace of the gate. Grandpa, finding her so engaged, assumed she was riding the gate for sport, and gave her, she recalls, "quite a scolding." She adds: "I have always thought of him as a grumpy old

Clytonville gate '65

man. Mama seemed to think I was right—at least in his attitude toward children."

Grumpy or not, grandpa in his nineties was still keeping up his vegetable garden as painstakingly as his son Cecil, now approaching the same age, does today. He ricked his wood neatly in his shed. He chopped kindling and logs, keeping abrim the woodboxes standing by all the fireplaces and stoves. He remained stubborn to the last; when he stumbled on a step and dropped his armload of wood, he would let no one help him to his feet, or even pick up his sticks for him. The humiliation bothered him more than the pain when he burned his hand trying to place a piece of wood "just so" in our nursery stove. (Pop inherited this "just so" approach; sometimes he worked at settling a log on the fire "just so" for so long that by the time he had it "just so," nothing remained of the log but cinders.)

Grandpa took ultimate salvation for granted. He had no fear of dying; he looked forward tranquilly to eternal bliss. When visitors dropped in, he would suggest that they join him in singing "Abide with Me," "Lead, Kindly Light," just as you or I might suggest having a martini or a Scotch and soda. His voice continued to override all others, as it had done for half a century. When alone, in his rocker, he would doze off singing hymns solo, between puffs on his pipe.

Grandpa died without premonition or pain on the morning of October 18, 1918. Relatives, friends, and business associates—white and red alike—came from as far away as Seattle and Portland to view his remains, lying in state in the parlor. Pop insisted on lifting Ed, Dale, and me—respectively nine, six, and seven years old—so that we could see him one last time. He appeared to me much as usual, though more serene. I must have felt a chill, never having seen a dead human before, when pop lifted me for that final look. I suspect, however, that I also experienced a secret gratification, knowing that at last I could examine grandpa carefully, certain that he would not shout at me. But I recall the appearance of the corpse less clearly than the uncomfortable fact that, while waiting, I had been sitting in short pants and half socks on a horsehair chair, and the horsehair had scratched the back of my legs.

the Espy plot, Oysterville, Washington

The day of the funeral was clear and cold. Aunt Kate held firm to her refusal to ride in an automobile, so the family, or at least its older members, walked to the graveyard. Ed, Dale, and I were sent with two cousins—Alice and Jewel, Uncle Will's children—to play on the bay shore. My knowledge of the funeral is confined to Mona's notes, scribbled that evening:

"It was a very large funeral, mama was disturbed by the $1,000 black casket, Will very emotional, papa wore his Prince Albert formal suit only time I ever saw him in tails. Could not locate a Baptist minister, had a terrible time finding one, ended with three, the result all three spoke. Papa insisted casket be opened at cemetery, mama said greatest tribute of all was Mr. Johnson (Indian) picking up a single rose and placing it in the casket at the cemetery. Mama was shocked the way the family sat around cracking jokes following the funeral. One I remember: 'If Mr. Lilly were alive Kate would marry again.'"

Aunt Kate lived another eight years, making her final trip to the cemetery, as she had predicted, in a motor-propelled hearse. She lies in the Espy family plot at grandpa's left side, with grandma at his right—too tranquil a triangle, I fear, ever to inspire a novelist.

Oysterville was grandpa's village until that morning of October 18, 1918. It was papa's village from then on.

Afterword

My mother died at Oysterville in 1954, and my father in the same bed five years later.

Of their offspring, three remain—Edwin, who recently retired as general secretary of the National Council of Churches of Christ; Dale, who lives with her husband, William Little, also retired, in the Oysterville home where she spent her first fourteen years; and myself.

The three of us left Oysterville to attend college—or, in Dale's case, high school—in 1926. We spent our summer vacations in Oysterville, but since then Ed and I have returned to the old homestead only for business, family reunions, funerals, or brief vacations.

As I age, however, Oysterville calls more insistently, and I find myself returning there more often. The village has changed remarkably little; even the goldfinches and sandpipers are back. God continues His gentle, eternal experimenting with the soft light bathing water, tidegrass, and hills. The sky behind the rain still shines silver.

In some ways, Oysterville is even more primitive than in my childhood. Woods have taken over the pastureland; coyotes and elk have migrated to the peninsula. We can hear the coyotes howling at night, and sometimes watch them hunting in the field. Deer are a nuisance. Oysterville still has no motor courts, no neon lights, no bowling alleys. Indeed, apart from two or three television antennae, automobiles are the only outward evidence of a more modern world. (All Oystervilleans, conditioned, perhaps, by winter storms, use their cars even to travel a hundred yards.) I do not believe a home has been built since the Depression.

When I visit Oysterville now, my first impulse is to stop by the cemetery on the ridge, where through a hole among the spruce trees I can watch the slow breathing of the bay, six hours in and six hours out. I pause by the gravestones—of grandpa and grandma and Aunt Kate; of papa and mama; of Nahcati and nameless sailors whose bodies washed ashore long ago; and I feel very much at home.

Then I drive west a mile to the ocean beach, which I am sorry to say has changed more than grandpa's village. When we made that journey in my boyhood, Dolly and Empress had to labor mightily to pull our wagon to the top of the innermost dune. Now my car does not notice the climb. The dunes still roll down to the ocean breakers, a quarter of a mile away; but they have grassed over, and real estate developers have built cottages and laid out roads and dug canals where there used to be only the gray or bone-white of sea gulls, driftwood, and sand.

Still, I have no reason to complain. When I walked in a mist the other night along the hard sand between high-water mark and the surf, the ocean was ablaze. The breakers rushed at me in ranks of yellow-green flame, and flung off sparks as they crashed. The wet sand was suffused with minute organisms of light; my footprints followed me in fire. Stars smaller than my fingernail hopped about me.

It is not everywhere, or every night, that a man can stride among constellations.

Documents

Uncle Cecil Espy house, Oysterville

Shoalwater Bay (Willapa Harbor)

The discharge of Shoalwater Bay into the Pacific Ocean is exceeded on the West Coast only by that of San Francisco Bay, the Columbia River, and Puget Sound. At mean high tide, the area of the bay covered by water is 110 square miles. At mean low tide, it is just over half of that—60 square miles. When the tide is ebbing, the average discharge of water into the ocean is a million cubic feet, or about seven and a half million gallons, per second, the reverse being true on a rising tide. The maximum discharge is 1,600,000 cubic feet per second, or almost twelve million gallons. The mean rate of ebb and flow is two and a half knots; the average rise and fall, six or seven feet with a maximum of twelve.*

The bay water is purer than that of any comparable estuary on the West Coast, and perhaps in the United States. The only noteworthy pollution, from some small sawmills at the mouth of the Willapa River near Leadbetter Bar, is generally carried out to sea rather than entering the bay proper.

---

*Statistics furnished by John Welsh, Water Resources Planner for the Seattle District, Corps of Engineers.

The Pine Creek
Declaration of Independence

Some historians deny that there ever was a written Declaration of Independence signed at Pine Creek on July 4, 1776. It is true that the two signed originals have both vanished. One, says legend, was dispatched to the Continental Congress, but the couriers were robbed of it along the way. The second was placed in a strongbox and buried in the stockade at Fort Horn, but was never recovered after the burning of the fort by Indians and Tories in the Great Runaway. As to the actuality of the document, however, Cousin Anna's word is good enough for me. According to a copy presumably made the day of the signing, the whole Declaration reads as follows:

Resolved—1. That whomever had directly or indirectly in any way, form or manner invaded the free exercise of Fair Play Men's rights, as has been attempted by all branches of the government of Great Britain, is our enemy, and an enemy to this country, and the liberty of of Mankind.

Resolved—2. That we the Committee and members of the Association of Fair Play Men, assembled this day, on ground we hold by virtue of being free men entitled to reside where we choose, do hereby dissolve any political bonds which may have heretofore connected us with the Old Country, or its provinces in America, and finally absolve ourselves of all allegiance to the Crown family of Great Britain, abandoning all practical connection with a nation that has persistently trampled on our rights and liberties as Americans and Fair Play Men, and inhumanly shed innocent blood of Americans, and in the case of ourselves, denied their right to protect us.

Resolved—3. We do hereby declare ourselves what we have long felt ourselves to be, a free and independent body of citizens, but ready at all times to assist our brothers who shed their blood at Lexington, and are, and intend to be a self-governing people under God's rule, the American Congress, and the Fair Play Association, to the furtherance of which independence we hereby pledge to each other our mutual cooperation, our lives, our possessions, and our honor as Fair Play Men.

Resolved—4. That we hereby accept and adopt as rules of life, all the Constitution of the Congress, as superseding in government the rules of conduct of the Fair Play Men's Association, to which we have remained loyal, and the Crown Family of Great Britain are served notice this day that they hereafter hold no rights, privileges, or indemnities amongst us whatsoever.

Resolved—5. That all officers, civil and armed under the Congress, and district, be entitled to exercise the same powers and authorities as was heretofore carried out by the Committee of Fair Play Men, but until 296 the government set up by the General Congress arrives among us, every member of the Committee of Fair Play Men shall continue to act as a civil officer, as a justice of the peace, to issue summonses, hear and decide controversies, pronounce sentence, according to the rules and regulations of the Fair Play Men's Association, [As this ends with a comma, possibly there were other "resolves" following or concluding the above.]

On the authority of *The Clinton Democrat,* issue of July 12, 1918, the names of the signers are:

Alexander Hamilton	Simon Kurtz
Hugh White	Hugh Nichols
Alexander Donaldson	Robert Covenhoven
John Clark	Thomas Francis
Adam Carson	Phillip Quigle
James Crawford	Robert Love
John Pfoutz	Thomas Nichols
Thomas Clark	Samuel Horn
Francis Clark	Henry McCracken
John Jackson	Peter Grove
William Campbell	Adam Dewitt
Peter Pentz	

Dr. William Bamford
and Robert Louis Stevenson

Dr. Bamford treated Robert Louis Stevenson during the latter's stay in the Bay area in 1879, and Mr. Stevenson was a frequent visitor at the Bamford home. For years the Bamfords' daughter Mary had in her possession a volume of Stevenson's "Travels With a Donkey," bearing the following inscription on the flyleaf:

My Dear Sir: Will you let me offer you this little book? If I had anything better, it should be yours. May you not dislike it, for it will be your own handiwork if there are other fruits from the same tree! But for your kindness and skill, this would have been my last book, and now I am in hopes that it will be neither my last nor my best.
You doctors have a serious responsibility. You recall a man from the gates of death, you give him health and strength once more to use or to abuse. I hope I shall feel your responsibility added to my own, and seek in the future to make a better profit of the life you have renewed to me. I am, my dear sir, gratefully yours,

ROBERT LOUIS STEVENSON.

April 1880.

Thomas, father of Robert Louis Stevenson, wrote Dr. Bamford the following letter:

17 Heriot Row, Edinburgh,
June 10, 1880.

Though I have not had the pleasure of meeting with you, will you allow me to express my grateful thanks for all the skill and kind attention which you bestowed on my son, Robert Louis Stevenson.
I have every reason to believe that under God we are indebted to you for his recovery from serious illness.
My wife and I join in wishing you God's blessings and all happiness. We beg your acceptance of the three books which Louis has published which we send by this mail.
Believe me, to remain ever truly obliged,

To Dr. William Bamford,   THOMAS STEVENSON.

References

Anderson, William Kyle. *The Robertson-Taylor Genealogy*. Detroit: Privately printed, 1900.

Baker, Rev. John Clap. *Baptist History of the North Pacific Coast*. American Publishing Society of Philadelphia and Boston, 1912.

Bliss, William Root. *Side Glimpses from the Colonial Meeting-House*. Boston and New York: Houghton, Mifflin and Company, 1894.

Commager, Henry Steele, and Morris, Richard B., eds. *The Spirits of 'Seventy-Six*. New York: Bobbs-Merrill, 1958.

Dixon, Mrs. Harold C., ed. *The Sou'Wester*. Vols. I–IX. Raymond, Wash.: Pacific County Historical Society.

Doddridge, Joseph. *Settlement and Indian Wars of Virginia and Pennsylvania*. Albany, New York: Joel Munsell, 1876.

Edmonds, Walter, D. *Drums Along the Mohawk*. Boston: Little, Brown and Company, 1936.

Feagans, Raymond J. *The Railroad That Ran by the Tide*. Berkeley, Calif.: Howell-North Books, 1972.

Fleming, Sanford. *God's Gold*. Philadelphia: Judson Press, 1949.

Ford, Henry Jones. *The Scotch-Irish in America*. Princeton: Princeton University Press, 1915.

Fuller, George W. *A History of the Pacific Northwest*. New York: Alfred A. Knopf, 1931.

Gibbs, James A., Jr. *Pacific Graveyard*. Portland, Ore.: Binfords & Mort, 1950.

Harvey, Oscar J. *A History of Wilkes-Barre*. Wilkes-Barre, Penn.: Ralder Press, 1930.

Hawthorne, Julian. *History of Washington*. New York: American Historical Publishing Company, 1893.

Jones, U. J. *History of the Early Settlement of the Juniata Valley*. Philadelphia: Henry B. Ashmead, 1850.

Levin, David, ed. *What Happened in Salem*. New York: Twayne Publishers, 1952.

Mayo, B. *Thomas Jefferson and His Unknown Brother Randolph*. Tracy W. Mc-Gregor Library, University of Virginia, 1942.

Miner, Charles. *History of Wyoming*. Philadelphia: J. Crissy, 1845.

Phillips, James D. *Salem in the Seventeenth Century*. Salem, Mass: The Essex Institute, 1933.

Riste, Carl Coke. "Carlota, A Confederate Colony in Mexico." *The Journal of Southern History*, 1945.

Roberts, Kenneth. *Northwest Passage*. New York: Doubleday, Doran & Company, 1937.

Rollo, Andrew F. *The Lost Cause*. University of Oklahoma Press, 1965.

Swan, James G. *The Northwest Coast; or, Three Years' Resistance in Washington Territory*. New York: Harper & Bros., 1857.

Taylor, Bayard. *El Dorado*. New York: Alfred A. Knopf, 1949.

Woodward, W. Elliott, compiler. *Records of Salem Witchcraft, Copied from the Original Documents*. 2 vols. New York: Da Capo Press & Plenum Publishers, 1969.

Thollander sketching
in Oysterville
drawn at the request of Wede Espy

EARL
THOLLANDER